DECISION
point

DECISION POINT

In accord with the *Code of Canon Law*, I hereby grant the *Imprimatur* ("Permission to Publish") for *Decision Point*.

> Most Reverend Dennis M. Schnurr
> Archbishop of Cincinnati
> Archdiocese of Cincinnati
> Cincinnati, Ohio
> April 4, 2014

The *Imprimatur* ("Permission to Publish") is a declaration that a book is considered to be free of doctrinal or moral error. It is not implied that those who have granted the Imprimatur agree with the contents, opinions, or statements expressed.

Design by: Shawna Powell
Illustration by: Jenny Miller & Hazel Mitchell

ISBN 978-1-937509-72-9

FIRST EDITION

Ninth printing, July 2017

Acknowledgments

This project began with a dream.

More than seven hundred people have poured their time, talent, and treasure into DECISION POINT. It is the result of years of research, development and testing. To everyone involved in every stage of the process: Thank you! May God bless you and reward you richly for your generosity.

Now we offer it to the Church as a gift, hopeful that it will help millions of young people encounter Jesus and discover the genius of Catholicism.

Special thanks goes to: Matthew Kiernan, Margie Rapp, Allen Hunt, Anita Hunt, Fr. Robert Sherry, Tim Nowak, Penny Giunta, Beth Rainford, Ashley Berger, and Fr. David Zink.

DECISION POINT was funded by a group of generous donors. It will now be made available at no cost to every parish in North America. This is one of the many ways that this program is unique.

Everything great in history has been accomplished by people who believed that the future could be better than the past. Thank you for believing!

TABLE of CONTENTS

Who ARE you?

WHAT ARE YOU here FOR?

What matters MOST?

WHAT MATTERS least?

It's time to start thinking about life's big questions.

This experience, this book, this program—this is an invitation to explore some of the most important questions in life. In the process you will discover the incredible dream that God has for you.

Don't say, "I'm too young!" Young people are capable of incredible things.

Now is your time. Live up to your potential.

Thank you for the privilege of making this journey with you.

Matthew Kelly

NOW IS YOUR Time. LIVE UP TO YOUR POTENTIAL

Life is

CHOICES

MY LORD GOD, I have no idea where I am going. I do not see the road ahead of me. I cannot know for certain where it will end. Nor do I really know myself. . . But I believe that the desire to please you does in fact please you. And I hope I have that desire in all that I am doing. Therefore I will trust you always though I may seem to be lost. . . I will not fear, for you are ever with me, and you will never leave me to face my perils alone.

Thomas Merton

1. LIFE IS CHOICES

Life is choices. Every day you make hundreds of choices.

What to eat. What to wear. What time to arrive. Whom to hang out with. Whether or not to listen. What to care about.

Many of these choices can seem inconsequential. But one choice builds upon another, and in the end our choices define who we become.

Choices matter.

1.1 YOUR *choices* MATTER

Learning to make great choices is one of the most practical skills you can develop. Decision making is central to everything we do.

You are so young and life is before you. Will you live it wisely or squander it?

Life is precious and beautiful. Ask a couple who have just welcomed their first child into the world—they will tell you how precious and beautiful life is.

Life is also fragile and fleeting. Ask someone who has just been told by his doctor that he has only three months to live—he will tell you how fragile and fleeting life is.

Life is before you. What will you do with your life?

This is what Joan of Arc wrote, just before she died at nineteen.

Learning to make great choices is essential.

James is seventeen years old and serving a life sentence in prison for murder. He lost his temper and shot a man who was disrespecting him. For a while James thought he was the victim of one bad decision. Over time he came to the realization that he was not the *victim* of a bad decision; he was the *author* of that bad choice. As a few more months passed, he came to understand that it was not *one* bad decision that led to that life-altering event; it was a long series of choices.

Mary made a choice. How much joy do you think it brought her?

"I know this now. Every man gives his life for what he believes. Every woman gives her life for what she believes. Sometimes people believe in little or nothing, and yet they give their lives to that little or nothing. One life is all we have and we live it as we believe in living it and then it's gone. But to surrender what you are and to live without belief is more terrible than dying—even more terrible than dying young."

He *chose* to hang out with gang members. He *chose* to join the gang. He *chose* to steal a gun. He *chose* to spend time in places where drugs and alcohol were used and abused. He *chose* not to go to school some days. He *chose* to start drinking. He *chose* to go out late at night. Then, one night, all these choices exploded together to change his life forever. He chose to lose his temper. He *chose* to pull the trigger.

Little choices matter.

Jessica is an incredible athlete and is about to graduate from Harvard at the top of her class.

She *chose* to be a conscientious student. She *chose* not to stay out late at parties. She *chose* to wake before sunrise and go to training. She *chose* not to smoke or drink. She *chose* to eat food that fueled her body. She *chose* not to hang out with people who were a bad influence. She *chose* to push herself harder than anyone else at training.

And all these choices have transformed her and her life.

James and Jessica both made many choices, but their choices were very different.

Little choices matter because they become the foundation for bigger decisions.

But sometimes it only takes one decision to change the direction of your life for better or worse.

Martin was an above average student. School didn't come easy to him, but he worked hard and his hard work paid off. During spring break of his freshman year in college he got drunk, went back to his hotel, slipped in the bathroom, broke his neck, and died.

When he chose to get drunk he probably didn't think he was making a life or death decision, but he was.

Sometimes it only takes one bad decision to destroy a life. Sometimes it only takes one bad decision to end a life.

That's the thing about choices. Sometimes what you think is a small decision could end up being the biggest decision of your life.

Every choice you make is proof that you are free.

Free will is one of God's greatest gifts to humanity.

WHO WAS JOAN OF ARC?

Joan was twelve years old when she had a series of supernatural experiences that included visions and hearing the voice of Saint Michael the Archangel. When she was seventeen, she led her first army and enjoyed a series of spectacular military successes with the French army. The following year she was captured by the British and placed on trial for heresy and witchcraft. In 1431, at nineteen years of age Joan of Arc was burned at the stake. Thirty years later she was exonerated of all charges and ultimately was canonized by Pope Benedict XV in 1920. Joan of Arc lived in France from 1412 to 1431. She is the patron saint of soldiers, and her feast day is May 30.

PEER PRESURE: PEOPLE CAN PRESSURE YOU TO DO THINGS, BUT THE ONLY ONE WHO MAKES THE DECISION IS YOU. THEY ARE NOT MAKING THE CHOICE – YOU ARE. OWN YOUR DECISIONS.

> **"HIS CONSCIENCE IS MAN'S MOST SECRET CORE AND HIS SANCTUARY. THERE HE IS ALONE WITH GOD WHOSE VOICE ECHOES IN HIS DEPTHS."**
>
> *VATICAN II - GAUDIUM ET SPES.*

To guide you in the use of this incredibly powerful gift, God has also given you **reason** and **conscience.**

rea•son (ree-*zh*un)

Reason is the capacity for logical, rational, and analytic thought.

con•science (con-sh*uh*ns)

Conscience is the inner voice that encourages you to do good and avoid evil. God speaks to us through our conscience (CCC 1776–1779).

Reason and conscience work together to help you distinguish good actions from bad ones. Reason and conscience work together to help you discover the best way to live.

All choices are not equal.

Some choices are good choices, and some are bad. And you usually know at the time if you are making a good or bad choice. The inner voice of conscience encourages you toward what is good and right.

Are you good at making decisions?

What's the best choice you made in the past twenty-four hours?

What's the worst choice you made in the past twenty-four hours?

How can you make better choices in the future?

God wants you to become a great decision maker. This is one of the reasons he sends us the Holy Spirit. Ask the Holy Spirit to guide you and counsel you—and you will find yourself making better choices.

Every day you make hundreds of choices. These choices determine the direction of your life. Sometimes you choose the-best-version-of-yourself and sometimes you choose a-second-rate-version-of-yourself.

Every time you say yes to something, it changes who you are forever.

It's time to start taking your choices seriously. Next time you need to make a decision, *ask the Holy Spirit to guide you.*

Discussion Questions

1) WHO DO YOU KNOW WHO IS A GREAT DECISION MAKER? WHAT MAKES THIS PERSON A GREAT DECISION MAKER?

_____

_____

_____

_____

_____

_____

2) DESCRIBE A TIME WHEN YOU IGNORED YOUR CONSCIENCE AND REGRETTED IT LATER. DESCRIBE A TIME WHEN YOU LISTENED TO YOUR CONSCIENCE AND FOLLOWED IT, EVEN THOUGH IT WAS DIFFICULT.

_____

_____

_____

_____

_____

_____

3) ARE YOU GOOD AT MAKING DECISIONS? ON A SCALE OF 1 TO 10 (10 BEING THE BEST), HOW GOOD DO YOU THINK YOU ARE AT MAKING DECISIONS? WHAT'S ONE PRACTICAL THING YOU COULD DO TO BECOME A BETTER DECISION MAKER?

_____

_____

_____

_____

_____

IF YOU DON'T KNOW WHO YOU ARE OR WHAT YOU ARE HERE FOR, IF YOU DON'T KNOW WHAT MATTERS MOST OR WHAT MATTERS LEAST, YOU MAY BE EXPERIENCING AN IDENTITY CRISIS. WE ALL EXPERIENCE THIS AT DIFFERENT TIMES IN OUR LIVES. BUT LET ME TELL YOU SOMETHING, **GOD WANTS TO SOLVE YOUR IDENTITY CRISIS.** I AM BEYOND IDENTITY CRISIS AND YOU WILL BE TOO THE DAY YOU REALIZE THAT YOU ARE A CHILD OF GOD, THAT GOD IS YOUR FATHER, AND THAT YOU ARE HIS SON OR DAUGHTER. YOU GET YOUR IDENTITY FIRST FROM GOD. UNTIL WE REALIZE THIS WE ARE LOST.

THE AVERAGE PERSON MAKES **4,000** DECISIONS A DAY. MOST OF THEM ARE SUBCONSCIOUS AND HABITUAL. THAT'S WHY IT IS CRITICAL TO BECOME A GREAT DECISION MAKER.

1.2 the BEST way to live

Everyone who loves you wants you to live your best possible life. But what is the best way to live?

This is the question that the great thinkers of every age grapple with. It is a question that we all wrestle with in a *deeply personal* way.

We are all searching for the best way to live.

Sometimes it is a conscious search and sometimes it is an unconscious search. We want to help you start searching consciously for the best way to live.

The best way to live is a big question. It's one of life's biggest questions. But you are not too young to start thinking about life's big questions.

Anne Frank was thinking about life's biggest questions when she wrote her diary at just thirteen years of age. You should read it.

It is *proof* that *young* people are capable of *incredible things*.

We want to help you discover the best way to live.

Why does this question matter? The question matters because you matter. It matters because your *happiness* matters.

In some ways the best way to live is different for every person. The best way for you to live might mean becoming a nurse. For the person next to you it might mean becoming a teacher. For the next person it might mean becoming a priest.

But at a foundational level, the best way to live is the same for us all.

Let's look at three **foundational principles** that demonstrate that the best way to live is, in some ways, the same for everyone.

What virtue do you most admire in Mary?

GET THE APP!

THE FIRST PRINCIPLE: THE-BEST-VERSION-OF-YOURSELF

People from different cultures and different countries and different religions may disagree on many things, but none propose that the best way to live is by trying to be something other than who you are.

No *religion* . . . no *culture* . . . no *country* says the meaning of life is to be the-*worst-possible*-version-of-yourself . . . or that the best way to live is by being a-*second-rate*-version-of-yourself.

God has not created you to be a-second-rate-version-of-yourself. Nor are you here to be another version of your parents, teachers, friends, or brothers and sisters. You are here to be yourself.

The best way to live is therefore in ways that help you become the-best-version-of-yourself.

This is true not just for you, but for everybody.

THE SECOND PRINCIPLE: VIRTUE

Show me a society that believes that lying and stealing from each other is the best way to live. There are no award ceremonies for the biggest liar or the biggest cheater. Somewhere deep inside we universally despise these things.

Virtue is at the heart of every good human experience.

Think about relationships. In the next decade you will spend enormous amounts of time and energy on relationships, but most people never realize a simple truth: Two patient people will always have a better relationship than two impatient people. Two generous people will always have a better relationship than two selfish people. Two courageous people will always have a better relationship than two cowardly people. Two humble people will always have a better relationship than two prideful people. Two honest people will always have a better relationship than two dishonest people.

Virtue is the best way to live for everyone.

TRUE FULFILLMENT CAN ONLY BE FOUND IN AND THROUGH JESUS CHRIST. YOU CANNOT BECOME THE-BEST-VERSION-OF-YOURSELF EXCEPT IN AND THROUGH JESUS.

THE GLORY OF GOD IS MAN FULLY ALIVE.

SAINT IRENAEUS

THE THIRD PRINCIPLE: SELF-CONTROL

The opposite of self-control is **slavery**. If we cannot control our ability to drink, then we are a slave to drink. If we cannot control our temper, then we are a slave to our temper. If we cannot control our ability to get started, then we are a slave to procrastination. If we cannot direct our ability to work hard, then we are a slave to laziness.

God made us free. Anything that enslaves us is *not* from God, and therefore not the best way to live.

At different times in history some people may have thought that it was OK for other people to be slaves, but *no man ever thought it was a good idea that he be made a slave.*

Freedom and self-control go hand in hand.

The person who has the self-control to do what is good and right—even when it is difficult or comes at great personal cost—is universally respected.

Self-control is the best way to live for everybody.

These are just three examples of how the best way to live is the same for us all. Throughout your life you will encounter people who say, "There are no absolute truths. What's true for you is not necessarily true for me!" This is **relativism**, and it is a lie.

Some things are true for everyone.

DISCUSSION

1. IN SOME WAYS THE BEST WAY TO LIVE IS THE SAME FOR US ALL. WHICH OF THE THREE PRINCIPLES HAD THE MOST IMPACT ON YOU (THE-BEST-VERSION-OF-YOURSELF, VIRTUE, OR SELF-CONTROL)?

2. HOW WOULD YOUR RELATIONSHIPS IMPROVE IF YOU STARTED TO REALLY LIVE THESE THREE PRINCIPLES?

3. IF AT THE END OF YOUR LIFE YOU COULD BE REMEMBERED FOR JUST ONE VIRTUE, WHICH WOULD YOU CHOOSE? WHY IS THAT VIRTUE IMPORTANT TO YOU?

Four Quotes. One Author.

HOW OLD DO YOU THINK THE AUTHOR WAS?

"LAZINESS MAY APPEAR ATTRACTIVE, BUT WORK GIVES SATISFACTION."

"HOW TRUE DADDY'S WORDS WERE WHEN HE SAID: ALL CHILDREN MUST LOOK AFTER THEIR OWN UPBRINGING. PARENTS CAN ONLY GIVE GOOD ADVICE OR PUT THEM ON THE RIGHT PATHS, BUT THE FINAL FORMING OF A PERSON'S CHARACTER LIES IN THEIR OWN HANDS."

"THE BEST REMEDY FOR THOSE WHO ARE AFRAID, LONELY OR UNHAPPY IS TO GO OUTSIDE, SOMEWHERE WHERE THEY CAN BE QUIET, ALONE WITH THE HEAVENS, NATURE AND GOD. BECAUSE ONLY THEN DOES ONE FEEL THAT ALL IS AS IT SHOULD BE."

"WHOEVER IS HAPPY WILL MAKE OTHERS HAPPY TOO."

All four quotes are from *The Diary of a Young Girl* written by Anne Frank, one of the six million Jewish victims of the Holocaust. The book, which was found and published after her death, documents her experiences hiding from the Germans during World War II. It is available in sixty–seven languages and has sold more than fifty million copies. Anne was thirteen when she began the diary.

M.Y. -T-H-O-U-G-H-T-S

ARE YOU LISTENING TO YOUR NAVIGATION?

1.3 God's DREAM FOR YOU

Have you ever met someone and discovered they were nothing like what you thought they would be?

Before you met them, you knew about them, but knowing about someone is not the same as *knowing* someone.

Everyone knows something about God, but when we really encounter God, most of us discover that he is not like we thought. You may know about God, but now it's time to get to *know* God. And you may discover that much of what you thought you knew was wrong. . . .

The first thing you discover when you really encounter God is that *God wants good things for you.*

Sometimes God wants better things for you than you want for yourself.

In 1 Corinthians 2:9 Paul teaches us, *"No eye has seen, no ear heard, nor the heart of man conceived, what God has prepared for those who love Him."*

What's Paul saying? You cannot even imagine what God has in mind for you.

God is the ultimate Father. You may have a great father here on earth, and you may not. But whether you do or you don't, you know a great father when you see one. God is that great Father. When earthly fathers shine, it is because they act like our heavenly Father.

Everything good in this world flows from the goodness of God.

God your Father created the universe for *you*. This world is his gift to you. He wants you to enjoy it and take care of it. He created all the beauty that surrounds you with you in mind. Then he looked at it and said, "It is good."

You too. God created you and he created you in his image. Deep in your heart you are good. But staying connected to that goodness is not always easy, and requires real effort.

Like any good father, God has dreams for his children. God has a dream for you. God wants you to become the-best-version-of-yourself.

He wants you to become all he created you to be—by living a good and full life. And God wants you to help everyone who crosses your path become the-best-version-of-themselves. But more than anything else, God wants to have a *dynamic relationship with you*.

1 CORINTHIANS 2:9

KNOW IT: What is Paul talking about?

THINK ABOUT IT: Do you want to go to Heaven?

LIVE IT: Are you living a life that leads to Heaven?

EVERYTHING MAKES
SENSE IN RELATION TO
GOD'S DREAM.
WHEN WE FEEL LIKE LIFE
IS NOT MAKING SENSE,
IT IS USUALLY BECAUSE
WE HAVE LOST SIGHT
OF GOD'S VISION FOR
OUR LIVES.

I never really understood this until my first child was born. After Walter was born I found myself yearning to be with him. He couldn't walk or talk. All he did was eat, and sleep, and need his diaper changed. But I loved being with him. When I was at the office I could not wait to get home to hold him or roll around on the floor with him. When I had to travel I missed him so much.

Over the years, that hasn't changed. As my wife and I have had more children, I yearn to be with each of them in the same way.

I love my children so much. It's crazy, really. And before I had children I just didn't understand. But as I began to think about this great love I have for my children, the love of God took on a whole new meaning. Because if I can love my children as much as I do, and I am broken and wounded and flawed and limited, *imagine how much God loves us.*

This was overwhelming to me and took my relationship with God to the next level. And it has made me take God's dream for me and my life even more seriously.

God wants you to become the-best-version-of-yourself. This is his dream for you and everything makes sense in relation to God's dream.

This is the idea that got me hooked on Catholicism. I was fifteen years old and nothing was making sense.

I grew up in a Catholic family, went to Catholic school, went to Mass every Sunday, but *I never really got it.* One day a friend of the family let me in on the secret. He talked about the **universal call to holiness**. He said that God calls everyone to live a holy life, and explained that some things I think, do, and say help me to grow in holiness and others don't. He also explained that I am happiest when I am doing the things that help me to grow in holiness.

There is a connection between happiness and holiness.

I finally got it. Catholicism finally made sense to me, because I started to see that everything the Church does is designed to help me become more perfectly the person God created me to be and everything I do each day matters.

Everything really does make sense in relation to God's dream for us.

What makes a good friend? Someone who helps you become the-best-version-of-yourself.

What makes a good meal? Food that helps you become the-best-version-of-yourself.

> THE DESIRE FOR GOD IS WRITTEN IN THE HUMAN HEART, BECAUSE MAN IS CREATED BY GOD AND FOR GOD; AND GOD NEVER CEASES TO DRAW MAN TO HIMSELF. ONLY IN GOD WILL HE FIND THE TRUTH AND HAPPINESS HE NEVER STOPS SEARCHING FOR:
>
> THE DIGNITY OF MAN RESTS ABOVE ALL ON THE FACT THAT HE IS CALLED TO COMMUNION WITH GOD. THIS INVITATION TO CONVERSE WITH GOD IS ADDRESSED TO MAN AS SOON AS HE COMES INTO BEING. FOR IF MAN EXISTS, IT IS BECAUSE GOD HAS CREATED HIM THROUGH LOVE, AND THROUGH LOVE CONTINUES TO HOLD HIM IN EXISTENCE. HE CANNOT LIVE FULLY ACCORDING TO TRUTH UNLESS HE FREELY ACKNOWLEDGES THAT LOVE AND ENTRUSTS HIMSELF TO HIS CREATOR.
>
> **(CCC #27)**

MODERN CULTURE'S NIGHTMARE

WHAT YOU DO NOW IS GOING TO MATTER LATER IN YOUR LIFE IN WAYS THAT YOU HAVE NOT EVEN BEGUN TO IMAGINE.

What makes a good book or movie? Those that inspire you to become the-best-version-of-yourself.

Why do your parents send you to school? To torture you! No, the word *education* comes from the Latin verb *educare*, which means "to draw out." Education at its best draws out the-best-version-of-you. Looking back on my life, I can see that the best teachers, mentors, coaches, and managers were all men and women who were trying to draw the best out of me.

What is the purpose of study? When you study hard you become a-better-version-of-yourself.

What is the meaning of work? Making money? No. This is a secondary outcome. The primary value of work is that when we work hard and pay attention to the details of our work, we develop character and virtue— and become the-best-version-of-ourselves.

What is the purpose of marriage? Husband and wife challenging and encouraging each other to become the-best-version-of-themselves, and raising children and encouraging them to become the-best-version-of-themselves.

Life is about saying yes to the things that help you become the-best-version-of-yourself, and no to the things that don't.

Next time you are confronted with a decision, simply ask yourself: What will help me become the-best-version-of-myself?

Everything makes sense in relation to God's dream. When we feel like life is not making sense, it is usually because we have lost sight of God's vision for our lives.

God wants you to become the-best-version-of-yourself. Will you choose God's dream or the modern culture's nightmare?

ANTHONY OF THE DESERT

GOD'S DREAM

1. HAVE YOU EVER MET SOMEONE AND DISCOVERED THAT PERSON WAS NOTHING LIKE WHAT YOU THOUGHT HE OR SHE WOULD BE LIKE?

_____

_____

_____

_____

_____

_____

2. WHO IN YOUR LIFE IS HELPING YOU BECOME THE-BEST-VERSION-OF-YOURSELF?

_____

_____

_____

_____

_____

_____

3. WHAT ARE TWO THINGS YOU CAN DO TO BECOME A-BETTER-VERSION-OF-YOURSELF THIS WEEK?

_____

_____

_____

_____

_____

_____

_____

WHAT'S ENSLAVING YOU?

MY THOUGHTS

Who Was MOSES?

Moses was born when his people were increasing in numbers and the Egyptian Pharaoh was starting to fear them. Moses' mother hid him when Pharaoh decreed that all newborn Hebrew boys be killed. The boy was found and adopted by the Egyptian royal family. After killing an Egyptian slave master, Moses fled across the Red Sea, where he encountered God in the burning bush. God sent Moses back to ask Pharaoh to set the Israelites free. After God sent ten plagues to convince Pharaoh to release the Israelites, Moses led their exodus out of Egypt and across the Red Sea toward Mount Sinai – where he received the Ten Commandments. But Moses never made it to the Promised Land. He died within sight of it after wandering in the desert for forty years. Moses was a murderer! But look what he went on to accomplish after he gave his life to God.

MOSES

1.4 be a REBEL

It's probably the last thing that you expected to hear at church, but I really want to encourage you to be a rebel. Jesus was a rebel.

But here's the thing: It's important to rebel against the right things.

Today's culture doesn't want you to become the-best-version-of-yourself. Today's culture doesn't want you to think too much about life. Today's culture doesn't want you to become hungry for the truth. Today's culture doesn't want you to develop your spiritual self. Today's culture doesn't want you to have a great relationship with God.

Modern culture just wants you to go along, be a good, obedient little consumer, and not ask too many questions about where the whole experiment is leading.

I want you to rebel against that. I want you to rebel against the modern culture.

Now, let's compare God's vision for you and your life with the modern culture's vision for you and your life.

God loves you deeply and wants you to become the-best-version-of-yourself. The culture doesn't care about you and usually leads you toward a-second-rate-version-of-yourself.

What drives God? Love. What's driving the culture? Consumption.

Almost everything that happens in today's culture is aimed at getting you to buy something, or feel inadequate, or both.

Everything has a brand on it today. What did we first use brands on? That's right: cattle. What did we next use brands on? Correct again: slaves. Do we own the brands or do the brands own us? Are we still the consumers or are we being consumed? We need to start thinking at a deeper level. Are we cattle and slaves or free men and women?

God sees us as his children. He created us *free* and wants to keep us free. The culture sees us as cattle and wants to turn us into slaves.

Do you want to be a child of God or a slave to the culture?

The problem is most of us spend a lot more time listening to the culture than we do listening to God.

It's time to rebel.

Reject the world's vision for your life, because it leads to emptiness and misery, in this life and the next life. *Embrace* and celebrate God's vision for your life, because it leads to joy and fullness, now and forever.

They say that every teenager goes through a rebellious stage. But we usually rebel against the wrong things. If you want to rebel against something, rebel against the culture that wants to rob you of your best self and enslave you. Rebel against the things that seek to make you less than who you really are.

The history of our great faith is full of examples of men and women who rejected the culture's vision for their life.

Anthony of the Desert inherited an enormous fortune as a young man when his parents died. The vision the culture had for him was to live a life of privilege and luxury as a wealthy landowner. He rejected the culture's vision for his life when he heard the words of Jesus: *"If you want to be perfect, go, sell what you possess and give to the poor, and you will have treasures in heaven; and come, and follow me."* (Matthew 19:21) Anthony sold or gave away all his land and possessions, gave the money for the care of the poor, and became a hermit. Over time he developed the monastic way of life, and he is now considered the father of all monks.

Now, this story may seem far from the world you live in. But reconsider it. Was Anthony's decision a difficult one? *Yes*. Was it a courageous decision? *Yes*. Did many of his friends think he was crazy? *Yes*. Did he have to overcome his own selfish desires? *Yes*.

Your world is not that different. When you decide to walk with God you will have to make tough choices, courageous decisions. Many of your friends will think you are crazy, and you too will need to overcome your selfish desires.

You and Anthony are not that different.

Reject the modern culture and the world's empty vision for your life. Embrace God. You will be happier.

VIRTUE IN FOCUS

pa·tience
[pey-shuh ns]

The capacity to accept or tolerate delay, trouble, or suffering without getting angry or upset.

Who are the most patient people you know?

How do they practice patience?

What are three ways you can become a more patient person?

MATTHEW 19:21

KNOW IT: The things of this world are fleeting and worthless compared to the treasures of the next world.

THINK ABOUT IT: If Jesus asked you to give up everything and follow him, what would be the hardest thing to give up?

LIVE IT: Go without something this week.

What do you think Mary's friends said about her?

Discussion Questions

1. WHEN WAS THE LAST TIME YOU WATCHED SOMETHING ON TV THAT HELPED YOU BECOME A-BETTER-VERSION-OF-YOURSELF?

2. IN WHAT WAYS DO YOU FEEL CALLED TO REBEL AGAINST TODAY'S CULTURE?

3. HOW IS THE PATH GOD IS CALLING YOU ALONG DIFFERENT AND BETTER THAN THE CULTURE'S WAY OF DOING THINGS?

My Thoughts

WHAT BRAND ARE YOU MOST ATTACHED TO?

(Draw logo here.)

> ## "DO NOT BE AFRAID."
> —JESUS CHRIST

1.5 DECISION point

One of the great figures in the Bible is Moses. He led the Israelites out of slavery in Egypt and toward the Promised Land.

When Moses was about to die he said to Joshua and the people of Israel, *"I have set before you today life and prosperity, death and adversity."* (Deuteronomy 30:15)

What was Moses saying to the people? *You choose*—life or death. *You choose*—prosperity or adversity.

Throughout our journey together you are going to face many decision points. They matter. They may not seem like life-or-death decisions, but they are.

Jesus said, *"I have come so that you may have life, and have it to the fullest."* (John 10:10)

Do you want to live life to the fullest? God will not force fullness of life on you. God has given you free will and he will let you use that free will to live a shallow and empty life if that is what you choose. What do you choose?

I have placed before you today God's incredible vision for your life and the world's empty vision for your life. Which do you choose?

The-best-version-of-yourself or some second-rate-version-of-yourself?

Freedom or slavery?

DEUTERONOMY 30:15

KNOW IT: Moses is telling the Israelites: "You are at a Decision Point."

THINK ABOUT IT: Are you choosing life or death, prosperity or adversity in your daily decisions?

LIVE IT: When you are deciding what to eat this week, choose life and prosperity.

JOHN 10:10

KNOW IT: God wants good things for you! Jesus wants to help you live life to the fullest!

THINK ABOUT IT: If you were living life to the fullest, how would your life be different?

LIVE IT: Do one thing today that will help you to live the incredible life God has imagined for you.

JOURNAL QUESTIONS

1. DO YOU WANT TO LIVE LIFE TO THE FULLEST? WHY OR WHY NOT?

_____
_____
_____
_____
_____
_____
_____

2. ARE YOU GOING TO CHOOSE GOD'S INCREDIBLE VISION FOR YOUR LIFE OR THE WORLD'S EMPTY VISION FOR YOUR LIFE?

_____
_____
_____
_____
_____
_____
_____

3. WHAT IS ONE MESSAGE FROM THIS SESSION THAT YOU ARE GOING TO SHARE WITH SOMEONE ELSE?

_____
_____
_____
_____
_____
_____
_____

Psalm 1: The Two Ways

[1] Blessed is the man who walks not in the counsel of the wicked, nor stands in the way of sinners, nor sits in the seat of scoffers;

[2] but his delight is in the law of the Lord, and on his law he meditates day and night.

[3] He is like a tree planted by streams of water, that yields its fruit in its season, and its leaf does not wither. In all that he does, he prospers.

[4] The wicked are not so, but are like chaff which the wind drives away.

[5] Therefore the wicked will not stand in the judgment, nor sinners in the congregation of the righteous;

[6] for the Lord knows the way of the righteous, but the way of the wicked will perish.

LIFE IS CHOICES

CROSSWORD PUZZLE

ACROSS

3. Rejecting the world's vision for your life

4. The opportunity or power to choose between two or more possibilities

6. The way you think, feel, act

8. The inner voice that encourages you to do good and avoid evil.

12. The capacity for logical, rational, and analytic thought

13. A good and moral behavior or character

14. The power of acting without the constraint of necessity or fate

15. Being content

16. Restraint exercised over one's own impulses, emotions, or desires

DOWN

1. A way of thinking, behaving, or working that exists in a place or organization

2. Opposite to self-control

5. Having a divine quality, being perfectly good.

7. What's driving the culture of the world

9. Not liking to work hard or to be active

10. The ability to make our own choices; one of God's greatest gifts to humanity

11. The ultimate Father

Answers on page 326

What's
HOLDING
you back?

O Lord my God, teach my heart this day where and how to see you, where and how to find you. You have made me and remade me, and you have bestowed on me all the good things I possess, and still I do not know you. I have not yet done that for which I was made. Teach me to seek you, for I cannot seek you unless you teach me, or find you unless you show yourself to me. Let me seek you in my desire, let me desire you in my seeking. Let me find you by loving you, let me love you when I find you. Amen.

St. Anselm

PAUL THE APOSTLE (AD 5–67) was originally named Saul of Tarsus. He was a persecutor of Christians until he experienced a vision of the risen Jesus on the road to Damascus and had a radical conversion (Acts 9:4). Paul became one of the most influential Christians of all time. Fourteen of the twenty-seven books of the New Testament are attributed to him. He knew well that what we spend our time thinking about tends to multiply in our lives. So, what did Paul encourage us to think about? "Finally, brethren, whatsoever things are true, whatsoever things are honest, whatsoever things are just, whatsoever things are pure, whatsoever things are lovely, whatsoever things are gracious: if there be any excellence, if there be any praise, think on these things." (Philippians 4:8)

2. WHAT'S HOLDING YOU BACK?

In Session 1 we talked about God's dream for you to become the-best-version-of-yourself. Nobody wants to be a-second-rate-version-of-themselves . . . so why do we find ourselves doing things that don't align with our best selves?

Have you ever noticed that sometimes you know something is wrong and bad for you . . . but you *still* desire it? *Not everything you desire is good.*

Or have you noticed that sometimes you know something is *not* good for you and you *don't* want to do it, but you find yourself doing it anyway?

The problem is, we enjoy things that don't help us become the-best-version-of-ourselves. This is a part of our **fallen nature**, the disordered desire that exists within every man and woman.

Paul wrote, "I do not do the good I want, but the evil I do not want is what I do." (Romans 7:19)

What was he saying? I want to be the-best-version-of-myself, but sometimes I find myself doing things that don't help me become the-best-version-of-myself—even though I don't want to do these things.

We don't always choose the-best-version-of-ourselves. We don't always choose virtue. We don't always choose self-control.

Let's take a look at what gets in the way, how we get deceived so easily, and what's holding us back.

2.1 THE Quest FOR HAPPINESS

We are all on a **quest for happiness**.

You have an enormous *desire for happiness*. This desire is an incredible gift, and God has placed this desire within you for a reason.

We all do certain things because we believe they will bring us happiness. Sometimes the things we choose bring us happiness, and sometimes they don't. We have all done things that we thought would make us happy, but that in fact left us feeling empty, unhappy, miserable, used, deceived, or worse.

We want to help you avoid this in the future by teaching you how to *choose wisely* the things that will truly bring you happiness.

We all want to be happy. The question is, how long do you want to be happy?

If you just want to be happy for an hour, take a nap.

If you want to be happy for two hours, have a great meal.

If you want to be happy for a whole day, go shopping.

If you want to be happy for a week, go fishing.

If you want to be happy for a month, take a long vacation—go down to Australia.

If you want to be happy for a year, inherit a fortune.

But the truth is, you want to be happy **forever.**

The good news is, God wants you to be happy forever too.

God has created us for happiness.

And not only does God want *you* to be happy; he wants to play an *active role* in your happiness. He doesn't just *hope* for your happiness from afar. He wants to *help* you find that happiness.

When it comes to happiness, the culture wants to sell you a poor substitute: **pleasure.** God wants you to be happy. The culture wants you to be a slave to pleasure. This is another reason to rebel against the culture.

The world tries to distract and confuse us with pleasure. Our culture says that pleasure and happiness are the same thing. It's *another lie.*

Pleasure is good and beautiful, and in the right context God wants us to experience much pleasure in this life. But pleasure is not happiness.

What is the difference between pleasure and happiness? Pleasure cannot be sustained beyond the activity producing it.

Let me give you an example. When we eat we feel pleasure. Stop eating and the pleasure stops. That's why we don't stop eating. Seventy-five percent of the time when we are eating we are not actually hungry. But we like the pleasure of eating, so we keep eating—that is the only way to maintain the pleasure. Pleasure cannot be sustained beyond the activity producing it.

How happy do you think Mary was when she held the child Jesus in her arms?

WHO WAS

Mother Teresa?

Mother Teresa (1910–1997) founded the Missionaries of Charity, a religious congregation made up of more than forty-five hundred religious sisters who are active in 133 countries. Their work consists of running homes and hospice facilities for those with HIV/AIDS, leprosy, and tuberculosis; soup kitchens; orphanages; family counseling programs; and schools. Members of the order take four vows: the traditional vows of poverty, chastity, and obedience, and a fourth vow, "To give wholehearted and free service to the poorest of the poor." Mother Teresa had an immense love for the unloved: "We think sometimes that poverty is only being hungry, naked, and homeless. The poverty of being unwanted, unloved and uncared for is the greatest poverty. We must start in our own homes to remedy this kind of poverty."

Happiness is different. Happiness is sustainable.

Here's another example. I come home from work one day next week, and it is my day to work out, but I don't really feel like working out. So I have to make a decision: Work out or plant myself in a recliner in front of my 127-inch idiot box with a six-pack of beer and a three-hundred-ounce bag of potato chips?

The choice is mine.

Now, suppose I force myself to work out even though I don't feel like it. The thing is, whenever I get done working out I am always glad—even if I had to force myself to do it. Happiness can be sustained beyond the activity producing it.

Happiness is more than pleasure. *Don't settle for an empty life of pleasure.* Choose more. Rebel against the culture of pleasure and start actively seeking the happiness God created you for.

So, what will really make you happy?

Happiness is the result of **right living**. Honesty leads to happiness; dishonesty leads to misery. Caring for others leads to happiness; selfishness leads to unhappiness. Patience leads to happiness; impatience will make you miserable.

There are right and wrong ways to live your life. The culture tells us that there is no right and wrong. The culture says that what's wrong for you might be right for me. This is nonsense. Hitler's way was wrong. Mother Teresa's way was right.

But how do you know what is the *right* thing to do?

At a basic level, you just know. One of God's great gifts to you is **conscience**. Your conscience guides you in the way of right living so that you can celebrate the-best-version-of-yourself, and live your best life.

Very often we say we don't know what we should do, but we are lying to ourselves (and to others), because our conscience is telling us the right course of action but we are trying to ignore it.

Our regrets are born when we ignore our conscience.

But there may be a handful of times in your life when you legitimately don't know what the right thing to do is. It is for these times more than any other that God has given you another of his great gifts: **reason**.

I had dinner last week with some friends, Mike and Samantha. They have been married for two years and have been trying to have a baby, but have not become pregnant. Their friends have been telling them about different types of fertility treatments, but they don't know if these treatments are part of God's dream for them. Mike and Samantha want to do the right thing, but they are not sure what the right thing to do is. This is a highly specialized and complex area of science and morality. To get to the truth they are going to need to study this issue.

This is a perfect example of why God gave you *a beautiful mind*. You have the ability to study an issue, search for the truth, think things through, seek out God's way, and act on the truth you discover.

If you want to make great decisions, *just do the next right thing*. Don't worry about what you have to do next week or next year; just do the next right thing right now.

Five, ten, fifty, one hundred times a day. Do the next right thing often enough and you will live a life uncommon, a life that is rich with inner peace and happiness.

WHO WAS Hitler?

Adolf Hitler (1889–1945) was the leader of the Nazi Party and Chancellor of Germany from 1933 to 1945. Hitler's was the diabolical mind behind the Holocaust; his regime was responsible for the deaths of six million Jews, as well as millions of others he and his followers considered racially or genetically inferior.

"THE TRUTH WILL SET YOU free" JOHN 8:32

JOHN 8:32

KNOW IT: God created you for freedom and wants you to be free. Jesus is telling us that truth is essential for freedom and happiness.

THINK ABOUT IT: What lies are enslaving you?

LIVE IT: Make a conscious effort to align your actions with the truth this week.

discussion questions

1. WHAT ARE SOME OF THE THINGS YOU DESIRE THAT ARE GOOD FOR YOU?

_____
_____
_____
_____
_____
_____
_____

2. WHAT IS SOMETHING YOU THOUGHT WOULD MAKE YOU HAPPY, BUT IN FACT LEFT YOU FEELING EMPTY, UNHAPPY, MISERABLE, USED, DECEIVED, OR WORSE?

_____
_____
_____
_____
_____
_____
_____
_____

3. DESCRIBE A TIME WHEN YOU HAD THE WISDOM AND COURAGE TO FOLLOW YOUR CONSCIENCE, AND YOU WERE GLAD YOU DID.

_____
_____
_____
_____
_____
_____
_____

2.2 STINKING THINKING

DISORDERED DESIRES: NOT ALL YOUR DESIRES ARE GOOD. IF THEY WERE, THEY WOULD DIRECT YOU TOWARD WHAT IS GOOD, RIGHT, JUST, AND NOBLE. BUT SOME OF YOUR DESIRES DIRECT YOU AWAY FROM WHAT IS GOOD. THESE DISORDERED DESIRES ARE PART OF OUR FALLEN NATURE AND THE RESULT OF ORIGINAL SIN. WHAT ARE YOUR DISORDERED DESIRES?

Even though God has given us incredible minds to reason with, we still do a lot of **stinking thinking**. Let's take a quick look at some of the paths that the world proposes for happiness.

Individualism. The creed of the individualist is: What's in it for me? Individualism is the philosophy of selfishness. The fruits of individualism are greed, selfishness, isolation, and exploitation.

Individualism is stinking thinking.

Hedonism. The creed of the hedonist is: Pleasure is the ultimate goal in life; if it feels good, do it! The fruits of hedonism are laziness, gluttony, procrastination, and lust.

Hedonism is stinking thinking.

Minimalism. The creed of the minimalist is: What's the least I can do? A minimalist is always seeking to exert the minimum effort and receive the maximum reward. Minimalism is the enemy of excellence and the father of mediocrity.

Minimalism is stinking thinking.

Relativism. The creed of the relativist is: There is no absolute truth; what's true for you may not be true for me! Relativism contradicts itself because it claims, "It is absolutely true for everybody that nothing is absolutely true for everybody." The fruits of relativism are disorientation, intellectual and spiritual confusion, and hopelessness caused by the loss of any meaning in life.

Relativism is stinking thinking.

Great thoughts are beautiful. Great actions are inspiring. Are any of these philosophies beautiful? I think not. When someone embraces these broken ways of thinking and living, do they inspire anything good? Absolutely not.

They may be convenient to your disordered desires and selfishness at a particular moment, but do they really suffice as a philosophy to live your life by?

JUST DO THE NEXT RIGHT THING.

Reject the world's vision for your life. *It will leave you empty and dissatisfied*. Rebel against the culture.

Reject these broken philosophies and watch out for people who live by them, because they will only use you for their own benefit and selfish gratification.

Beyond yourself, these philosophies also mean doom for communities of any size.

What would happen to a community—a family, a parish, or a nation—if everyone lived by these self-centered philosophies? Those communities would grow apart, fall apart, and self-destruct.

In many ways this is what we are witnessing in world affairs today. As modern cultures and nations become increasingly secular, rejecting God and his ways, they begin to implode. *Anything that stands against God and his truth cannot last.*

Truth, beauty, and goodness: These are what your soul is thirsty for. The philosophies the world wants to pass off to you are deficient in all three.

VIRTUE IN FOCUS

Cour·age
[kur·ij]

Mental or moral strength to venture, persevere, and withstand danger, fear, or difficulty.

What has been the most courageous moment of your life?

Who is the most courageous person you know?

In what situations would you like to have more courage?

DISCUSSION QUESTIONS

1. HOW IS "STINKING THINKING" HOLDING YOU BACK FROM BECOMING THE PERSON GOD CREATED YOU TO BE?

_____

_____

_____

_____

_____

2. INDIVIDUALISM, HEDONISM, MINIMALISM, RELATIVISM: WHICH OF THESE ARE THE BIGGEST TEMPTATIONS FOR YOU AT THIS TIME IN YOUR LIFE?

_____

_____

_____

_____

_____

3. DESCRIBE A TIME WHEN YOU EMBRACED ONE OF THESE BROKEN PHILOSOPHIES. WHAT WAS THE OUTCOME? HOW DID YOU FEEL AFTERWARD? DID YOU BECOME A-BETTER-VERSION-OF-YOURSELF?

_____

_____

_____

_____

_____

_____

_____

WHAT IS WISDOM?

Wisdom is not the amassing of knowledge. The sheer volume of information available on the Internet is enough to boggle the mind, and experts say the amount of data will soon double every day. But information is not **wisdom**. In fact, even if you could commit all this information to memory and claim it as knowledge, knowledge is not **wisdom**. So, what is **wisdom**? **Wisdom** is truth lived.

2.3 HUNGRY FOR THE TRUTH

One of the beautiful things about young people is *you are hungry for the truth*. And because of this hunger for the truth, you *hate being lied to*.

The broken philosophies we just explored and the stinking thinking that comes with them lead to the lie that there is no truth—and if there is no truth, there is no right and wrong. This is among the most absurd claims modern culture makes.

This kind of stinking thinking makes happiness impossible.

The good news is *there is truth*. Some things are true for everybody. There is such a thing as right and wrong.

You know this already from your own experience. Tell a lie and you will feel uncomfortable with yourself. You will also notice that lying makes you more anxious and less joyful. Anxiety represents the world. Joy represents God. Every lie takes you further away from God and his joy, and deeper into the anxiousness of the world.

If someone else lies to you, you feel that they have wronged you in some way. How can they wrong you if there is no right and wrong?

You're smarter than the culture. Rebel against it.

There is such a thing as truth—not this rubbish of *your* truth and *my* truth, but **universal truth**. Truth is bigger than you and me; truth is bigger than everyone. There is such a thing as right and wrong. And you will only ever be happy to the extent that you align your life with truth, and make choices based upon what is right.

Truth and happiness are connected.

Ever since Adam and Eve were in the Garden of Eden, God has been trying to lead us in this truth, and we have been rebelling. When we walk with God in his truth we find happiness and fulfillment. When we rebel against God and turn our backs on his truth, we find misery and discontent.

In the book of Exodus we read the story of Moses leading the people out of slavery in Egypt and into the Promised Land. Every person and every culture has questions about what is right and wrong. This is how God answered the Israelites' questions:

1. **You shall love the Lord your God and serve him only.**
2. **You shall not take the name of the Lord your God in vain.**
3. **Keep holy the Sabbath.**
4. **Honor your father and your mother.**
5. **You shall not kill.**
6. **You shall not commit adultery.**
7. **You shall not steal.**
8. **You shall not bear false witness.**
9. **You shall not covet your neighbor's wife.**
10. **You shall not covet your neighbor's goods.**

I know, it may seem a little old-fashioned, but *wisdom is never old-fashioned*. Let me suggest an exercise. Watch the news tomorrow night with this list in front of you. As each story is presented you will notice that most of the news is bad news. (The culture focuses on what is bad. God invites you to focus on what is good.) After each story is presented in the news program, ask yourself, which of the Ten Commandments was broken?

The truth is, the list is brilliant. It is pure genius. Wherever you find injustice and misery in this world, you will discover that at least one of the Ten Commandments has been broken.

Now ask yourself: How would the world be different if we just lived by the Ten Commandments?

Imagine all the misery and heartache that could be avoided if we all just lived by these ten nuggets of life-giving wisdom.

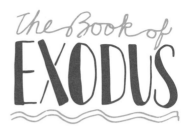

The Book of EXODUS

The Book of Exodus is the second book in the Old Testament. It tells the story of how the people of Israel, led by Moses, left slavery in Egypt. They journeyed through the wilderness to Mount Sinai, where God promised them the land of Canaan ("the Promised Land") in return for their faithfulness. Israel entered into a covenant with God, who gave them laws to live by and instructions for the Tabernacle. It was in the Tabernacle that God promised to live among them, lead them to the Promised Land, and give them peace.

What do you think was Mary's favorite Scripture passage?

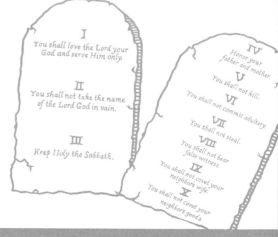

I
You shall love the Lord your God and serve Him only.

II
You shall not take the name of the Lord God in vain.

III
Keep Holy the Sabbath.

IV
Honor your father and mother.

V
You shall not kill.

VI
You shall not commit adultery.

VII
You shall not steal.

VIII
You shall not bear false witness.

IX
You shall not covet your neighbor's wife.

X
You shall not covet your neighbor's goods.

Discussion QUESTIONS

1. **DESCRIBE A TIME WHEN YOU WERE NOT "HUNGRY FOR TRUTH," WHEN YOU DIDN'T WANT TO KNOW THE TRUTH. WHY WERE YOU AVOIDING IT?**

2. **THINK ABOUT A DISTURBING STORY YOU HAVE SEEN IN THE NEWS RECENTLY. WHAT HAPPENED? WHICH OF THE TEN COMMANDMENTS WERE BROKEN?**

3. **WHEN WE EXAMINE THE TEN COMMANDMENTS, THE OBVIOUS WAYS OF VIOLATING THEM ARE APPARENT, BUT WHAT ARE SOME OF THE MORE SUBTLE WAYS WE CAN BREAK THEM?** For example, most people will never be in a situation in which they are tempted to break the Fifth Commandment (You shall not kill). But most of us have killed someone's reputation with gossip. Go through the commandments one by one and discuss the not-so-obvious ways each can be broken.

2.4 THIS IS ▷ Personal

This discussion may seem very theoretical—but it isn't. This is deeply personal. What's holding *you* back? What's getting in the way of you becoming the-best-version-of-yourself? Disordered desires? Stinking thinking? Wrong friends? Bad habits? Drugs? Alcohol? Sex? An eating disorder?

Let me tell you a story to put all this in context.

HOPE

"HOPE IS THE THEOLOGICAL VIRTUE BY WHICH WE DESIRE THE KINGDOM OF HEAVEN AND ETERNAL LIFE AS OUR HAPPINESS, PLACING OUR TRUST IN CHRIST'S PROMISES AND RELYING NOT ON OUR OWN STRENGTH, BUT ON THE HELP OF THE GRACE OF THE HOLY SPIRIT."

(CCC 1817)

Once upon a time there was a Native American Indian boy. It was the custom of his tribe to send the boys out into the wilderness around the time they were becoming young men. For thirty days they had to take care of themselves. They had to find their own food, defend themselves against wild animals, and find somewhere safe and sheltered each night to sleep. After the thirty days had past, all the men in the tribe would come searching for the boy and when they found him, he would be initiated into the tribe as an adult.

For several days everything was fine. The boy found plenty of food to eat and a place to sleep each night. But around the fifth and the sixth day food became scarce. On the seventh day the boy couldn't find any food at all, and this went on for almost a week. Finally, the boy woke up starving the morning of the thirteenth day. He hadn't eaten in almost a week.

That morning as he wandered in the wilderness, the boy noticed a mountain in the distance. He thought to himself, "Perhaps I will find food up on the mountain."

The boy walked in the direction of the mountain, and around the middle of the day he reached it and began to climb it. He soon discovered a path and followed it toward to the top, but still no food.

Late in the afternoon, just as the boy was stumbling upon the pinnacle of the mountain, starving and exhausted, a rattlesnake slithered across the path in front of him.

The boy froze.

The boy looked at the snake and the snake looked at the boy. Then the boy slowly began to back away from it. But just as he did, the snake said to the boy, "Boy, I am lost up here in the mountains and I cannot find my way down. But I know you know the way down. Please, will you lead me down the mountain?"

The boy replied, "No. I know what you are. You're a rattlesnake. At any moment you could strike out and hurt me, even kill me."

The rattlesnake said to the boy, "You look hungry, boy."

"Ahh," the boy groaned, "I'm starving. I haven't eaten in almost a week."

The snake said to the boy, "I know where we can find food. If you lead me down the mountain I will lead you to food."

The boy said, "No. You're a rattlesnake and you could hurt me."

The snake said to the boy, "If you lead me down the mountain, I promise I will lead you to food and I promise I will not hurt you."

The boy thought for a moment, and then he said to the snake, "Do you promise?"

"I do," replied the snake.

So the boy led the snake down the mountain, and when they got to the bottom the snake led the boy to food. The snake laid before the boy every type of food he could imagine, a banquet fit for a king. The boy ate and he drank, and he felt like a king.

Then the snake began to dance, and when the snake danced it was beautiful. So, the boy began to dance also. The boy danced and the snake danced, and they ate some more and drank some more, and then all of a sudden the snake struck out and bit the boy.

The boy fell to the ground screaming and crying. The snake slithered over to the boy. The boy looked at the snake, and the snake looked at the boy, and the boy screamed, "You promised! You promised you wouldn't hurt me."

The snake looked deep into the boys eyes, smiled and laughed, and said, "You knew what I was when you picked me up."

In a world filled with so much cynicism, the **SUPERNATURAL VIRTUES** –*Faith, Hope,* and *Love*– are often laughed at and dismissed as foolish and naive. Some people say that hope only sets you up for disappointment, and because of that hope is a bad thing.

Hope is a good thing, maybe the best of things. Hope is one of those things that you can't buy, but that will be freely given to you if you ask. Hope is the one thing people cannot live without. Hope is a thing of beauty.

What is it that sooner or later is going to turn on you and bite you?

And what are you going to do about it?

The rattlesnakes we encounter in life are always making promises they cannot keep. It is the very nature of these things to turn on us and strike us down.

Life is a journey. Where is your journey taking you at the moment? Is it time to make a change? If it is, I hope you will have the **courage** to make the change.

Courage is a prerequisite for the life God has envisioned for you.

Everything in life requires courage. Whether it is playing football or coaching football; crossing the room to ask a woman on a date, or rekindling a love that has grown old; whether it's your first day at college or your first day back at college after twenty years, life requires courage. It takes courage to say yes at the right times and it takes courage to say no at the right times. Your first day at work or starting a business, battling a potentially fatal disease, getting married, struggling to overcome an addiction, apologizing for something you have done, or coming humbly before God in prayer and asking: God, what do you think I should do? All require courage.

Life requires courage. Courage animates us and is therefore essential to the human experience.

The most dominant emotion in our society today is **fear**. We are afraid. Afraid of rejection and failure, afraid of certain parts of town, afraid of certain types of people, afraid of criticism, afraid of suffering, afraid of change, afraid to tell people how we really feel, afraid of losing the things we have worked hard to buy, afraid of what our friends will think . . . We are afraid of so many things. Often, we are afraid to be the-best-version-of-ourselves.

But before too long we are going to meet someone who will *banish our fears* and fill us with courage to *live an incredible life.*

GET THE
APP!

Discussion Questions

1. WHAT DID THE STORY ABOUT THE RATTLESNAKE MAKE YOU THINK?

2. WHAT DOES THE RATTLESNAKE REPRESENT FOR YOU? WHO OR WHAT IS HOLDING YOU BACK? WHAT IS IT THAT SOONER OR LATER IS GOING TO TURN ON YOU AND STRIKE YOU DOWN? HOW WOULD YOUR LIFE BE BETTER IF YOU COULD WALK AWAY FROM THAT RATTLESNAKE?

3. IF YOU HAD MORE COURAGE, WHAT GOOD THING WOULD YOU DO?

If you ask people **what the main message is in the Bible,** they might tell you IT'S *Love* OR F O R G I V E N E S S. BUT WHAT IS THE PHRASE THAT APPEARS MORE TIMES **than any other message in the Bible?**

DO NOT BE AFRAID. OVER AND OVER throughout history, GOD'S MESSAGE TO HUMANITY HAS OVERWHELMINGLY BEEN *Do not be afraid.* *This phrase (or some variation of it) appears more than* **one thousand times** in the Bible. → **WHY?** ← BECAUSE GOD SENSES THAT WE ARE IN FACT AFRAID. *AFRAID TO TRUST HIM.* **Afraid to love others.** *Afraid to love ourselves.* Afraid to embrace and celebrate THE-BEST-VERSION-OF-OURSELVES. **Afraid to ask the big questions and see where they might lead us**. **AFRAID.**

GOD WANTS TO *liberate* YOU FROM THESE FEARS.

> "HE WHO HAS OVERCOME HIS FEARS WILL TRULY BE FREE."
>
> –ARISTOTLE

THE BOOK OF JUDGES

The Book of Judges is the seventh book of the Bible. It tells the stories of a series of divinely inspired leaders (judges). These judges were sent by God to help the Israelites live faithful lives. Gideon was one of these leaders. There is a pattern to the stories: The people are unfaithful to God and thus fall into the hands of their enemies. The people repent and call on God for mercy. God's merciful response is to send them a new leader (a judge), who delivers the Israelites from oppression, and they prosper again. But before too long, they get carried away with their prosperity, forget their promises to God, become unfaithful, and repeat the cycle.

2.5 DECISION point

In the book of Judges we read about how the Israelites had turned away from God, choosing idolatry and immorality. As a result they fell into slavery again. Then God called on Gideon and he had to make a choice.

Gideon was a young man that God chose to free the people of Israel from their worship of idols.

Gideon was asked to tear down the altar of Baal and to build an altar to the Lord. Was he afraid? *Yes*. Did he have doubts? *Yes*. Was he concerned what his friends would think? *Yes*.

But . . . he listened to the voice of God—above his doubts, fears, and friends. He trusted in God's word. And he chose good over evil, right over wrong, and bravery over cowardice.

So Gideon, under God's instructions, destroyed the altar of Baal. This is where the Israelites were worshiping false gods.

The Israelites had:

- Gone looking for happiness in the wrong places
- Fallen into stinking thinking
- Turned their back on the truth
- Been too proud to admit their wrongdoing

Life is choices. Today's culture wants to build an altar of Baal in your heart. In fact, the construction of this altar probably started long ago. I know, because I tore down that altar many years ago, and yet it is amazing how often I notice that the world has started building a new altar to Baal in my heart, and I have to tear it down all over again.

Because like the Israelites, we have all:

- Gone looking for happiness in the wrong places
- Fallen into stinking thinking
- Turned our back on the truth
- Been too proud to admit our wrongdoing

Just like with Gideon, a **decision point** is before you today. God is asking you to tear down the altar of Baal that the culture has built in your heart. *Tear it down*.

And *now*, build in your heart an *altar to the Lord*.

Anyone or anything that doesn't help you become the-best-version-of-yourself is just too small for you.

Decide *today* not to let anything get in the way of becoming the-best-version-of-yourself.

Don't let anything hold you back from becoming the person God created you to be.

GIDEON

How much courage did Mary need to say yes to God?

1. IF GOD CALLED YOU TO A GREAT MISSION LIKE HE DID GIDEON, DO YOU THINK YOU
   WOULD SAY YES? WHY? WHY NOT?

_____
_____
_____
_____
_____

2. LIKE THE ISRAELITES, WE HAVE ALL: GONE LOOKING FOR HAPPINESS IN THE WRONG
   PLACES, FALLEN INTO STINKING THINKING, TURNED OUR BACKS ON THE TRUTH, AND
   BEEN TOO PROUD TO ADMIT OUR WRONGDOING. WHEN WAS THE LAST TIME YOU ACTED
   LIKE THE ISRAELITES?

_____
_____
_____
_____
_____

3. WHAT DOES OUR CULTURE WORSHIP?

_____
_____
_____
_____
_____
_____
_____

·PSALM 62·

[1]For God alone my soul waits in silence;
from him comes my salvation. [2]He only is my rock and my
salvation, my fortress; I shall not be greatly moved.

[3]How long will you set upon a man to shatter him, all of you,
like a leaning wall, a tottering fence? [4]They only plan to thrust
him down from his eminence. They take pleasure
in falsehood. They bless with their mouths,
but inwardly they curse.

[5]For God alone my soul waits in silence, for my hope is from
him. [6] He only is my rock and my salvation, my fortress;
I shall not be shaken. [7]On God rests my deliverance and
my honor; my mighty rock, my refuge is God.

[8]Trust in him at all times, O people; pour out your heart
before him; God is a refuge for us.

[9]Men of low estate are but a breath, men of high estate
are a delusion; in the balances they go up; they are together
lighter than a breath. [10]Put no confidence in extortion,
set no vain hopes on robbery; if riches increase,
set not your heart on them.

[11]Once God has spoken; twice have I heard this: that power
belongs to God; [12] and that to thee, O Lord, belongs steadfast
love. For thou dost requite a man according to his work.

WHAT'S HOLDING YOU BACK?

CROSSWORD PUZZLE

ACROSS

2. A philosophy centered on the question, "What's in it for me?"

6. Disordered desire that exists in every person.

8. A philosophy that believes pleasure is the ultimate goal in life.

10. The moral strength to venture, persevere, and withstand danger, fear, or difficulty

12. Happiness is the result of

13. The mistaken belief that what is true for one person might not be true for everyone.

DOWN

1. The power of the mind to think and understand in a logical way.

3. The idea that some things are true for everybody.

4. You have an enormous desire for

5. Poor short-term substitute for happiness.

7. A philosophy focused on doing only the bare minimum.

9. The dominant emotion in our culture today

11. To desire something good and expect it with confidence.

Answers on page 326

The JESUS Question

Lord, catch me off guard today. Surprise me with some moment of beauty or pain. So that at least for the moment I may be startled into seeing that you are here in all your splendor, always and everywhere, barely hidden, beneath, beyond, within this life I breathe. Amen.

Frederick Buechner

IF **YOU** COULD PERFORM ONE OF JESUS' **MIRACLES,** WHICH WOULD YOU **CHOOSE?**

WHY? WHAT'S YOUR **MOTIVE** FOR THE ONE YOU CHOSE?

HOW **CLOSE** CAN YOU GET TO PRODUCING THE **OUTCOME** OF THAT MIRACLE WITHOUT **PERFORMING** THE MIRACLE?

3. THE JESUS QUESTION

Every time I start thinking seriously about Jesus, I come to the same conclusion: *I don't know him anywhere near as well as I should.*

Jesus is the one who changed everything. Lots of people talk about changing the world, but *Jesus did.*

All of human history revolves around him. It is impossible to measure his impact on the world. And your life will *never really make sense* until you place *Jesus* at the center of it.

Jesus made the lame walk, taught the simple, set captives free, gave sight to the blind, fed the hungry, healed the sick, comforted the afflicted, and afflicted the comfortable. Then, in the ultimate act of love, Jesus laid down his life for us—dying on the cross for our sins. Then he did something that nobody had ever done before, and nobody has done since—he rose from the dead.

The more I get to know Jesus, the more I get to know my true self. And this is what I discover:

I am the *lame* that Jesus makes walk.

I am the *simple* that Jesus patiently teaches.

I am the *captive* that Jesus wants to set free.

I am the *blind* that Jesus wants to give sight to.

I am the *hungry* that Jesus wants to feed.

I am the *sick* that Jesus wants to heal.

I am the *afflicted* that Jesus wants to comfort, and at other times,

I am the *comfortable* that he wants to afflict.

Jesus is the *healer of my soul* . . . and *my soul needs healing.*

I think if you are honest with yourself, you will discover that *your soul needs healing too.*

Jesus is the friend you have been yearning for your whole life.

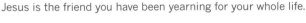

3.1 WHO IS JESUS?

Who is Jesus? The first thing to get really clear about is that Jesus walked the earth. This is indisputable. The culture tries sometimes to present Jesus in the same category as Santa Claus and the Easter Bunny. This is ludicrous. You are smarter than that. We need to start thinking about Jesus on a deeper level than the popular culture.

How do we know Jesus actually existed?

The most comprehensive presentation of Jesus' life is in the Gospels, and the Scriptures clearly establish Jesus as living at a particular time and place in history. They are not vague about when he lived or where he lived. They go to great lengths to establish his birth in the context of world history.

But the best evidence to establish that Jesus walked the earth is not in Christian writings, but in secular writings and other religious traditions.

Secular historians of his time wrote about Jesus, and Jewish writers agree that Jesus walked the earth at the same time and place that the Gospels establish.

It is also worth noting that the other major world religions all acknowledge Jesus. This is important because all these other religions are rivals of Christianity. The easiest way for these rival religions to disprove Christianity would be to demonstrate that Jesus never actually lived. But they are unable to do that.

Jesus is not a figment of Christian imagination. He lived in a place and time, walking the earth just as you do today.

But let's go deeper.

Who was Jesus?

One day as Jesus was walking down the road with his disciples, he asked them two questions.

The first question: "Who do people say that I am?"

His disciples replied, "Some say you are John the Baptist returned from the dead; others say you are Elijah, or one of the other prophets."

The second question: "Who do you say that I am?"

I call this **The Jesus Question**, and everyone has to answer it for themselves. You cannot avoid the question—not answering the question is an answer.

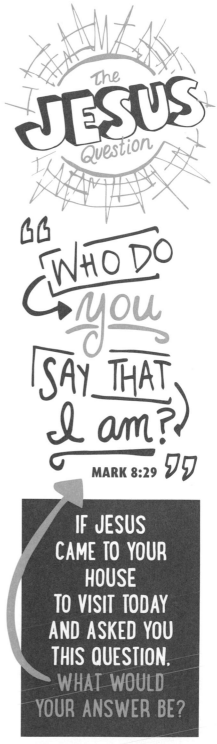

"WHO DO you SAY THAT I am?"

MARK 8:29

IF JESUS CAME TO YOUR HOUSE TO VISIT TODAY AND ASKED YOU THIS QUESTION, WHAT WOULD YOUR ANSWER BE?

WHO IS

THE Messiah

-?-

THROUGHOUT THE OLD TESTAMENT, REFERENCES ARE MADE TO THE MESSIAH, THE HOLY ONE OF GOD, WHO WOULD COME AND SAVE GOD'S PEOPLE. AS CHRISTIANS WE BELIEVE THAT JESUS IS THE MESSIAH.

Notice Jesus didn't ask the disciples who they thought he was the first day he met them. By the time he asked, they had been at his side for almost three years.

So perhaps before you answer the Jesus question, we should take another look at Jesus, who he is, why he came, what he really taught, and what all of that means to you in the modern world.

The culture wants to reduce Jesus to just a *nice guy*. This is tragic. So, who is Jesus?

There are many ways to answer the question. He is a Galilean. A Jew. A carpenter. An itinerant preacher. A miracle worker. The Son of God. The King of Kings. The Christ. The Savior of the world. The chosen one. The Messiah.

C. S. Lewis, one of the great Christian writers of the twentieth century and the creator of the Narnia series, says we only really have three choices when it comes to Jesus: He is a either a liar, a lunatic, or the Messiah he claims to be.

Other major world religions acknowledge Jesus as a great teacher or a great prophet—which seems very accommodating and tolerant—but there are several problems with this position.

First, Jesus never claimed to be a great teacher or a great prophet. He claimed to be the long-awaited Messiah. If he isn't the Messiah, he is either a liar or a lunatic—but not a great teacher and prophet. *These things are incongruent.*

Let's get clear. If Jesus is not the Messiah, *he is the biggest liar who ever lived.* You cannot be the biggest liar in history and still be a great teacher and prophet. These things are incongruent.

And more than being a liar, if Jesus is not the Christ, he perpetrated *the biggest fraud in human history*.

There is the option that he was a lunatic, that he was mentally ill. Asylums are full of people with the "Messiah complex," but there is no historic record of anyone of any credibility claiming to be the Messiah before Jesus, and I suspect you cannot name someone who has claimed to be the Savior of the world since. The Messiah complex is a post-Jesus phenomenon.

If Jesus was a lunatic, could the early Christians have kept that a secret? The scale of the conspiracy that would be required to conceal Jesus as a lunatic makes it more than improbable. And if he was just a lunatic, they could have easily proved that and simply locked him up. There would have been no need to crucify him, as he would have been easily discredited. If they could have proved he was a lunatic, they would have had no reason to feel threatened by him, and no reason to kill him. But he was considered by both the secular and the religious authorities of his time to be much more dangerous than a simple lunatic.

Who is Jesus? He is the Galilean carpenter who became an itinerant preacher, who turned water into wine, made the lame walk and the blind see, walked on water, multiplied a handful of loaves and fishes to feed thousands, got under the skin of secular and religious leaders of the day, was executed on a cross, was buried in a borrowed tomb, and three days later rose from the dead. Jesus wasn't a great teacher; he was the greatest teacher. He wasn't a great prophet; he was the greatest prophet. But more importantly, Jesus is the Christ, the long-awaited Messiah.

Now let's take a look at what all this means to you.

WHAT IS A PROPHET?

A PERSON WHO ANNOUNCES THE WILL OF GOD.

discussion questions

1. HOW DID THIS SESSION CHANGE THE WAY YOU SEE JESUS?

_____
_____
_____
_____
_____
_____

2. HOW DID JESUS CHANGE THE WORLD?

_____
_____
_____
_____
_____
_____

3. THE JESUS QUESTION IS, "WHO DO YOU SAY THAT I AM?" (MARK 8:29) IF JESUS CAME TO YOUR HOUSE TO VISIT TODAY AND ASKED YOU THIS QUESTION, WHAT WOULD YOUR ANSWER BE?

_____
_____
_____
_____
_____
_____
_____
_____

SIN MAKES US SELFISH. THE MORE WE SIN, THE MORE WE FOCUS ON OURSELVES—ONLY OURSELVES, THINKING ALWAYS ABOUT OURSELVES.

THE MORE WE SIN, THE LESS CAPABLE WE BECOME OF DOING GOOD—BEING GENEROUS, CHARITABLE, AND VIRTUOUS.

JESUS WANTS TO TURN YOUR LIFE UPSIDE DOWN, AND THEN IT WILL BE RIGHT SIDE UP.

3.2 the PROBLEM and the SOLUTION

Watch the evening news and you will quickly come to the conclusion that the world is a bit of a mess. I don't know anyone who would say the world is moving in a great direction. Parents are concerned about the world their children will inherit. Grandparents try not to think about it because it makes them too anxious. They have seen enough of the change to recognize just how disturbing the trends are.

How did the world get to be a mess? Do you want the *truth* or some sugarcoated answer?

Lots of people could give you lots of different reasons, answers, and excuses, but most of them would focus on one aspect of the mess. They will talk about suffering and death, the collapse of the family, poverty and economic turmoil, or environmental breakdown. But these are all just symptoms. What's the disease?

If you get the flu, your symptoms may be a sore throat, a hacking cough, a fever, a runny nose, and aches and pains. But the only way to fix the symptoms is to cure the disease.

Suffering and death, the collapse of the family, poverty and economic turmoil, environmental breakdown, and whatever else you want to add to this list are all just symptoms.

But let's get back to the question: How did the world get to be a mess?

The big answer to the question, the macro answer, is that people are sinful and they turn their backs on God.

Sin is the disease. And the truth is, sin makes us unhappy.

God never intended for us to suffer and die. His original idea was for us to live in paradise forever. God's original plan was for ever-reigning peace between God, man, and the environment, and harmony between all men and women (CCC 374–379, 384, 400).

Suffering and death are a direct result of sin.

In Session 2 we talked about Gideon from the book of Judges. This whole book of the Bible is a series of stories that illustrate the Israelites' turning away from God, and then turning back to God. Each time they embraced sin and turned away from God their lives became miserable. Each time they turned their backs on God they fell into another form of slavery.

Sin always leads to slavery of one kind or another.

But each time the Israelites turned back to God they experienced peace and prosperity.

The same thing happens to us. When we turn away from God our lives become miserable. Sure, there may be pleasure to be had in the moment, but the pleasure is fleeting, it's not sustainable, and after the pleasure of sin has faded there is just the misery it inevitably leaves behind. And every sin makes the world a little bit more of a mess.

Sin and evil are real. And they are not something that is "out there." They are in you and me. We each have the capacity for tremendous virtue and good, but we also have the capacity for sin and evil. These things are in us and we have to come to terms with them if we are going to live life to the fullest the way God wants us to.

So, what is sin?

Sin is usually spoken about as a behavior that is wrong or immoral. And it is, but the only way to truly understand sin is in the context of the relationship between God and humanity.

"God is infinitely good and all his works are good." (CCC 385) It is out of his goodness that God created us in his image and for good (Genesis 1:27–31).

Sin is more than just bad behavior. It is the rejection or destruction of something good. You cannot reject or destroy something that is good without rejecting *goodness itself*. God is goodness, and so, every sin is in some way a rejection of God. This is why the most devastating dimension of sin is separation from God (CCC 385–390). Sin breaks down our relationship with God, puts obstacles between us and Him.

We have a long history of turning away from God, offending God, and rejecting his goodness—this is where Jesus enters the story.

The central claims of Christianity are that God became man in Jesus, that he died on the cross to atone for our sins, and that he rose from the dead to liberate us from death. But Jesus also came to show us **the best way to live**. Nobody can teach you more about the best way to live than Jesus.

— **BE HONEST** —
WITH YOURSELF:
SIN MAKES YOU
UNHAPPY.

"I AM THE WAY, THE TRUTH, AND THE LIFE."

–Jesus Christ

THE TRINITY

God, the Father, is the first person of the Trinity. The Father is kind, merciful, and loving, and he gives in abundance. By calling God Father, the language of faith indicates two main things: that God is the origin of everything, and that he is goodness and loving care for all his children. (CCC 239)

Jesus, the Son, is the second person of the Trinity. The Son is one person with two natures: divine and human. He is true God and true man. (CCC 464)

The Holy Spirit is the third Person of the Trinity. He is the one whom Jesus promised the Father would send to guide and encourage us. When you think of it, the Holy Spirit is incredibly practical. How often in your life do you need guidance and encouragement?

In the Scriptures God is revealed as the Father, who created us (Genesis 1); his Son, who redeemed us (Matthew 1); and the Holy Spirit, who inspires us (Acts 1). The whole history we find in the Bible is the story of God's ongoing concern for the human family, and for each of us as his children.

Try this. Read the Gospel of Matthew. As you read about what Jesus taught, ask yourself, are these the solutions to the mess the world is in today? I think you will discover that Jesus has the antidote to the world's mess. Jesus is the solution.

What does this mean to you and me?

It is easy to say that the world is a mess. But the thing is, the more I become aware of who I really am, the more I discover that I'm a bit of a mess too. I do things every day that don't help me to become the-best-version-of-myself. And most of the time I don't actually want to do these things. Just like Paul wrote, "I do not do the good I want, but the evil I do not want is what I do"(Romans 7:19).

I am capable of incredible good, but sometimes I turn my back on God and his goodness. Sometimes I do it because I am stubborn and other times because I am lazy. Sometimes I turn my back on God and his goodness because the right path just seems too hard, and other times because I am selfish and just want what I want.

The truth is, I am a sinner, and sinners need a Savior. The world is a mess and I am a mess, but Jesus came to fix the mess. That's good news.

If you could have lunch with Mary, what would you ask her about Jesus?

DISCUSSION QUESTIONS

1. IN MANY WAYS THE WORLD IS AN INCREDIBLE PLACE, BUT IN LOTS OF OTHER WAYS IT IS A MESS. IN WHAT WAYS IS THE WORLD A MESS?

_____

_____

_____

_____

_____

_____

2. HOW DID THE WORLD GET TO BE SUCH A MESS?

_____

_____

_____

_____

_____

_____

3. WHAT IS SIN? HOW DOES IT AFFECT YOU?

_____

_____

_____

_____

_____

_____

_____

THE JESUS PROPHESIES

There have been lots of famous people throughout history. Neil Armstrong was famous for being the first man to walk on the moon. Rosa Parks was famous for standing up for justice. Pablo Picasso was famous for his paintings. Mozart and Beethoven were famous for their music. Christopher Columbus was famous for discovering the Americas. Shakespeare, Dickens, Tolstoy, and Austen were famous for their writings. But all their fame came during their lives or after they died. And it was largely the result of what they did.

Jesus was famous before he was born, and he was famous because of who he was—the long-awaited Messiah. Lots of people get written about while they are alive or after they die, but Jesus was written about hundreds of years before he was born.

ISAIAH 11 PROPHESIED that the Messiah would be a descendant of David. **MATTHEW 1:1** shows that this prophecy was FULFILLED.

GENESIS 49 PROPHESIED that the Messiah would be born of the tribe of Judah, one of the twelve tribes of Israel. **MATTHEW 1:** FULFILLED.

MICAH 5 PROPHESIED that the Messiah would be born in Bethlehem. **MATTHEW 2:** FULFILLED.

ISAIAH 7 PROPHESIED that the Messiah would be born of a virgin mother. **LUKE 1:** FULFILLED.

PSALM 72 PROPHESIED that kings would come and adore the Messiah. **MATTHEW 2:** FULFILLED.

PSALM 41 PROPHESIED that the Messiah would be betrayed. **MATTHEW 26:** FULFILLED.

ZECHARIAH 11 PROPHESIED that the Messiah would be sold for thirty pieces of silver. **MATTHEW 26:** FULFILLED.

Jesus was FAMOUS before He was BORN!

IF YOU DECIDED TO COMMIT YOUR WHOLE LIFE TO DOING GOOD, WHAT WOULD YOU DO?

AGAPE IS SELFLESS, SACRIFICIAL, UNCONDITIONAL LOVE. THIS IS THE LOVE WE ALL YEARN FOR AND USUALLY GO LOOKING FOR IN ALL THE WRONG PLACES. JESUS LAID DOWN HIS LIFE FOR OTHERS—FOR US. THAT IS A MONUMENTAL LOVE, A GENEROUS LOVE THAT PLACES THE GOOD OF THE OTHER PERSON ABOVE ANY SELFISH DESIRE.

3.3 JESUS WAS A *Radical*

If you really want to work out who Jesus is and discover what that means for you and your life, you need to delve deeply into his life and teachings.

Sometimes when you get familiar with something, you stop seeing it for what it really is. Jesus and his teachings have been a victim of this familiarity. Every Sunday we go to church and we hear a reading from the Gospel. Over time this can create the illusion that we know the Gospel, when in truth, most of us have barely scratched the surface of the life and teachings of Jesus Christ.

Once we really get into his life and teachings we discover quickly that *Jesus was a radical*. If you haven't encountered Jesus the radical lately, I'd encourage you to *take another look*. His life was radical. His teachings were radical. His love is radical. His invitation is radical.

His teachings were radical two thousand years ago, and they are just as radical now. Radical as they may be, they contain the answer to the question we began to explore in Session 1: What is the best way to live?

Even if you could prove to me indisputably that Jesus never existed, there is no God, and there is no life after death, no Heaven to look forward to, I would still believe that the teachings of Christianity (and those of Catholicism in particular) are the best way to live. I am absolutely convinced that there is no surer path to happiness in this life than embracing the teachings of Jesus Christ as set forth by the Catholic Church.

The radical nature of Jesus' life, teachings, and love is a constant source of inspiration. Let's explore some examples.

"You have heard that it was said, 'You shall love your neighbor and hate your enemy.' But I say to you, love your enemies and pray for those who persecute you." (Matthew 5:43–44)

This was radical teaching two thousand years ago. What was the teaching before this? An eye for an eye and a tooth for a tooth (Exodus 21:24, Leviticus 24:20, Deuteronomy 19:21).

Jesus came along and with one sentence on some dusty road or in a crowded synagogue wiped away the justification of revenge, and the moral, ethical, and spiritual development of humanity took a right turn.

This teaching is still radical two thousand years later. When was the last time you went out of your way to love someone who despises you, opposes you, or makes your life difficult?

And we are all persecuted in different ways by different people. Bullying is persecution. Excluding people is persecution. Ridicule, sarcasm, and negative humor are all persecution. When we are persecuted, our first reaction is probably not to pray for the person who is persecuting us. Our natural reaction is most likely some form of revenge. But Jesus wants to raise us above our natural reactions, and teach us to respond with grace.

In preparing the way for Jesus, John the Baptist said, "Whoever has two coats must share with anyone who has none; and whoever has food must do likewise." (Luke 3:11)

Think about that when you look in your wardrobe to get dressed tomorrow. Then consider that there are seven billion people on the planet today, one billion don't have enough clothes and more than two billion of them are hungry just for bread. On our watch!

Speaking of radical, you probably have lots of people talking to you about chastity and encouraging you not to have sex before marriage. In our hypersexual culture these messages might seem radical, but Jesus' teaching is much more radical.

"You have heard that it was said, 'You shall not commit adultery.' But I say to you that everyone who looks at a woman with lust has already committed adultery with her in his heart." (Matthew 5:27–28)

Guys, think about it—how often do you look at a girl lustfully? Ladies, how often do you look at a guy lustfully? Jesus said that to look at someone lustfully is to commit adultery in our hearts. That's radical.

Jesus calls us to a freedom that gives us the self-control to direct every aspect of our being—including where we turn our gaze and what we ponder when we look at something or someone.

These are just a few of the many examples of Jesus' radical teachings. But what was most radical was what he taught us about *love*. He taught us this not only with words, but also with his life.

The world portrays love as a selfish thing, there for our own pleasure and satisfaction. Jesus presents *agape*. Agape is selfless, sacrificial, unconditional love. This is the love we all yearn for and usually go looking for in all the wrong places. He laid down his life for others—for us. That is a monumental love, a generous love that places the good of the other person above any selfish desire.

John the Baptist was an itinerant preacher who lived around the time of Jesus. His main message is found at the beginning of the third chapter of Matthew's Gospel: "Repent, for the kingdom of heaven is at hand." (Matthew 3:2) Some people thought John the Baptist may have been the Messiah, but he made it clear that he was not, explaining that he had come to prepare the way for the Messiah. He said, "I baptize you with water for repentance, but he who is coming after me is mightier than I, whose sandals I am not worthy to carry; he will baptize you with the Holy Spirit." (Matthew 3:11) John baptized Jesus (Matthew 3:13–17). He also upset many of the leaders of his time by speaking out against their injustice and hypocrisy. John the Baptist was beheaded under orders from Herod, who had him killed to impress a woman. **Have you ever done something to impress a girl (or a guy)?**

John's central message of repentance is always needed. **To repent means to turn back to God.** Have you turned away from God in some area of your life? Is it time for you to turn back to God?

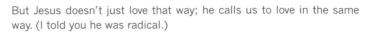

"I am the Way, the Truth, and the Life." John 14:5-7

KNOW IT: What three things did Jesus say he is?

THINK ABOUT IT: Would you be a-better-version-of-yourself if you followed Jesus' WAY, accepted his TRUTH, and embraced his LIFE?

LIVE IT: Allow Jesus to direct what you do sometime today!

But Jesus doesn't just love that way; he calls us to love in the same way. (I told you he was radical.)

On Sunday at Mass, after the Gospel has been read, I ask myself, "If I lived this one Gospel reading 100 percent, how much would my life change?" The answer is the same every week: radically.

There is a gap between my life and the life God invites me to live. There is a gap between the person I am and the person God created me to be. I have a long way to go. But I have started and I hope you will join me in the journey.

Most people think they are pretty good Christians. I even know non-Christians who think they are pretty good Christians. But compared to what? Compared to Jesus? No, most people don't use that as their measuring stick. Compared to the Gospel? Most people don't use that as their measuring stick either. Most compare themselves to what they see on television or to their peers. In most cases today this can be setting the bar very low indeed.

If you really want to explore the question of the best way to live, I recommend you get yourself a Bible and just start by reading the Gospel of Matthew. Read it slowly. Think about what you're reading. This way you will save yourself a lot of heartache and discover the path that leads to lasting happiness in this life and eternal happiness with God in the next life.

Along the way you will also discover the real Jesus, and you might discover he is very, very different to what you had previously thought.

ask yourself...

IF I LIVED THIS ONE Gospel READING 100%, HOW MUCH WOULD MY LIFE CHANGE?

RADICALLY.

DISCUSSION QUESTIONS

1. WHO DO YOU KNOW WHO TAKE THE TEACHINGS OF JESUS SERIOUSLY, ALLOWING THOSE LESSONS TO DIRECT THE WAY THEY LIVE THEIR LIVES?

_____

_____

_____

_____

_____

_____

2. HOW DO THE TEACHINGS OF JESUS CHALLENGE YOU TO RADICALLY CHANGE YOUR LIFE?

_____

_____

_____

_____

_____

_____

3. WHAT IS AGAPE LOVE? HOW IS IT DIFFERENT FROM THE WAY MOVIES, MUSIC, AND THE MEDIA PORTRAY LOVE?

_____

_____

_____

_____

_____

_____

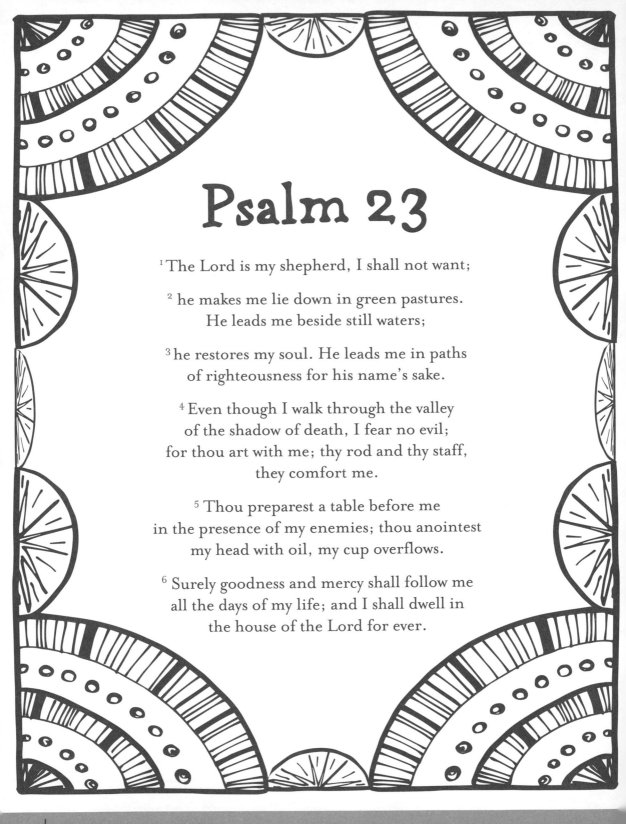

Psalm 23

¹ The Lord is my shepherd, I shall not want;

² he makes me lie down in green pastures.
He leads me beside still waters;

³ he restores my soul. He leads me in paths
of righteousness for his name's sake.

⁴ Even though I walk through the valley
of the shadow of death, I fear no evil;
for thou art with me; thy rod and thy staff,
they comfort me.

⁵ Thou preparest a table before me
in the presence of my enemies; thou anointest
my head with oil, my cup overflows.

⁶ Surely goodness and mercy shall follow me
all the days of my life; and I shall dwell in
the house of the Lord for ever.

"DO NOT BE AFRAID."
—JESUS CHRIST

GRACE IS THE HELP GOD GIVES US TO RESPOND TO HIS CALL AND TO DO WHAT IS GOOD AND RIGHT.

How do you think Mary felt when people mistreated Jesus?

3.4 SECOND ★ CHANCES

We spoke earlier about God's dream for you to become the-best-version-of-yourself. We also spoke about how sometimes we want to do the right thing, but we find ourselves doing the complete opposite.

You may be too young right now, but there will come a time in your life when you will try to overcome a bad habit but cannot. You will try and try again, but over and over you will fail. And then you will discover that some things cannot be done merely by willpower and your own strength and abilities. On this day you will discover your need for **grace**.

What is grace? Grace is the help God gives us to respond to his call, and to do what is good and right.

Grace gets us beyond the Paul dilemma: "I do not do the good I want, but the evil I do not want is what I do."

Ask an alcoholic who has tried to stop drinking and he will tell you that he tried and tried on his own, and failed. Finally, he surrendered to God, and *grace* allowed him to quit drinking and stay sober.

We all come up against bad habits we cannot shake at different times. These are the great intersections of our lives, the moments when we choose to surrender to God's grace or hold on stubbornly to our old self-destructive ways.

The truth is, you cannot become the-best-version-of-yourself on your own. You need grace. The fullness of the invitation is to become the-best-version-of-yourself in Jesus.

Without grace nothing is possible.

With all the talk of sin in the previous section, you may not be feeling so good about yourself. That's good. Seriously, that's really good. It means that you are in touch with your conscience. This is a sign of spiritual life.

Fortunately as Christians we believe in the forgiveness of sin. This is where grace and sin intersect.

We all need a fresh start from time to time.

One of the greatest sources of grace is the sacrament of **Reconciliation**. I am not going to give you a long lecture about it. I am just going to encourage you to go to Reconciliation . . . and to go regularly.

I try to go once a month. I need the grace. I need to take an honest look at myself. I need to be held accountable; it brings the best out of me. I need the spiritual coaching and guidance that I get in the sacrament of Reconciliation.

It's good for me and I love the peace that fills my heart when the priest says the words of absolution:

"God, the Father of mercies, through the death and resurrection of his Son has reconciled the world to himself and sent the Holy Spirit among us for the forgiveness of sins; through the ministry of the Church may God give you pardon and peace, and I absolve you from your sins in the name of the Father, and of the Son, and of the Holy Spirit. Amen."

The peace that comes from having our sins forgiven is a peace the world cannot give us. Do you have that peace? If you don't, maybe it's time you made a good confession.

VIRTUE IN FOCUS

Joy [joi]

A state of happiness that is independent of situations or circumstances

What brings you joy?

Who is the most joyful person you know?

What can you do to increase your capacity for joy and to bring more joy to others?

D·I·S·C·U·S·S·I·O·N
QUESTIONS

1. GRACE IS THE HELP GOD GIVES US TO RESPOND TO HIS CALL AND TO DO WHAT IS GOOD
   AND RIGHT. IN WHAT PART OF YOUR LIFE DO YOU NEED GOD'S GRACE MOST TODAY?

2. HOW DO YOU IMAGINE YOU WOULD BE DIFFERENT IF YOU WENT TO RECONCILIATION
   ONCE A MONTH?

3. WE ALL NEED TO BE FORGIVEN BY GOD AND OTHERS, AND WE ALL HAVE PEOPLE WE
   NEED TO FORGIVE. IN THE OUR FATHER WE PRAY, "FORGIVE US OUR TRESPASSES AS
   WE FORGIVE THOSE WHO TRESPASS AGAINST US." WHOM IS GOD CALLING YOU TO
   FORGIVE TODAY?

JESUS IS THE HEALER OF MY SOUL

THE GOSPEL OF Matthew

Matthew's Gospel is one of the four Gospels and the first book of the New Testament. Scholars believe it was written between AD 70 and 110, and that it was written by a Jewish author, for a Jewish Christian audience. The way Matthew tells the story of Jesus draws on many symbols from Jewish tradition to emphasize that Jesus is the long-awaited Messiah.

3.5 DECISION point

The Gospel of Matthew is my favorite. Maybe it is because my name is Matthew. Maybe it's because so many times I decided I would read the New Testament from start to finish and didn't get much past Matthew, so it is the Gospel I am most familiar with. But I think the reason is because the images, parables, and practicality of Matthew's Gospel resonate with me deeply.

In the ninth chapter we come across the story of the call of Matthew. It simply says:

"As Jesus was walking along, he saw a man called Matthew sitting at the tax booth; and he said to him, 'Follow me.' And he got up and followed him." (Matthew 9:9)

Matthew woke up and went to work as a tax collector that day just like he did on any other day. He didn't know his whole life was about to change. That's how God works. Our God is a God of surprises.

Jesus' invitation to Matthew is one he makes to us all. There is no great fanfare; he simply says, "Follow me."

Will you?

Will you follow Jesus?

Maybe you're not ready to make that decision. That's OK. But if that is the case, you have a responsibility to learn more about who Jesus is, so that you can decide to follow him or not. If you are really not sure if you want to follow Jesus, read the Gospel of Matthew, and get to know him more.

But don't just avoid the question. God doesn't like that. We read in the book of Revelation, "You are neither hot nor cold... So, because you are lukewarm, and neither hot nor cold, I am about to spew you out of my mouth." (Revelation 3:15–16)

Like Matthew the tax collector, today might feel like a regular day for you. But it isn't. Deciding to follow Jesus—or not to follow Jesus—is one of the biggest **decision points** you will come to in your life.

Invite Jesus into your heart and into your life, decide today to follow him, and many years from now, you will look back and know that today was a turning point in your life.

JOURNAL
QUESTIONS

1. HOW IS THIS SESSION CALLING YOU TO CHANGE?

_____
_____
_____
_____
_____
_____

2. ARE YOU GOING TO READ THE GOSPEL OF MATTHEW? WHY? WHY NOT?

_____
_____
_____
_____
_____

3. WHO IS YOUR FAVORITE EXAMPLE FROM HISTORY OF A PERSON WHO HAS FOLLOWED JESUS?

_____
_____
_____
_____
_____
_____
_____

ONE SOLITARY LIFE

BY JAMES ALLAN FRANCIS

He was born in an obscure village
The child of a peasant woman
He grew up in another obscure village
Where he worked in a carpenter shop
Until he was thirty when public opinion turned against him

He never wrote a book
He never held an office
He never went to college
He never visited a big city
He never traveled more than two hundred miles
From the place where he was born
He did none of the things
Usually associated with greatness
He had no credentials but himself

He was only thirty three

His friends ran away
One of them denied him
He was turned over to his enemies
And went through the mockery of a trial
He was nailed to a cross between two thieves
While dying, his executioners gambled for his clothing
The only property he had on earth

When he was dead
He was laid in a borrowed grave
Through the pity of a friend

Nineteen centuries have come and gone
And today Jesus is the central figure of the human race
And the leader of mankind's progress
All the armies that have ever marched
All the navies that have ever sailed
All the parliaments that have ever sat
All the kings that ever reigned put together
Have not affected the life of mankind on earth
As powerfully as that one solitary life

MY THOUGHTS

THE JESUS QUESTION
CROSSWORD PUZZLE

ACROSS

1. Purity and self-control in thought, conduct, and intention in the area of sexuality

4. Sexual relations with someone who is not your spouse

6. God wants to flood our hearts with _____

10. A state of pain or distress

11. Being treated unfairly because of your beliefs

12. The help God gives us to respond to his call, and to do what is good and right

13. The first four books of the New Testament that share the life and teachings of Jesus Christ

DOWN

2. To offend God by rejecting what is good, right, and true

3. Selfless, sacrificial, unconditional love

5. The new and countercultural teachings of Jesus were _____

7. The long-awaited Messiah

8. Devoid of connection to things religious or spiritual

9. Profoundly immoral

14. The Sacrament God gives us for the ongoing forgiveness of our sins

Answers on page 326

The
PRAYER
Process

God, grant me the serenity to accept the things I cannot change, courage to change the things I can, and wisdom to know the difference. Living one day at a time, enjoying one moment at a time, accepting hardships as the pathway to peace, taking, as Jesus did, this sinful world as it is, not as I would have it, trusting that you will make all things right, if I surrender to your will, so that I may be reasonably happy in this life, and supremely happy with you forever in the next. Amen.

— *The Serenity Prayer* —

> **PRAYER HELPS US TO DISCOVER WHO WE ARE AND WHAT WE ARE HERE FOR.**

4. THE PRAYER PROCESS

Some things help you to become the-best-version-of-yourself and some things don't. Prayer is one of the things that help.

Prayer may sound boring to you, but I can assure you if you feel that way you have never really experienced prayer.

As a human being you are a delicate composition of body and soul. You are not just a body. You have a soul, and throughout your life you will decide to fill your soul with something. The question is: What are you going to fill your soul with? God or the world? Joy or misery? Peace or turmoil?

Once again, you get to decide.

The world denies your spiritual self and treats you as if you are just a body. I want you to rebel against that lie.

In this session I simply want to encourage you to nurture your spiritual self, to pay attention to it in a world full of distractions, and to set aside a few minutes each day to spend in quiet prayer.

I want to convince you to *feed your soul*.

4.1 Why PRAY?

feed your soul.

Why pray? The answer is actually very simple: because you want to be happy. If there is a God, and if that God has a plan for your life, then trying to find happiness outside of that plan is impossible. Discovering God's beautiful plan for your life is essential to your happiness—and should be your *highest priority.*

I know you have lots of other priorities at the moment, but a day will come in your life when you'll realize that everything you thought was important is second to discovering God's plan for your life. The sooner that day comes, the better your life will be.

You will never be happy doing something other than God's will. So the question becomes: How do we discover God's will for our lives?

One of the ways we discover God's will is through regular prayer.

In the summer of 1845, Henry David Thoreau left Concord, Massachusetts, because he believed it had become too busy and too noisy. He built himself a little hut out by Walden Pond and began a two-year experiment in living a simple life. During his time there in the woods, he wrote these words:

"I went to the woods because I wanted to live life deliberately . . . I wanted to live deep and suck out all the marrow of life . . . to put to rout all that was not life . . . and not, when I came to die, discover that I had not lived."

In some ways, I pray for the same reason Thoreau went to the woods. I pray because I want to live life deliberately. I pray because I want to live life deeply and suck all the marrow out of life! I pray because I want to work out what really matters in this life and spend my time on those things. I pray because I don't want to come to the end of my life and discover that I have not really lived.

I have tried life with and without prayer, and found that life without prayer is unbearable. Without prayer, life doesn't make sense. I don't know how people live without prayer. I don't know how you could remain sane in this crazy, noisy, busy world without prayer. Living without prayer is like choosing to be blind, lame, deaf, and dumb.

But I didn't always feel this way. It all changed for me when I was about fifteen.

IF YOU TOLD ME YOU WANTED TO GET REALLY GOOD AT BASKETBALL OR FOOTBALL OR GOLF OR TENNIS.

I WOULD TELL YOU TO STUDY THOSE WHO HAVE BEEN THE BEST IN HISTORY. WHEN IT COMES TO PRAYER. MY ADVICE DOES NOT CHANGE. STUDY THE SAINTS: THEY WERE CHAMPIONS OF PRAYER.

"PRAYER GIVES US STRENGTH FOR GREAT IDEALS, FOR KEEPING UP OUR FAITH, CHARITY, PURITY, GENEROSITY; PRAYER GIVES US STRENGTH TO RISE UP FROM INDIFFERENCE AND GUILT, IF WE HAVE HAD THE MISFORTUNE TO GIVE IN TO TEMPTATION AND WEAKNESS. PRAYER GIVES US LIGHT BY WHICH TO SEE AND TO JUDGE FROM GOD'S PERSPECTIVE AND FROM ETERNITY. THAT IS WHY YOU MUST NOT GIVE UP ON PRAYING!"

—POPE JOHN PAUL II

Discussion Questions

1. WHOM DO YOU TALK TO EVERY DAY? WHY?

_____

_____

_____

_____

_____

_____

_____

2. DO YOU PRAY? HOW OFTEN? HOW DO YOU FEEL AFTER YOU PRAY?

_____

_____

_____

_____

_____

_____

_____

3. DO YOU THINK YOU WOULD BE HAPPIER IF YOU MADE TIME TO PRAY EACH DAY?

_____

_____

_____

_____

_____

_____

_____

My Thoughts

WHAT IS PRAYER?

AN EXPRESSION OF THANKS OR A SOLEMN REQUEST FOR HELP FROM GOD.

"PRAYER IS THE RAISING OF ONE'S MIND AND HEART TO GOD OR THE REQUESTING OF GOOD THINGS FROM GOD."

—SAINT JOHN DAMASCENE

4.2 THE BIG QUESTION

My life changed one Sunday afternoon when I was about your age. I didn't know it at the time. It seemed like another ordinary day, and the guy who changed my life I found pretty annoying at the time. This is what happened. . . .

At the time I was in high school. Everything at school was going very well—I had a great group of friends, a wonderful girlfriend, and a good part-time job. On the outside everything seemed fine, but on the inside a growing restlessness was building up.

One Sunday afternoon I was at a barbecue with some of my mates when I bumped into a family friend. He asked me how school was going. "Fine," I replied. But he was a doctor and doctors are good at asking questions, and he just kept asking me questions. Each question and each answer led us a little closer to his diagnosis. Then after about fifteen minutes, he paused briefly, looked deep into my eyes, and said, "You're not really happy, are you, Matthew?"

He knew it and I knew it, but I was ashamed to admit it at first. But our lives seem to flood with grace at unexpected moments, and I began to tell him about the emptiness and restlessness I was experiencing. After listening to me carefully he suggested I stop by my church for ten minutes each morning on the way to school.

I listened, smiled, nodded politely, and immediately dismissed him as some sort of religious fanatic. As he expanded on his idea and how it would transform my life, I wondered to myself, *how is ten minutes of prayer each day going to help me?* Before he had finished speaking I had resolved to completely ignore everything he said.

In the coming weeks I threw myself into my studies, my work, and my sporting pursuits with more vigor than ever before. I had done this to appease my restless heart at other times in my life. But achievement in these areas no longer brought the fulfillment it once had.

One morning about six weeks later the emptiness had become so great that I found myself stopping by church on the way to school. I crept quietly into the church, sat near the back, and began to plan my day. Just planning the day ahead of me lifted the clouds of hurried confusion. For the first time in my life I tasted a few drops of that wonderful tonic we call peace—and I liked it.

The next day, and every day, I returned. Each morning I would simply sit toward the back of the church and move through the events of the day in my mind. With each passing day a sense of peace, purpose, and direction began to fill me.

Then one day as I sat there it occurred to me that "planning my day" wasn't really prayer. So I began to pray: *God, I want this . . . and I need this . . . and could you do this for me . . . and help me with this . . . and let this happen . . . and please, don't let that happen. . . .*

For the next few weeks, this is how it went. Every morning I would stop by church, sit toward the back, plan my day, and tell God what I wanted. For a while this was the depth of my prayer life. And then one day I had a problem. That morning I came to the church and with a simple prayer in my heart, I looked up toward the tabernacle and began to explain, *God, I've got this problem. . . . This is the situation. . . . These are the circumstances. . . .* Then I stumbled onto the question that would change my life forever: *God, what do you think I should do?*

With that question my life began to change. Asking that question marked a new beginning in my life. Before that day, I had only been interested in telling God what *my* will was. Now for the first time I was asking God to reveal his will.

God, what do you think I should do? I call this the **Big Question.** It is the question that changed my life forever, and the question that continues to transform my life on a daily basis when I have the courage to ask it.

There is only one question and one course of action that leads to lasting happiness in this changing world: God, what do you think I should do? It is a mistake to think that we can find happiness without asking this question.

Our lives change when our habits change. Are you ready for your life to change?

TO **PRAY** IS TO **TALK TO GOD** ABOUT **ANYTHING THAT IS IN YOUR *heart:*** the things that bring you *joy* and the things that bring you ***sorrow;*** the **SUCCESSES** you experience and the **FAILURES** you encounter; *your strengths* and *talents;* **YOUR FAULTS** and **WEAKNESSES; YOUR HOPES** and **DREAMS.** In prayer you **TALK TO GOD** ABOUT *everything*.

What do you think Mary prayed for?

1. DESCRIBE A TIME WHEN SOMEONE CHALLENGED YOU TO DO SOMETHING THAT WOULD
   HELP YOU BECOME THE-BEST-VERSION-OF-YOURSELF. HOW DID YOU RESPOND?

_____

_____

_____

_____

_____

_____

_____

2. HAVE YOU EVER ASKED GOD THE BIG QUESTION: "WHAT DO YOU THINK I SHOULD DO?"
   IF YOU HAVE, WHAT HAPPENED? IF YOU HAVE NEVER ASKED GOD THE BIG QUESTION,
   WHY NOT?

_____

_____

_____

_____

_____

_____

_____

3. IF YOU SPENT TEN MINUTES A DAY IN PRAYER EVERY DAY FOR THE NEXT MONTH, HOW
   DO YOU THINK YOU MIGHT BE DIFFERENT A MONTH FROM NOW?

_____

_____

_____

_____

_____

_____

_____

4.3 The ⟶ PRAYER Process

Isaac Newton's first law states: An object at rest stays at rest and an object in motion stays in motion at the same speed, unless acted on by an external force.

The hard part is getting started. Have you ever noticed that when you sit down to start writing a paper, you get distracted by a million things? You remember three things you needed to do, you decide you are hungry and go to the fridge, you need to go to the bathroom, etc.

Getting started on anything can be excruciating. A space shuttle uses 96 percent of its fuel at takeoff.

It can be very difficult at first to take prayer seriously too. I don't say that to discourage you. I tell you this so that when you experience the difficulty you will realize it is normal and you will persevere.

The hardest things to do are those that have never been done before. The first time man went to the moon was incredibly difficult because everything had to be learned from scratch. Prayer isn't like that. Great men and women have been practicing prayer for thousands of years, and we can learn a lot from them.

Most people either don't pray at all or don't pray very much, because nobody has ever really taught them how to pray. In this session I am going to teach you **The Prayer Process.** I developed The Prayer Process a few years ago after studying hundreds of methods of prayer, because I wanted to give people a simple process that they could use every day to guide their conversation with God.

After all, that is what prayer ultimately is: a conversation with God.

The Prayer Process is designed to be very simple, yet deeply personal. It is made up of seven simple steps.

1. GRATITUDE: Begin by thanking God in a personal dialogue for whatever you are most grateful for today.

2. AWARENESS: Revisit the times in the past twenty-four hours when you were and were not the-best-version-of-yourself. Talk to God about these situations and what you learned from them.

3. SIGNIFICANT MOMENTS: Identify something you experienced in the past twenty-four hours and explore what God might be trying to say to you through that event (or person).

GETTING STARTED

The hardest part of anything is getting started. Prayer is no different. If you are having trouble, use the Psalms to pray. The Psalms are a powerful collection of prayers. Use them to get started— they will teach you how to pray, and before too long your own words will begin to flow.

4. PEACE: Ask God to forgive you for any wrong you have committed (against yourself, another person, or Him) and to fill you with a deep and abiding peace.

5. FREEDOM: Speak with God about how He is inviting you to change your life so that you can experience the freedom to be-the-best-version-of-yourself.

6. OTHERS: Lift up to God anyone you feel called to pray for today, asking God to bless and guide them.

7. Pray the Our Father.

The Prayer Process is quite simple and, like most things, easy to talk about. But the best way to understand it is to practice it!

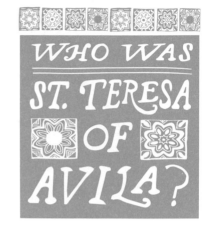

TERESA OF AVILA (1515–1582) WAS A CARMELITE NUN. SHE WAS A GREAT CATHOLIC AUTHOR AND MYSTIC, AND A CHAMPION OF PRAYER. TERESA WROTE EXTENSIVELY ABOUT THE IMPORTANCE OF HAVING INTIMATE AND PERSONAL CONVERSATION WITH GOD IN PRAYER. THIS IS KNOWN AS MENTAL PRAYER. HER FEAST DAY IS OCTOBER 15.

Want to learn more? Read *Conversation with Christ*, by Peter Rohrbach. It is a fabulous introduction to prayer.

A space shuttle uses 96% of its fuel at takeoff.

DISCUSSION QUESTIONS

1. HAS ANYONE EVER TAUGHT YOU HOW TO PRAY? WHO? WHEN?

_____
_____
_____
_____
_____
_____
_____

2. WHICH OF THE SEVEN STEPS IN THE PRAYER PROCESS INTRIGUED YOU THE MOST? WHY?

_____
_____
_____
_____
_____
_____
_____

3. IF YOU WERE GOING TO SET ASIDE TEN MINUTES TO PRAY AT THE SAME TIME EVERY DAY, WHAT TIME OF DAY WOULD BE BEST FOR YOU?

_____
_____
_____
_____
_____
_____

My Thoughts

THE **5** TYPES **OF PRAYER**

1 ADORATION

2 PETITION

3 INTERCESSION

4 THANKSGIVING

5 PRAISE

To learn more,
read CCC 2623–2643.

learn to LISTEN

EVERY RELATIONSHIP IMPROVES WHEN WE REALLY START TO LISTEN.

Søren Kierkegaard wrote, "Praying does not mean listening to yourself speak; praying means calming down and being still and waiting until you hear God."

4.4 The Best Way to learn

You get good at riding a bicycle, not by reading a book about bikes or listening to a lecture about riding techniques, but by actually riding a bicycle. Sure, the book and the lecture can be helpful, but ultimately you will hone your skills by spending time on the bike.

The same is true for prayer. It's good to talk about it and to read books about it, but at some point the best thing to do is just try it and see what you learn from actually praying.

There are two reasons most people don't pray: nobody ever taught them and they don't know where to start. The Prayer Process solves both of these problems. It teaches us how to pray and it gives us a simple step-by-step process, so we know exactly where to start.

What I would like to do now is to walk you through the process while you actually practice it. I'll keep talking to you, guiding you through the process, but there won't be anything to watch here on the screen. So, let's start by closing our eyes.

Now, get comfortable, so that you can be still and quiet for a few minutes, and take some deep breaths. Breathe in deep, and breathe out any stress or anxiety that you have in your life today.

Now, let's begin...

In the name of the Father, and of the Son, and of the Holy Spirit. Amen.

The first step in The Prayer Process is... GRATITUDE: Begin by thanking God in a personal dialogue for whatever you are most grateful for today.

> What are you grateful for at this time in your life? Talk to God about that. Don't just think about it. Have a mental conversation with God about everyone and everything you are grateful for today...

The second step in The Prayer Process is... AWARENESS: Revisit the times in the past twenty-four hours when you were and were not the-best-version-of-yourself. Talk to God about these situations and what you learned from them.

> Recall a time in the past twenty-four hours when you were the-best-version-of-yourself, even if it was just for a moment... Talk to God about that situation... tell him if it was easy or difficult... and how you felt...
>
> Now bring to mind a time in the past twenty-four hours when you were not the-best-version-of-yourself... Talk to God about why you

did what you did... tell him how you felt at the time... and how you felt after... and talk to him about how you are going to try to handle situations like that differently in the future...

The third step in the process is... SIGNIFICANT MOMENTS: Identify something you experienced in the past twenty-four hours and explore what God might be trying to say to you through that event (or person).

How have you experienced God in the past twenty-four hours? Did you sense that God was trying to tell you something through a person or something that happened? Talk to God about that now... again, try to go beyond just thinking about these things and have a mental conversation with God...

The fourth step in the process is... PEACE: Ask God to forgive you for any wrong you have committed (against yourself, another person, or Him) and to fill you with a deep and abiding peace.

Are you carrying around guilt or shame over something? God is your Father and he loves you deeply, ask him right now to forgive you and fill you with a deep, deep peace.

The fifth step in The Prayer Process is... FREEDOM: Speak with God about how He is inviting you to change your life so that you can experience the freedom to be the-best-version-of-yourself.

God loves you as you are today, but he loves you too much to let you stay this way. How do you sense God is calling you to change and grow? Talk to him about that... now ask him to give you the courage and strength to make this change in your life...

The sixth step in the process is... OTHERS: Lift up to God anyone you feel called to pray for today, asking God to bless and guide them.

Who do you want God to bless in a special way today? Talk to God about each of these people... and vocalize the specific ways you would like God to bless them... Take your time... Slowly pray for the people in your life... one at a time...

The final step of The Prayer Process is to pray the Our Father. It is a prayer most of us have been praying all our lives, but if we really comprehended the words of this prayer we would not be able to finish it without weeping for joy. So, let's pray it together, out loud, slowly and deliberately...

Our Father...

VIRTUE IN

FOCUS

Per·se·ver·ance
[pur-*suh*-**veer**-*uh* ns]

Continued effort to do or achieve something despite difficulties, delays, failure, or opposition.

Developing a dynamic prayer life requires perseverance more than anything else. **Just keep showing up.** Some days you will feel like praying and many days you will not, but if you keep showing up you will develop a phenomenal friendship with God.

PRAY
WITHOUT
CEASING
(1 Thessalonians 5:17)

We cannot pray every minute of every day. We have things to do. *What was Paul saying?* He was encouraging us to transform every moment of every day into a prayer. *How?* By offering each hour of study or work to God as a prayer, offering inconveniences and suffering to God as a prayer, and offering everything we do each day to God, we transform the ordinary realities of everyday life into prayer.

When I was a child I was taught to start my day by offering everything that was going to happen that day to God. This prayer is called a morning offering. There are many different versions; this is the one I was taught:

O Jesus, through the most pure heart of Mary, I offer you the prayer, works, joys, and sufferings of this day, for all the intentions of your divine heart.

Amen.

There is genius in Catholicism. It may not always be apparent on the surface, but behind each and every Catholic tradition are glimpses of the genius of Catholicism.

You can open your eyes now. Thanks for praying with me. For four years I have been working on this Confirmation program, and for four years I have been praying for you – the young men and women from all over the world who will experience it. I'm going to continue to pray for you every day. And I hope you will pray for me, and all the team at Dynamic Catholic, as we continue to work to develop resources to help you and others to have powerful encounters with God.

FEED YOUR SOUL

DISCUSSION

QUESTIONS

1. WHAT ARE YOU MOST GRATEFUL FOR TODAY?

_____

_____

_____

_____

_____

_____

2. WHAT SURPRISED YOU THE MOST AS YOU PRACTICED THE PRAYER PROCESS?

_____

_____

_____

_____

_____

_____

3. NOW THAT YOU HAVE BEEN TAUGHT HOW TO PRAY, WHAT IS MOST LIKELY TO GET IN THE WAY OF DEVELOPING PRAYER AS A DAILY HABIT IN YOUR LIFE?

_____

_____

_____

_____

_____

_____

STEP 1 GRATITUDE

Begin by thanking God in a personal dialogue for whatever you are most grateful for today.

STEP 2 AWARENESS

Revisit the times in the past twenty-four hours when you were and were not the-best-version-of-yourself. Talk to God about these situations and what you learned from them.

STEP 3 SIGNIFICANT MOMENTS

Identify something you experienced in the past twenty-four hours and explore what God might be trying to say to you through that event (or person).

STEP 4 PEACE

Ask God to forgive you for any wrong you have committed (against yourself, another person, or Him) and to fill you with a deep and abiding peace.

STEP 5 FREEDOM

Speak with God about how He is inviting you to change your life so that you can experience the freedom to be the-best-version-of-yourself.

STEP 6 OTHERS

Lift up to God anyone you feel called to pray for today, asking God to bless and guide them.

STEP 7 PRAY THE OUR FATHER

MY
THOUGHTS

4.5 DECISION point

MARK 1:35
MATTHEW 14:23
LUKE 5:16
LUKE 9:28

And LOTS OF OTHERS . . .

KNOW IT: Over and over we read about Jesus going off to quiet places to pray.

THINK ABOUT IT: If Jesus needed time to reflect and pray, how much more do you and I need it?

LIVE IT: Develop the daily habit of finding a quiet place to connect with God.

"MENTAL PRAYER IS NOTHING ELSE THAN AN INTIMATE FRIENDSHIP, A FREQUENT *heart-to-heart* CONVERSATION WITH HIM BY WHOM WE KNOW OURSELVES *to be loved.*"

–Saint Teresa of Avila

Over and over throughout the Gospels we read about Jesus going to quiet places to pray.

Mark 1:35: "In the morning, while it was still dark, he got up and went out to a deserted place, and there he prayed."

Matthew 14:23: "After he had dismissed the crowds, he went up a mountain by himself to pray."

Luke 5:16: "Now more than ever the word about Jesus spread abroad; many crowds would gather to hear him and be cured of their diseases. But he would withdraw to deserted places and pray."

Luke 9:28: "Jesus took with him Peter, James, and John, and went up on a mountain to pray."

Why did Jesus withdraw so often to pray? He was God, right? True. But he was also man. Imagine the distractions. The fame. The people who were trying to convince him to be a political or worldly leader. The people who were trying to use him for their own benefit. He withdrew to pray so that he could stay focused on his mission, to remember what really mattered.

We all get confused about what really matters from time to time. Prayer helps us to keep things in perspective.

We live in a noisy, busy world. If you are going to work out *who you are* and *what you are here for,* you need to step back from it all for a few minutes each day to reconnect with yourself and with God.

What place does prayer have in your life today? Is prayer at the center of your life or on the periphery of your life? Give prayer a central place in your life. Place prayer at the center of your life and amazing things will begin to happen.

Find a place where you can spend a few minutes with God each day. Set aside a time at the same time each day for prayer. Make this place and time a sacred part of your day, and God will fill you with his wisdom so you can make great decisions every day.

To pray or not to pray? That's your **decision point** today.

Here's my challenge for you: Practice The Prayer Process every day for thirty days. After thirty days I hope you are convinced that prayer should remain a daily habit for the rest of your life.

JOURNAL QUESTIONS

1. OVER AND OVER IN THE SCRIPTURES WE READ ABOUT JESUS GOING OFF TO A QUIET PLACE TO PRAY. DO YOU HAVE A QUIET PLACE WHERE YOU CAN PRAY EACH DAY? WHERE?

_____

_____

_____

_____

_____

_____

2. DO YOU HAVE A FAVORITE QUIET PLACE YOU LIKE TO GO WHEN YOU NEED TO MAKE BIG DECISIONS?

_____

_____

_____

_____

_____

_____

3. DID YOU DO ANYTHING TODAY THAT WAS MORE IMPORTANT THAN SPENDING A FEW MINUTES WITH GOD IN PRAYER?

_____

_____

_____

_____

_____

_____

THE GEOGRAPHY OF PRAYER

Do you pray only for yourself? If so, your geography of prayer is pretty small—tiny, in fact! As Christians, we believe we are called to pray for the whole world, and as such, the geography of our prayer should take in the whole world. When I was in high school I was given a rosary. Each of the five decades was a different color and represented a different region of the world. The idea was to offer each decade for the people in those different regions, thus praying for the whole world.

First decade (green beads): Pray for Africa

Second decade (red beads): Pray for the Americas

Third decade (white beads): Pray for Europe

Fourth decade (blue beads): Pray for the South Pacific

Fifth decade (yellow beads): Pray for Asia

Prayer is powerful. If we love our neighbor, we will pray for our neighbor. As Catholics, the geography of our prayer even reaches beyond this world when we pray for our loved ones who have died, that they may be united with God in paradise.

The geography of prayer is just one of millions of beautiful realities that make up our faith.

Psalm 42

As a hart long for flowing streams, so longs my soul for thee, O God. ²My soul thirsts for God, for the living God. When shall I come and behold the face of God? ³My tears have been my food day and night, while men say to me continually, "Where is your God?"

⁴These things I remember, as I pour out my soul: how I went with the throng, and led them in procession to the house of God, with glad shouts and songs of thanksgiving, a multitude keeping festival. ⁵Why are you cast down, O my soul, and why are you disquieted within me? Hope in God; for I shall again praise him, my help ⁶and my God.

My soul is cast down within me, therefore I remember thee from the land of Jordan and of Hermon, from Mount Mizar. ⁷Deep calls to deep at the thunder of thy cataracts; all thy waves and thy billow have gone over me. ⁸By day the Lord commands his steadfast love; and at night his song is with me, a prayer to the God of my life.

⁹I say to God, my rock: "Why hast thou forgotten me? Why go I mourning because of the oppression of the enemy?" ¹⁰As with a deadly wound in my body, my adversaries taunt me, while they say to me continually, "Where is your God?" ¹¹ Why are you cast down, O my soul, and why are you disquieted within me? Hope in God; for I shall again praise him, my help and my God.

ACROSS

2. The absence of noise

3. A state of great unhappiness that comes from turning our backs on God

5. A state of being thankful and showing appreciation

6. The immense happiness that comes from walking with God in all things

11. People, besides yourself, whom you feel inspired to pray for

12. A conversation with God

13. The spiritual or immaterial part of a human being

14. Something that is more important than other things and needs to be done first

DOWN

1. The ability to perceive what is really happening within us and around us

4. To do something again and again to get good at it

7. A state of being that is free from stress and anxiety

8. A state of great disturbance, confusion, or uncertainty

9. The strength of character to do what is good and right

10. Important, meaningful

Answers on page 326

SESSION FIVE

The BIBLE

Loving Father, Thank you for this day and thank you for this opportunity to explore your Word in the Scriptures. Inspire me to live with passion and purpose. Help me to discover the genius of your ways. Quiet my mind and open my heart so that I can hear exactly what you are trying to say to me today. Give me wisdom to embrace your ways with joy; give me courage to walk with you at every moment; give me strength when the world makes me weary; and help me to remember that I can always find rest and renewal in the Scriptures. Amen.

Matthew Kelly

5. THE BIBLE

Albert Einstein said, "I want to know the thoughts of God, the rest are details."

The Bible is not just another book. It's the Word of God. You have probably heard that a lot. But what does it really mean? For one thing, words have value based on who speaks them. If you knew someone who was always telling lies and he told you something, you would discount what he said because you know from experience that he has a habit of lying.

Some people's words should be discounted. But this here—the Bible, the Word of God—is not to be discounted. God should be taken at his word. The Bible should be taken very seriously. Your happiness in this life and the next life depends in large part on how seriously you take the Word of God.

Here's the mysterious thing about the Bible: It has the power to transform our lives. That's why so many people don't read it! Seriously.

God wants to transform *you* and *your life*. Too often when we pray, we pray for *tweaking*. We want God to *tweak* this and *tweak* that. But God is not interested in tweaking. God is in the business of *transformation.* He wants to turn your life upside down, which as it turns out is right side up. He wants to transform the way you think about yourself, he wants to transform the way you think about relationships, he wants to transform the way you think about money and career, and he wants to transform the way you think about the world and the culture.

If you want to see something incredible, *start praying for transformation*. Ask God to transform you and your life. Most people have never prayed a prayer of transformation.

The truth is, your happiness depends upon discovering God's will for your life, and the Bible can help you with that. But too often we are not interested in discovering the will of God. Usually we are more interested in "my will be done" than "thy will be done." Think about it: When was the last time you actively sought out God's will in a situation?

The Bible leads us to God's mysterious and fabulous plan for our lives— and that is always transformational. This is not just another book.

5.1 A Map for the Journey

Many years ago, I read an article in a travel magazine about the Camino. The Camino is a pilgrimage, a five-hundred-mile walk that begins in the South of France, crosses the Pyrenees into Spain, and then works its way west across northern Spain, finishing in Santiago de Compostela—where Saint James, one of the twelve apostles, is buried.

I remember reading the article and thinking that it would be an amazing adventure . . . but I also remember thinking that it was the kind of thing that I would never do. Why? Two main reasons: I am not really the outdoors type and I didn't figure I would ever take a month off. But ten years later, I decided to make the pilgrimage.

A pilgrimage is a spiritual journey to a holy place. Sometimes people go on a pilgrimage in search of answers to questions, and sometimes they do it to thank God for a special favor. I was going for both reasons. I was grateful for all the blessings God had given me, but I had questions about what I should do with the rest of my life.

I blocked a whole month on my schedule (a year in advance) and began to research everything I needed to know for the trip. I read books, studied the route, looked into where to eat and where to stay along the way, what the weather would be like, what clothes to bring and what boots to wear, what to pack and what to leave behind, and I talked to people who had made the journey.

My biggest question was: How will I know if I am going the right way? I had read that an image of a seashell was used to direct pilgrims along the path. But I had also heard that in many places this symbol was faded, which often caused pilgrims to take the wrong path.

Then, I met a couple who had made the pilgrimage seven times. They said to me, "You've got to get a copy of this particular guidebook! It's the bible of the Camino." I immediately ordered a copy.

The book was amazing. It had maps and routes, suggested starting and ending points for each day, elevations and distances. It showed you where fresh water was available to fill your water bottle, and warned you not to drink the water in certain places. It showed you options for where to stay and where to eat. It marked spots on the map where the signs were faded, and gave specific instructions about what to do in those places. And at every step along the way, it told you how far to the next place for food, water, or sleep. That guidebook was invaluable. It gave me confidence for the journey.

The Bible is that guidebook for your life.

WHAT IS A PILGRIMAGE?

A spiritual journey to a holy place.

TOP TEN CATHOLIC PILGRIMAGES

1. St. Peter's Basilica, the Vatican
2. Jerusalem, Israel
3. Lourdes, France
4. Fatima, Portugal
5. Camino de Santiago, Spain
6. Ephesus, Turkey
7. Guadalupe, Mexico
8. Czestochowa, Poland
9. Assisi, Italy
10. Knock, Ireland

"A thorough knowledge of the Bible is worth more than a college education."

THEODORE ROOSEVELT

WHAT IS A HOLY PLACE?

A PLACE SET APART FOR GOD BECAUSE OF SPECIAL RELIGIOUS SIGNIFICANCE. JERUSALEM IS A HOLY PLACE BECAUSE JESUS LIVED, TAUGHT, DIED, AND ROSE FROM THE DEAD THERE. YOUR LOCAL PARISH CHURCH IS A HOLY PLACE BECAUSE IT IS THE CENTER OF WORSHIP FOR YOUR COMMUNITY.

WHAT IS YOUR FAVORITE HOLY PLACE?

Whether you realize it or not, you are on a sacred journey. Life is a pilgrimage and you are a pilgrim. Remember, a pilgrimage is a spiritual journey to a holy place. A pilgrim is someone on a journey to a holy place. The holy place we are journeying toward is Heaven.

The world doesn't want you to be a pilgrim on a spiritual journey. The world wants you to be a tourist. A pilgrim travels with purpose. A tourist travels only for pleasure. You have to decide—do you want to be a tourist or a pilgrim?

There is more to life than life. You will die one day and it is healthy to think about that from time to time. If you died today and had to account to God for the way you have lived your life, how would you fare?

God wants you to live a rich, full, and happy life—and he provides the Bible as a map for that.

Where do you think was Mary's favorite place to pray?

DISCUSSION QUESTIONS

1. DO YOU THINK OF THE BIBLE AS A GUIDEBOOK? IF NOT, WHAT IS YOUR PERCEPTION OF THE BIBLE?

_____
_____
_____
_____
_____
_____

2. IN WHAT WAYS ARE YOU A TOURIST AND IN WHAT WAYS ARE YOU A PILGRIM?

_____
_____
_____
_____
_____
_____

3. HOW COMFORTABLE WOULD YOU BE IF YOU DIED TODAY AND HAD TO ACCOUNT FOR THE WAY YOU HAVE LIVED YOUR LIFE?

_____
_____
_____
_____
_____
_____

Gud är kärlek

Bog yest' lyubov'

ANG DIYOS AY PAG-IBIG

GOD IS LIEFDE

GOTT · IST · DIE · LIEBE

amor

DEUS É AMOR

DEUS CARITAS EST

GOD IS LOVE

UPENDO

MUNGU NI

Dios · es · amor

Hami wai aideari

DDUW YW CARIAD

Amore

Dio è

Elohim ahavah

Allah Adalah Kasih

Dieu est amor

5.2 INTRODUCTION TO THE BIBLE

One of the ways God loves us is by revealing himself to us. He does not remain a distant, anonymous God; he allows us to know him. Not only does God reveal himself to us but he also reveals his loving plans. We call this Divine Revelation.

There are many things we can know just by observing the natural world, such as the law of gravity and the regularity of the seasons from one year to the next. But there are some things we can only know because God reveals them to us; for example, the Trinity, the fact that God is three persons in one: Father, Son, and Holy Spirit. We only know this because God has revealed it to us.

God reveals himself to us in two ways, through Sacred Scripture and through Sacred Tradition. Sacred Scripture is the Bible. Sacred Tradition is the teachings that have been handed down from the apostles to their successors through preaching, example, and life of worship, even before the New Testament was written.

Both Scripture and Tradition make up the Word of God, and both were entrusted to the Church to interpret and share with the people of every place and time. If you separate the Scriptures from Tradition, the Scriptures begin to die. They are kept alive through their connection with Sacred Tradition. Separate the Scriptures from Tradition and it becomes very easy to misinterpret them.

The first generation of Christians didn't have a written New Testament; the Church existed before it was written. The New Testament itself is the fruit of Sacred Tradition, and a beautiful demonstration of the role Tradition has always played in the lives of Christians from the very beginning. It is impossible to truly appreciate the Bible unless we understand the connection between the Bible and the Sacred Tradition of the Catholic Church.

The Bible is made up of seventy-three books—forty-six in the Old Testament and twenty-seven in the New Testament. The Old Testament can be divided into three sections: the Historical Books, the Wisdom Books, and the Prophets. The New Testament can be divided into five sections: the Gospels, the Acts of the Apostles, the Letters of Saint Paul, the Catholic Letters, and the book of Revelation.

The books of the Bible are:

THE OLD TESTAMENT

THE HISTORICAL BOOKS

Genesis
Exodus
Leviticus
Numbers
Deuteronomy
Joshua
Judges
Ruth
1 Samuel
2 Samuel
1 Kings
2 Kings
1 Chronicles
2 Chronicles
Ezra
Nehemiah
Tobit

Judith
Esther
1 Maccabees
2 Maccabees

THE WISDOM BOOKS

Job
Psalms
Proverbs
Ecclesiastes
Song of Solomon
Wisdom
Sirach (Ecclesiasticus)

THE PROPHETS

Isaiah
Jeremiah
Lamentations
Baruch
Ezekiel
Daniel
Hosea
Joel
Amos
Obadiah
Jonah
Micah
Nahum
Habakkuk
Zephaniah
Haggai
Zechariah
Malachi

THE NEW TESTAMENT

THE GOSPELS

Matthew
Mark
Luke
John

THE ACTS OF THE APOSTLES

THE LETTERS OF SAINT PAUL

Romans
1 Corinthians
2 Corinthians
Galatians
Ephesians
Philippians
Colossians
1 Thessalonians
2 Thessalonians
1 Timothy
2 Timothy
Titus
Philemon
Hebrews

THE CATHOLIC LETTERS

James
1 Peter
2 Peter
1 John
2 John
3 John
Jude

REVELATION (APOCALYPSE)

ARE·YOU·READY·FOR
GOD'S
Amazing
PLAN
FOR·YOUR·LIFE?

The Bible was originally written in Hebrew and Greek, and has been translated into more languages than any other book. It was written by hundreds of different authors between approximately 1500 BC and 100 AD.

In the Old Testament God reveals himself as the Creator who is deeply interested in a relationship with humanity. In the New Testament he reveals his mercy and overwhelming desire that all people experience his love—more proof of God's incredible yearning for a relationship with us.

If you want to get a sense of what the Old Testament is all about, read Genesis. The book of Genesis demonstrates that there is a great cause-and-effect relationship between obedience to God and happiness, and between disobedience and misery. Genesis shows us, over and over again, what happens if you follow the ways of God and what happens if you follow the ways of the world. In Genesis we see an in-depth study of the human condition.

The New Testament presents the life and teachings of Jesus Christ and the life of the early Church.

All this might lead you to ask, where did the Bible come from?

It did not fall from Heaven as a single book. Nor did God dictate it mechanically to scribes. God chose certain people whom he inspired to write down what he wanted to convey to humanity. The Bible came together over the course of more than sixteen hundred years, and hundreds of authors were involved in writing the Bible as we know it today.

You could spend your whole life just studying Sacred Scripture and it would be a life well spent. And truth be told, very few lives are really well spent. I hope you spend yours well and I hope this program is helping to prepare you for that.

But if you did spend your whole life studying the Bible you would discover that it is not just a theological book. The Bible is immensely practical. It can show you how to get to Heaven, but it can also show you how to live on earth. In many ways it is a guide to a happy life.

> "ANYONE WHO SEEKS TRUTH SEEKS GOD, WHETHER OR NOT HE REALIZES IT."
>
> Saint Edith Stein

What do you think were Mary's hopes and fears?

discussion questions

1. WHAT NEW THING DID YOU LEARN ABOUT THE BIBLE IN THIS SECTION?

_____

_____

_____

_____

_____

_____

2. WHAT'S YOUR FAVORITE BOOK IN THE BIBLE? WHY?

_____

_____

_____

_____

_____

_____

3. IF YOU COULD BE ONE PERSON IN THE BIBLE, WHO WOULD YOU WANT TO BE? WHY?

_____

_____

_____

_____

_____

_____

YOU MAY BE SAYING TO YOURSELF,
"I am too young
to be thinking about all this serious stuff!"
BUT THAT WOULD BE A MISTAKE.
MOZART *was* EIGHT *years old*
when *he wrote* his first *symphony.*
JESUS was **TWELVE** years old
WHEN HE FIRST TAUGHT IN THE TEMPLE.
ANNE FRANK *was* THIRTEEN
——— *when she wrote her diary.* ———
RALPH WALDO EMERSON was
FOURTEEN when he enrolled at Harvard.
JOAN *of* ARC *was* SEVENTEEN
WHEN SHE LED THE FRENCH ARMY.
BILL GATES was **NINETEEN**
——— when he co-founded Microsoft. ———
YOU ARE NOT TOO YOUNG
TO START THINKING ABOUT THESE THINGS.
You are not too young
to start thinking seriously about your life.

5.3 HOW SHOULD I USE THE IBLE?

When it comes to reading the Bible, the first rule is: Don't be intimidated. So many people never read the Bible because they get intimidated. If you come across something you don't understand, just press on. Don't get bogged down.

Don't be intimidated by the Bible. This is our book. It lays out a blueprint for happiness. It helps us to know the heart of God, and his incredible dreams for us. And the Bible teaches us how to listen to the voice of God in our own lives.

So, where to start?

I would like to recommend that you start with three books.

1. The Gospel of Matthew.

First, as we discussed in Session 3, read the Gospel of Matthew. This will help you to delve deeply into the life and teachings of Jesus.

2. The book of Genesis.

Next read Genesis. This will give you incredible insight into the human condition, show you what happens when we walk with God and what happens when we turn our backs on him, and help you to see that the world is a bit of a mess and the Gospel is the antidote.

3. The book of Psalms.

Finally, read the Psalms; better still—pray them! This is the most beautiful collection of prayers. Here you will find a prayer for every occasion in your life. You will encounter every emotion in the Psalms: joy, sorrow, hope, desperation, trust, fear, confusion, clarity, and many more.

Begin by reading one chapter a day. It will take you twenty-eight days to work your way through Matthew and fifty days to make your journey through Genesis. If you then pray three Psalms a day it will take you fifty days to make your way through all 150 Psalms.

In just 128 days you will have a good sense of what the Bible is all about.

> "LOOK, THE VIRGIN SHALL CONCEIVE AND BEAR A SON, AND THEY SHALL NAME HIM EMMANUEL, WHICH MEANS 'GOD IS WITH US.'"
> Matthew 1:23

KNOW IT: At every moment of every day God is with us.

THINK ABOUT IT: Do you recognize and acknowledge God's presence in your daily life? Or are you oblivious to him by your side?

LIVE IT: Today when you are moving from one activity to another, use those gaps in your day to talk to God about what just happened or what is about to happen.

When you read your chapter, approach it with an open heart, listening for what God is saying to you. As you read, identify a word, phrase, or idea in each chapter that jumps out at you, something that taps you on the shoulder.

For example, you might be reading the first chapter of Matthew's Gospel. The first seventeen verses are the genealogy of Jesus—not the most interesting reading for a Bible rookie. But the phrase that often strikes me when I read this first chapter of Matthew is verse 23: "Look, the virgin shall conceive and bear a son, and they shall name him Emmanuel, which means 'God is with us.'"

"God is with us." There may have been times in your life when God has felt very far away. There have almost certainly been times when you have wandered far from God. I hope there have also been some times in your life when you have felt God was near. But here is the elemental truth: God is with us.

And each day, before you begin reading the Bible, pray asking God to help you to listen to what he is trying to say to you. It could be something as a simple as:

"Loving Father, I know you have good plans for me. Open my heart and my mind so that I can hear clearly what you are trying to say to me through the Scriptures today."

The process is quite simple.

1. Begin with a short prayer.

2. Read a chapter of the Bible.

3. Pick out a word, phrase, or idea that jumps out at you.

4. Talk to God about it.

If you read the same chapter many times, you might be drawn to different phrases or ideas on different days.

Even if you pick the same phrase, you may have very different conversations with God about that same phrase. Perhaps you pick the phrase "God is with us." You may have a conversation with God about how you sense his presence guiding you and encouraging you. But you may come back in a couple of years and read the same chapter, pick out the same phrase, and have a conversation with God about how he feels far from you at that time.

Talk to God about the word or phrase that strikes you, and listen for what he is trying to say to you through it. Just as we discussed with The

THE PROCESS IS QUITE SIMPLE.

Begin with a short prayer.

Read a chapter of the Bible.

Pick out a word, phrase or idea that jumps out at you.

Talk to God about it.

"GOOD. BETTER. BEST. NEVER LET IT REST. TILL YOUR GOOD IS BETTER AND YOUR BETTER IS BEST."

SAINT JEROME

SAINT JEROME (347–420) was a priest, confessor, theologian, and historian. He is most famous for translating the Bible into Latin. It took him twenty-three years to complete the translation. Can you imagine translating the whole Bible? Jerome wrote,

"IGNORANCE OF SCRIPTURES IS IGNORANCE OF CHRIST."

He is the patron saint of librarians and his feast day is September 30.

Prayer Process, it is important that you don't just sit there and think about it. The point is to have a conversation with God about whatever that particular Scripture stirs in your heart.

Another great way to connect with the Scriptures is to bring your Bible to Mass. Sure, most churches have those booklets that have the readings in them, but there is something very powerful about holding a Bible. It's different. Try it and you will see.

This requires some advance preparation. I like to mark the readings with Post-it notes before I go to Mass. Otherwise, I am distracted looking for the readings in my Bible during Mass. Next week's readings are usually published in the bulletin, or you can find them online.

Spend some time preparing for Mass next week, and bring your Bible— you will have a completely different experience.

I also want to encourage you to bring your Bible to these classes. Throughout the rest of this program we will be referring to passages from the Bible. Each time we do, find the passage in your Bible and mark it with an asterisk or underline it.

Don't be afraid to write in your Bible. It's yours. It's there to help you learn and grow spiritually, and sometimes highlighting a passage or underlining a phrase can be very helpful. This will also help you over time to see what parts of the Bible you have spent time with.

The last thing I want to encourage you to do in this section is to identify some favorite Bible passages. Memorize them. These will be of great comfort and guidance to you throughout your life.

Here are some of mine:

"Be still and know that I am God." Psalm 46:10

Life is busy and noisy and distracting, and that can all be overwhelming at times. Sometimes it helps just to sit down, be quiet, sit still, and recognize God's presence.

Another of my favorite Scripture passages is:

"Seek first the kingdom of God and his justice, and all else will be given in addition." Matthew 6:33

You will be amazed the clarity that this one line of Scripture can bring to decision-making. We are making hundreds of choices every day, and each choice celebrates the kingdom of God or rejects it. Happiness comes from seeking God and his kingdom. If we put that first in our decisions, so many of the other things of this world will take care of themselves.

"What does the Lord require of you? But to live justly, love tenderly, and to walk humbly with your God." Micah 6:8

This is almost like a mini-Gospel. We could spend our whole lives just reflecting on this one passage, examining ourselves each day: Am I living justly? Am I loving tenderly? Am I walking humbly with my God?

Finally, I would like to encourage you to have a favorite Psalm. Read it often, but also memorize it. There will be times in your life when you are too tired, too distracted, or too conflicted to form your own words for prayer. At these times you will find yourself praying your Psalm.

My favorite is Psalm 23: *"The Lord is my shepherd, there is nothing I shall want . . ."*

There are a hundred ways to invite the Scriptures into our lives. I hope you will make reading the Bible part of your daily routine. If you do, I am confident you will find it a life-changing habit.

IF YOU DON'T HAVE TIME TO PRAY AND READ THE SCRIPTURES, YOU ARE BUSIER THAN GOD EVER INTENDED YOU TO BE.

What do you think Mary looked forward to each day?

1. HOW DO YOU FEEL ABOUT THE CHALLENGE TO READ THE BIBLE FOR A FEW MINUTES EACH DAY?

_____
_____
_____
_____
_____
_____

2. HOW DO YOU THINK YOUR LIFE WOULD CHANGE IF YOU DID READ THE BIBLE FOR A FEW MINUTES EACH DAY?

_____
_____
_____
_____
_____
_____

3. OTHER THAN READING THE BIBLE, WHAT OTHER HABITS COULD HELP YOU BECOME THE-BEST-VERSION-OF-YOURSELF?

_____
_____
_____
_____
_____
_____

VIRTUE IN FOCUS

Kind·ness
[kahynd-nis]

The act of being friendly, generous, and considerate

Has anyone shown you kindness today? Who? How?

How does it make you feel when someone is kind to you?

Who is one person in your life whom God is calling you to be kinder to?

5.4 THE POWER OF HABIT

Albert Einstein also said, "Compound interest is the most powerful force in the universe." You might be thinking, what on earth does compound interest have to do with the Bible. Let me explain.

To demonstrate the power of compound interest, let's take a look at an example.

If from your eighteenth birthday you saved just three dollars a day, every day, until your sixty-fifth birthday, you would have saved $51,465. But if you invested that money at a compounding interest rate of 10 percent, you would have more than a million dollars—$1,017,046, to be exact.

But most people don't retire with anywhere near that much money. In fact, the latest data shows that at age sixty-five the average American has a net worth of just $66,740. Most people never engage the power of compounding interest. Most wait until far too late in life to start saving for retirement—and it matters.

In the example we discussed, if everything else remained the same except you waited until you were thirty to start saving your three dollars a day, instead of retiring with more than a million dollars, you would have just $316,115.

What's the lesson here? The earlier you start saving the better.

Habits are even more powerful than compounding interest, and they have the same powerful compounding impact on our lives. The earlier you develop some foundational positive habits, the better.

What are your habits? What are the things you do every day or every week with unrelenting consistency? Are they helping you or hurting you?

Tell me what your habits are and I will tell you what your future looks like. Thoughts become choices, choices become actions, actions become habits, habits become character, and your character is your destiny. Your life is running in the direction of your habits much faster than you might think.

Life is choices. Make a choice often enough and it will become an ingrained habit.

You can, of course, be on the wrong side of compound interest. Run up some credit card debt that you can't pay off and you will discover that many of those cards have 21 percent interest rates. You will then find yourself very much on the wrong side of compounding interest.

The same can happen with habits. No drug addict or alcoholic ever set out to become a slave to their addiction. It happened one step at a time, one choice at a time, and before they knew it they were trapped. Habits are incredibly powerful—for better or for worse.

How would you like your life to be different this year than it was last year? Our lives change when our habits change. If you want your life to be different this year, change your habits. If you want to do better academically, change your habits. If you want to do better in a sport, change your habits. If you want to have more fulfilling relationships, change your habits.

You may be quite content with your life today, but there will be times when you will encounter profound discontentment. When you come to those moments, I want you to remember: Our lives change when our habits change.

Throughout this program I am trying to help you to establish some foundational habits in your life. In Session 4 we explored the habit of daily prayer. Now I want to encourage you to add the habit of reading the Bible for a few minutes each day. Perhaps you could start your day reading a chapter from the Bible and end your day with The Prayer Process. There are going to be a few defining foundational habits in your life. I hope prayer and reading the Bible are among them.

There are so many habits, good and bad, that can impact the direction of your life. You know the habits that will help you become the best-version-of-yourself and the ones that will not.

What will be the defining habits of your life?

Let me share with you something I have learned from trying to read the Bible each day for twenty years: It is never convenient. It is always inconvenient. There are always other things you could be doing, and often there will be other things you would rather be doing. There will be those days when you yearn to read the Bible and talk with God about what you discover. But those days will likely be quite rare. There are going to be times when you feel like you are getting nothing out of it. When you encounter those times I want to encourage you to persevere. At those times I want you to hear me whispering into your ear, "Press on. Press on. The effort will be worth it in the long run."

One day you will be glad you did. I promise you.

WHO WAS Saint James?

James was one of Jesus' twelve apostles. He was the son of Zebedee and Salome, and the brother of John the Apostle. Jesus sent the disciples to preach the Gospels to the ends of the earth, and James did just that, traveling to the region along the western coast of Spain to share the Good News with anyone who would listen. Saint James is buried in the cathedral in Santiago de Compostela, the famous destination of the Camino. Pilgrims have been walking that path for hundreds of years. Saint James is the patron saint of Spain and his feast day is July 25.

"SEEK FIRST THE KINGDOM OF GOD AND HIS JUSTICE, AND ALL ELSE WILL BE GIVEN IN ADDITION."

MATTHEW 6:33

The inconvenience of having the discipline to read the Bible daily is a microcosm of a much larger truth: Christianity is inconvenient. But it will bring you a joy that you have not even imagined yet. So embrace the life and teachings of Jesus like you would a good friend whom you have not seen for a long time. Embrace the genius of Catholicism and you will live a life uncommon.

You matter, your happiness matters, and that's why habits matter.

You may be saying to yourself, "I am too young to be thinking about all this serious stuff!" But that would be a mistake. Mozart was eight years old when he wrote his first symphony. Jesus was twelve years old when he first taught in the Temple. Anne Frank was thirteen when she wrote her diary. Ralph Waldo Emerson was fourteen when he enrolled at Harvard. Joan of Arc was seventeen when she led the French army. Bill Gates was nineteen when he co-founded Microsoft. You are not too young to start thinking about these things. You are not too young to start thinking seriously about your life.

KNOW IT: God's priorities are clear.

THINK ABOUT IT: How clear are you about your priorities? Are they good priorities?

LIVE IT: Do something today that puts God's priorities at the center of your life.

DISCUSSION QUESTIONS

1. WHO DO YOU KNOW WHO HAS GREAT HABITS? WHAT ARE THOSE HABITS?

_____

_____

_____

_____

_____

_____

2. HAVE YOU EVER SEEN BAD HABITS DESTROY A PERSON'S LIFE?

_____

_____

_____

_____

_____

_____

_____

3. WHAT WILL BE THE BIGGEST OBSTACLE TO YOU ESTABLISHING THE HABIT OF READING THE BIBLE FOR A FEW MINUTES EACH DAY?

_____

_____

_____

_____

_____

_____

_____

Psalm 119

⁸⁹ For ever, O Lord, thy word
is firmly fixed in the heavens.

⁹⁰ Thy faithfulness endures to all
generations; thou hast established
the earth, and it stands fast.

⁹¹ By thy appointment they stand
this day; for all things are thy
servants.

⁹² If thy law had not been my
delight, I should have perished
in my affliction.

⁹³ I will never forget thy precepts;
for by them thou hast given me
life.

⁹⁴ I am thine, save me; for I have
sought thy precepts.

⁹⁵ The wicked lie in wait to
destroy me; but I consider thy
testimonies.

⁹⁶ I have seen a limit to
all perfection, but thy
commandment is exceedingly
broad.

⁹⁷ Oh, how I love thy law!
It is my meditation all the day.

⁹⁸ Thy commandment makes me
wiser than my enemies, for it is
ever with me.

⁹⁹ I have more understanding
than all my teachers, for thy
testimonies are my meditation.

¹⁰⁰ I understand more than the
aged, for I keep thy precepts.

¹⁰¹ I hold back my feet from every
evil way, in order to keep thy
word.

¹⁰² I do not turn aside from
thy ordinances, for thou hast
taught me.

¹⁰³ How sweet are thy words to my
taste, sweeter than honey to my
mouth!

¹⁰⁴ Through thy precepts I get
understanding; therefore I hate
every false way.

¹⁰⁵ Thy word is a lamp to my feet
and a light to my path.

Psalm 119: 89–105

5.5 DECISION point

Thirty minutes to speak about the most important book in the world is nothing. So as I prepared to speak to you about the Bible, I asked myself, "What do you hope to accomplish with this session?" I came to the conclusion that I could teach you very little about the Bible in such a short time. So I set out with two objectives:

1. To give you a starting point so that you would feel comfortable picking up the Bible and beginning to read it.
2. To give you an appetite for reading the Bible.

So, I want to encourage you to get yourself a good Bible and make reading it a part of your day. When you go looking for a Bible, remember, not all Bibles are the same—so get yourself a good Catholic Bible. The Catholic Bible has seventy-three books, but many other Christian Bibles have removed books and those Bibles usually contain only sixty-six. Visit DynamicCatholic.com and we will help you find a good Catholic Bible.

If you really want to surprise your parents, ask them to get you a Bible as an early Confirmation gift.

Last week I was speaking to my friend Brian in San Diego, and he was talking about his Bible. He has had it for years, reads from it every day, and it is well worn. Something he said to me struck me particularly: "You need a good Bible to do life with."

Here's my challenge: Wear out a Bible in your lifetime. Get a really good one, and wear it out with prayer and reflection.

Dozens of voices are influencing you and the direction of your life every day. But how often do we pause and allow God to speak into our lives? Reading the Bible for a few minutes each day is a great way to allow the voice of God to speak into the situations and circumstances we are dealing with.

If I were going to spend the rest of my life on a deserted island and I could only take one book with me, I would take the Bible. I hope in time you will come to feel the same way.

The Bible is a map and an instruction manual, but it is also an invitation to get to know God and his Church. Will you accept the invitation to get to know God? Or will you reject it? What role are you going to allow the Bible to play in your life?

You get to decide.

Get yourself a Bible. Take a few minutes each day to read it. I'm telling you, it will change your life in the most incredible ways.

"BE STILL AND KNOW THAT I AM GOD."

PSALM 46:10

KNOW IT:
To be still and quiet is really good for us.

THINK ABOUT IT:
When was the last time you sat down and gave yourself the gift of a few still, quiet minutes?

LIVE IT: Make time today to be quiet and still.

JOURNAL QUESTIONS

1. WHAT ARE THE MAJOR VOICES INFLUENCING THE DIRECTION OF YOUR LIFE?

_____

_____

_____

_____

_____

_____

2. WHEN WAS THE LAST TIME YOU ACCEPTED OR REJECTED AN INVITATION FROM GOD?

_____

_____

_____

_____

_____

_____

_____

3. ARE YOU OPEN TO GOD'S DIRECTION IN YOUR LIFE?

_____

_____

_____

_____

_____

_____

_____

THE BIBLE
CROSSWORD PUZZLE

ACROSS

1. The twenty-seven books of the Bible that tell the story of the life of Jesus and his followers and include the Gospels, Catholic Letters, Acts of the Apostles, and Letters of Saint Paul

4. A picture or chart used to find one's way that shows rivers, mountains, streets, etc.

6. A pattern of behavior that is acquired through frequent repetition

10. A thorough or dramatic change

14. A spiritual journey to a holy place

DOWN

2. The course or path in which someone is moving

3. The teachings that have been handed down from the apostles to their successors

5. The first of Saint Paul's Letters

7. God reveals himself to us in two ways, through Sacred _____ and through Sacred Tradition.

8. The first forty-six books of the Bible

9. What God wants us all to experience after we die

11. Father, Son, and Holy Spirit

12. Every day you make thousands of_____.

13. The Word of God

Answers on page 326

RELATIONSHIPS

Lord of all pots and pans and things, since I've no time to be a great saint by doing lovely things, or watching late with thee, or dreaming in the dawnlight, or storming heaven's gates, make me a saint by getting meals, and washing up the plates. Warm all the kitchen with thy Love, and light it with thy peace; forgive me all my worrying, and make my grumbling cease. Thou who didst love to give men food, in room, or by the sea, accept the service that I do, I do it unto thee. Amen.

— Brother Lawrence —

6. RELATIONSHIPS

My father died of cancer when I was thirty. It was very painful, but I have many great memories of him. He was a wise and patient man who always had practical insights into the situations of my life. I often find myself thinking about some of the unforgettable conversations we had. One of those conversations was about friendship.

One Saturday we were watching one of my brothers play soccer, and the stands were quite empty. Dad asked me how things were going at school and I was telling him about some problems I was having with a friend.

I remember as if it happened yesterday: He turned to me, held up his hand, stretched out his fingers, and said, "Matthew, true friendship is rare. Much rarer than most people think. If you find five true friends in this life you will be a very blessed man."

At the time I thought to myself, "Five! I've got tons of friends." But as time has passed, life has revealed the wisdom in my father's words. True friendship is incredibly rare.

We all need a few great friends to do life with. We need friends who will challenge us when we need to be challenged, encourage us when we need to be encouraged, and be genuinely happy for us when we succeed. We all need a handful of friends who can help us to become the-best-version-of-ourselves.

Finding that handful of friends is not just going to happen. It requires patience, self-control, trust, and some great decisions. God wants to help you to develop fabulous relationships.

The truth is, a great deal of your happiness and a great deal of your misery in this life will probably come from relationships—so it is important to get this right!

6.1 WHAT IS THE PURPOSE?

Developing great relationships is like constructing a great building. The first stage is design, and design is driven by purpose. The best warehouse in the world would not serve very well as a family home, and the best family home in the world would not serve very well as a warehouse.

Everything has a purpose. If you want to succeed at something, the first thing you need to get really clear about is purpose. The purpose of golf is to shoot your lowest possible score, the purpose of football

WHO WAS JOHN the APOSTLE?

Saint John the Apostle (AD 6–100) was one of the Twelve Apostles of Jesus. He was also the brother of James. The Church Fathers generally identify him as the author of five books of the Bible: the Gospel of John, three epistles of John, and the book of Revelation. He was the only male follower of Jesus at the foot of the cross with Mary. How many of your friends would stay with you as John stayed with Jesus? John is the patron saint of friendship and his feast day is December 27.

is to score more points than the other team, the purpose of business is to be profitable by adding value to your customers' lives so that they will continue to purchase your products and services, and the ultimate purpose of life is to get to Heaven.

But what is the purpose of relationships?

The sad thing is, too many people never really explore this question. As a result, when we look around society today we don't see too many dynamic and healthy relationships.

Lots of people think the purpose of relationships is just to have fun. Relationships should be fun, but they are not going to be fun all the time, and fun is not the main purpose. If you think it is, you will fail in relationships.

So, what is the purpose of relationships?

To answer this question, we must first revisit the purpose of life.

We have already spoken about God's dream for us to become the-best-version-of-ourselves. Everything makes sense in relation to God's dream for us—including relationships. In our discussion of the Bible we talked about being pilgrims. This world is not our final destination; we are just passing through here. We have talked time and time again about God's overwhelming desire for a relationship with us. God wants us to walk with him in this life and be with him for eternity in Heaven.

God gives us relationships to help us become the-best-version-of-ourselves. He gives us relationships so that we can help each other get to Heaven.

My number one job in my marriage is to help my wife Meggie get to Heaven. My number one job as a parent is to help my kids to know and love God and get to Heaven. My number one job as a friend is to help my friends get to Heaven. My number one job here, right now, is to help you get to Heaven. So each day I encourage my wife, my children, and my friends to become a-better-version-of-themselves. Why? Because it is impossible to grow in virtue and character and not draw nearer to God. It is impossible to become a-better-version-of-yourself and not be one step closer to Heaven.

The purpose of every relationship is two people helping each other become the-best-version-of-themselves. It doesn't matter if a relationship is between husband and wife, boyfriend and girlfriend, brother and sister, parents and children, manager and employee, coach and player, teacher and student. The purpose of every relationship is to help each other become the-best-version-of-ourselves. I am here to help you become the-best-version-of-yourself, and you are here to help me become the-best-version-of-myself.

YOU WILL LEARN MORE FROM YOUR FRIENDS THAN YOU EVER WILL FROM BOOKS. CHOOSE YOUR FRIENDS WISELY.

Matthew 7:24-27

KNOW IT: There is a difference between the wise and the foolish.

THINK ABOUT IT: Are you building your life on a solid foundation like the wise man?

LIVE IT: What one thing can you do each day to strengthen the foundation you are building your life upon?

Why do you think we know so little about Mary?

The world says that the secret to having great relationships is common interests. Common interests are good, but they are not the key to great relationships. Your interests ten years from now will most likely be very different from your interests today. Throughout our lives our interests are constantly changing and evolving. And if you build a relationship on common interests, if you make common interests the most important thing, and your interests change—the relationship will change. And it will very often fall apart.

Purpose matters. The foundation you choose to build your relationships upon matters. Think about the story from Matthew's Gospel. Jesus said:

"Every one who hears these words of mine and does them will be like a wise man who built his house upon the rock; and the rain fell, and the floods came, and the winds blew and beat upon that house, but it did not fall, because it had been founded on rock. And every one who hears these words of mine and does not do them will be like a foolish man who built his house upon the sand; and the rain fell, and the floods came, and the winds blew and beat against that house, and it fell; and great was the fall of it." (Matthew 7:24–27)

Fun is great, but it is not enough. Common interests are fabulous, but they are not enough. Building relationships upon fun or common interests is like building a house on sand. Great relationships need common *purpose*. Building relationships upon the common purpose of helping each other become the-best-version-of-ourselves is like building a house on rock.

If you want to build your relationships on sand, choose your friends based on whether or not they are good-looking, fun, athletic, rich, and popular. If you want to build your relationships on rock, choose friends of good character, who are striving for virtue, who help you become the-best-version-of-yourself, and lead you closer to God.

The more closely we align ourselves with the purpose of anything, the more success we will have. Relationships have a purpose. God gives us relationships to help us become the-best-version-of-ourselves.

The beautiful thing about the purpose of relationships is that it is unchanging. Like the rock that the wise man built his house on, common purpose is a solid foundation to build your relationships upon. Many things may change in your life over the next month, year, or decade, but the purpose of relationships will not.

Are you ready to start building your relationships on a solid foundation?

1. WHO ARE THE MOST IMPORTANT PEOPLE IN YOUR LIFE? WHY?

_____

_____

_____

_____

_____

_____

_____

_____

2. WHAT IS THE PURPOSE OF RELATIONSHIPS?

_____

_____

_____

_____

_____

_____

_____

_____

_____

3. WHAT ARE YOU PRETENDING NOT TO KNOW ABOUT YOUR APPROACH
   TO RELATIONSHIPS?

_____

_____

_____

_____

_____

_____

_____

_____

NOTHING IS MORE PRACTICAL
THAN FINDING GOD,
than falling in Love
IN A QUITE ABSOLUTE, FINAL WAY.
What you are *in love* with,
WHAT SEIZES YOUR IMAGINATION,
will affect **EVERYTHING.**
It will decide what will get you
OUT OF BED *in the morning,*
WHAT YOU DO WITH YOUR EVENINGS,
how you spend your weekends,
WHAT YOU READ, WHOM YOU KNOW,
what ***breaks your heart,***
and what amazes you with
JOY *and* GRATITUDE.
Fall in love, STAY IN LOVE,
AND IT WILL DECIDE EVERYTHING.

> "There is nothing I would not do for those who are really my friends. I have no notion of loving people by halves, it is not my nature."
>
> *—Jane Austen*

"THERE IS NOTHING ON THIS EARTH MORE TO BE PRIZED THAN TRUE FRIENDSHIP."

-SAINT THOMAS AQUINAS

6.2 Choose your friends wisely

Many of the most important decisions you will make in your life will be around relationships. Here are five examples:

1. FRIENDS. The friends you choose to surround yourself with now and throughout your life will have an enormous impact. Sooner or later, we all rise or fall to the level of our friendships. If your friends take their studies seriously, chances are you will too. If your friends get into drugs and alcohol, chances are you will also. If your friends waste endless hours sitting around playing video games, chances are you will too. Friends are a powerful habit, for better or for worse. Are your friends helping you become the-best-version-of-yourself? Are you helping them to become the-best-version-of-themselves?

You are going to make a lot of friendship decisions throughout your life. Get into the habit now of asking the Holy Spirit to guide your friendship decisions.

2. PARENTS. Your relationship with your parents is a central relationship in your life. It is now, and it always will be. My dad has been dead for ten years, and there are still days when I think to myself, "I should call Dad and tell him that . . ." and then I catch myself and remember he is not with us anymore. A week does not pass when I don't think about my dad and how he would advise me in a situation. Whether they are alive or not, whether you live with them or not, your bond with your parents is powerful.

This relationship is so important that it is the first human relationship to be mentioned in the Ten Commandments. The Fourth Commandment is: Honor your father and your mother. I heard a great story a couple of weeks ago that made me realize how powerfully and practically God uses his commandments to lead us to happiness and the fullness of life he desires for us.

Caitlin was fifteen years old when her parents thought it would be a good idea for her to go on a mission trip to serve the hungry and the homeless. She didn't want to go and didn't want to hear why her parents thought she should. Finally, her parents came to her one night and said, "We have prayed about it and we have a strong sense that you should go on this mission trip." That Saturday as they put her on the bus she was sobbing in anger because they were making her go. A week later, when she got back, she was happier than her parents had ever seen her. Her eyes had been opened to how difficult life is for so many, but she had also met Scott. Caitlin and Scott dated all through high school, all through college, and just three weeks ago, they got married. Her parents had a strong sense that Caitlin should be on that trip because God was inspiring them to send her.

Caitlin was resistant to her parents' guidance. Little did she know that God was working through them.

God works in powerful ways through his commandments. So next time your parents ask you to do something, or encourage you to consider something, you may want to politely and humbly say yes.

3. MARRIAGE. Some of you will become priests or enter religious life, but most of you will get married. Whom you decide to marry will have an enormous impact on your life and happiness. What criteria will you use to make that decision? Looks? Personality? Character? Looks matter to a certain extent. It is important that you be attracted to the person you marry. Personality matters more. But character matters most. Is this person committed to growing in godly character? Are you committed to growing in godly character? If not, then the truth is, sooner or later your marriage will most likely find itself in a very difficult place.

Marriage is a beautiful thing. It really is, and I didn't fully understand that until I was married. But marrying the right person for the right reasons is critical. Marriage may seem like something in the very distant future for you, but what I want you to know *now* is that the decisions you are making around relationships today will affect your marriage, no matter how far it is in the future.

4. COMMUNITY. We all need people to do life with—friends, family, and community to encourage us and challenge us. When we are young we find ourselves involved in various communities—school, parish, sports, and neighborhood. But as we get older we have to actively seek out community. Part of the genius of Catholicism is the parish community. Parish life provides a natural and powerful opportunity for us to encourage, challenge, and support each other.

I'm not going to lie to you. Some parish communities are better than others. But I want to encourage you to get involved in your parish more each year. Join the youth group, become a reader or a Eucharistic Minister, or get involved in any of the many groups and ministries that make up your parish community. You might say, "The youth group is lame at our parish!" Maybe it is. So do something about it. Get involved and make it better. It is easy to criticize from the sidelines.

Don't ask what your parish can do for you; ask what you can do for your parish. It is through service and sacrifice that we are very often led to the beautiful plan God has for our lives.

5. GOD. I put your relationship with God last on the list, but it is the most important. Unless you make your relationship with God a priority, your chances of getting the other relationship decisions right are next to zero.

Good·ness
[goo d-nis]

The quality of being good, having virtue, character, and moral excellence.

Are you striving for goodness?

How do you feel when you behave in ways that are good, virtuous, and morally excellent?

Who is one person in your life that models goodness for you?

The Trinity—Father, Son, and Holy Spirit—is the most dynamic relationship, and your relationship with God will have an enormous influence on every other relationship in your life.

Every yearning you have for good things is in some way a yearning for God. Your longing for relationship is a yearning for God. God is relationship. So, no wonder you yearn for relationships so much.

Throughout your life you are going to make lots of relationship decisions. You are already making dozens every day. Are you making good relationship decisions? What can you do to make better relationship decisions? Do you understand how some of the decisions you make today will impact your life in the future?

There is a great Scripture I want to invite you to reflect upon today. When we really think about what it takes to have great relationships, it can be overwhelming. In John's Gospel, Jesus says, "the Holy Spirit, whom the Father will send in my name, will teach you everything. . ." (John 14:26) The Holy Spirit will teach you everything . . . including how to have great relationships.

Open yourself up to the Holy Spirit's guidance. Try it. Don't take my word for it. At least once a day for the next week, pray to the Holy Spirit and ask him to guide you in a specific situation. Follow your conscience and the guidance of the Holy Spirit and you will notice that you are less anxious and more joyful.

This Catholic stuff really works. It's real. It's true. It's just that most people have never really given it a chance in their life. Give the genius of Catholicism a chance in your life. You will be glad you did.

John 14:26

KNOW IT: God, the ultimate Father, wants to teach you everything you need to know to live a rich and full life.

THINK ABOUT IT: Are you really opening yourself up to the Holy Spirit's guidance?

LIVE IT: Each time you need to make a decision, ask the Holy Spirit to guide you.

Love REARRANGES OUR PRIORITIES

D·I·S·C·U·S·S·I·O·N
QUESTIONS

1. WHAT'S THE BEST FRIENDSHIP DECISION YOU HAVE MADE IN THE PAST TWELVE MONTHS?

_____

_____

_____

_____

_____

2. HOW DO YOU FEEL GOD IS CALLING YOU TO IMPROVE YOUR RELATIONSHIPS WITH YOUR PARENTS?

_____

_____

_____

_____

_____

_____

3. ARE YOUR FRIENDS HELPING YOU TO BECOME THE-BEST-VERSION-OF-YOURSELF? ARE YOU HELPING THEM TO BECOME THE-BEST-VERSION-OF-THEMSELVES?

_____

_____

_____

_____

_____

_____

PSALM 25

To thee, O Lord, I lift up my soul.

2 O my God, in thee I trust, let me not
be put to shame; let not my enemies
exult over me.

3 Yea, let none that wait for thee be
put to shame; let them be ashamed
who are wantonly treacherous.

4 Make me to know thy ways,
O Lord; teach me thy paths.

5 Lead me in thy truth, and teach me,
for thou art the God of my salvation;
for thee I wait all the day long.

6 Be mindful of thy mercy,
O Lord, and of thy steadfast love,
for they have been from of old.

7 Remember not the sins of my youth,
or my transgressions; according to thy
steadfast love remember me,
for thy goodness' sake, O Lord!

8 Good and upright is the Lord;
therefore he instructs sinners
in the way.

9 He leads the humble in what is right,
and teaches the humble his way.

10 All the paths of the Lord are
steadfast love and faithfulness, for
those who keep his covenant and his
testimonies.

11 For thy name's sake, O Lord, pardon
my guilt, for it is great.

12 Who is the man that fears the Lord?
Him will he instruct in the way
that he should choose.

13 He himself shall abide in prosperity,
and his children shall possess
the land.

14 The friendship of the Lord is for
those who fear him, and he makes
known to them his covenant.

15 My eyes are ever toward the Lord,
for he will pluck my feet
out of the net.

16 Turn thou to me, and be gracious to
me; for I am lonely and afflicted.

17 Relieve the troubles of my heart, and
bring me out of my distresses.

18 Consider my affliction and my
trouble, and forgive all my sins.

19 Consider how many are my foes,
and with what violent hatred
they hate me.

20 Oh guard my life, and deliver me;
let me not be put to shame,
for I take refuge in thee.

21 May integrity and uprightness
preserve me, for I wait for thee.

22 Redeem Israel, O God,
out of all his troubles.

MY THOUGHTS

6.3 WHAT IS Love?

How did Mary love?

1 JOHN 4:7-21

KNOW IT: To know God is to love God.

THINK ABOUT IT: How well do you know God?

LIVE IT: Do something today that puts God's priorities at the center of your life.

JOHN 3:16

KNOW IT: God loves you more than you could ever imagine.

THINK ABOUT IT: Think about all the love you have for everyone in your life, and multiply it by infinity. God loves you more than that.

LIVE IT: How can you share the love of God with others?

What is love? This is one of life's biggest questions. We all yearn for opportunities to love and be loved. Love matters. You matter. Whom and what you decide to love matters.

"What you are in love with, what seizes your imagination, will affect everything. It will decide what will get you out of bed in the morning, what you do with your evenings, how you spend your weekends, what you read, whom you know, what breaks your heart, and what amazes you with joy and gratitude. Fall in love, stay in love, and it will decide everything." These are the words of Father Pedro Arrupe (1907–1991). Whom and what you decide to love is going to have an enormous impact on your life. So let's take a look at what love is and is not.

One of the most beautiful passages in the Bible is in the First Letter of John, Chapter 4:7–21. From this passage we get one of the most quoted phrases of all time: "God is love." These three words are usually quoted on their own. But the whole verse reads, "Whoever does not love does not know God, for God is love." If you read this carefully you discover that God gives us a fabulous clue right here.

John tells us that people who don't love don't know God. He implies that if they knew God they would love. Which tells us that getting to know God is the best way to learn how to love. So, what does God teach us about love?

The most quoted verse in the Bible is John 3:16. At baseball games and football games, you will often see someone holding up a sign that says JOHN 3:16. That verse reads, "For God so loved the world that he gave his only son, so that everyone who believes in him may not perish but may have eternal life." This is the love of God the Father.

Then, there is the love of the Son. What does Jesus teach us about love? The first thing he teaches us is the position love has in the whole scheme of things. When he was asked, "Which is the greatest of the commandments?" he replied, "You shall love the Lord your God with all your heart, and all your soul, and all your mind." This is the greatest and the first commandment. And the second is like it: "You shall love your neighbor as yourself." (Matthew 22:36–39) Love is the most important thing.

Jesus also teaches that the essence of love is self-donation: "No one has greater love than this, to lay down one's life for one's friends." (John 15:13) He teaches us further that love is not words, but action, by laying down his life for us on the cross. He backs up his words with action. Jesus doesn't just talk about love; he models it for us. Love is selfless.

Finally, he instructs us on how we should love: "This is my commandment, that you love one another as I have loved you." (John 15:12) Notice Jesus didn't say, "This is my suggestion to you . . . ." It wasn't a suggestion; it was a command. He commands us to love one another in the same way he loves us—that is, by laying down our lives for each other. But it is important to point out that he didn't lay down his life so that we could have more of our selfish desires and worldly pleasure; Jesus laid down his life so that we could have eternal life. In the same way, he wants us to lay down our lives for others in ways that lead them to eternal life. You will come across many people in your life who want you to make sacrifices so that they can have more of their selfish desires and worldly pleasure. That's not love. That's manipulation.

God's vision of love is beautiful, selfless, and radical. By contrast, the world's vision of love places a disproportionate focus on physical pleasure and having fun. God's vision of love is others-focused selflessness; the world's vision of love is me-focused selfishness.

More than anything, the world tells us that love is a feeling. God tells us that love is a choice. In my marriage there are times when I feel overwhelmingly in love with my wife, but there are also times when I don't feel that way. It's when I don't have those fabulous feelings that I really prove my love for Meggie. It is in those moments when I don't have those fabulous feelings that I choose to love her. Love is a choice, not a feeling – and it's a choice that proves itself with action. Feelings are fleeting, while love lives on.

Love rearranges our priorities. It shows us what really matters, and in the process, banishes selfishness.

The world pretends that love is a mutual giving and taking. But that is not love. In love there is no taking, just giving and receiving. There is a beautiful reflection by Bruce Barton that illustrates this point. It is called "Two Seas."

There are two seas in Palestine. One is fresh, and fish are in it. Splashes of green adorn its banks. Trees spread their branches over it and stretch out their thirsty roots to sip of its healing waters. Along its shores the children play, as children played when He was there. He loved it. He could look across its silver surface when He spoke His parables. And on a rolling plain not far away He fed five thousand people.

The River Jordan makes this sea with sparkling water from the hills. So it laughs in the sunshine. And men build their houses near to it, and birds their nests; and every kind of life is happier because it is there.

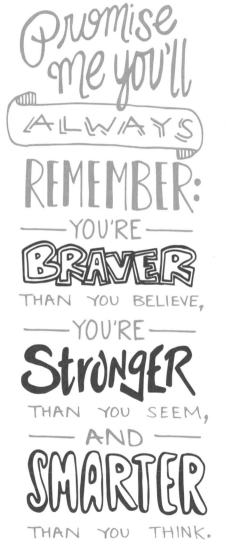

Promise me you'll ALWAYS REMEMBER: YOU'RE BRAVER THAN YOU BELIEVE, YOU'RE Stronger THAN YOU SEEM, AND SMARTER THAN YOU THINK.

—Christopher Robin to Pooh

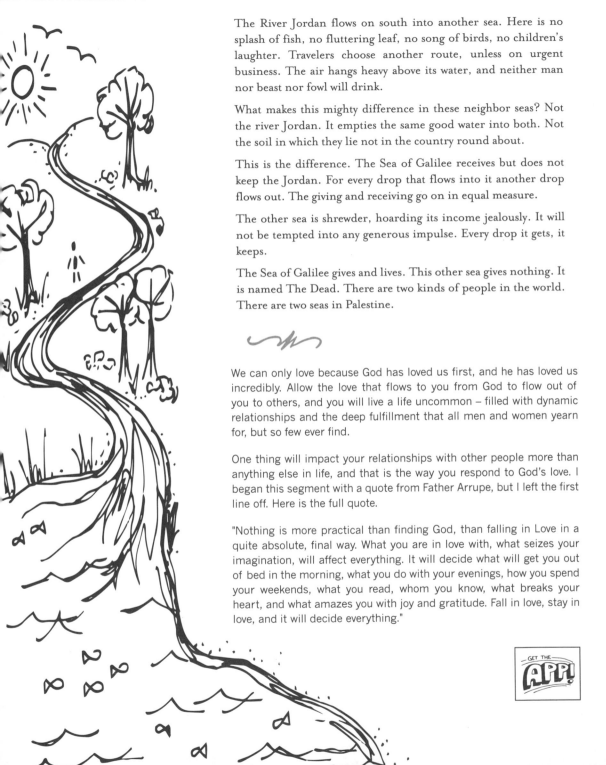

The River Jordan flows on south into another sea. Here is no splash of fish, no fluttering leaf, no song of birds, no children's laughter. Travelers choose another route, unless on urgent business. The air hangs heavy above its water, and neither man nor beast nor fowl will drink.

What makes this mighty difference in these neighbor seas? Not the river Jordan. It empties the same good water into both. Not the soil in which they lie not in the country round about.

This is the difference. The Sea of Galilee receives but does not keep the Jordan. For every drop that flows into it another drop flows out. The giving and receiving go on in equal measure.

The other sea is shrewder, hoarding its income jealously. It will not be tempted into any generous impulse. Every drop it gets, it keeps.

The Sea of Galilee gives and lives. This other sea gives nothing. It is named The Dead. There are two kinds of people in the world. There are two seas in Palestine.

We can only love because God has loved us first, and he has loved us incredibly. Allow the love that flows to you from God to flow out of you to others, and you will live a life uncommon – filled with dynamic relationships and the deep fulfillment that all men and women yearn for, but so few ever find.

One thing will impact your relationships with other people more than anything else in life, and that is the way you respond to God's love. I began this segment with a quote from Father Arrupe, but I left the first line off. Here is the full quote.

"Nothing is more practical than finding God, than falling in Love in a quite absolute, final way. What you are in love with, what seizes your imagination, will affect everything. It will decide what will get you out of bed in the morning, what you do with your evenings, how you spend your weekends, what you read, whom you know, what breaks your heart, and what amazes you with joy and gratitude. Fall in love, stay in love, and it will decide everything."

GET THE
APP!

Discussion Questions

1. WHAT DID YOU LEARN ABOUT LOVE IN THIS SESSION?

_____

_____

_____

_____

_____

_____

_____

2. WHO MODELS SELFLESS LOVE IN YOUR LIFE?

_____

_____

_____

_____

_____

_____

_____

_____

3. HOW DOES YOUR RELATIONSHIP WITH GOD INFLUENCE YOUR RELATIONSHIPS WITH OTHER PEOPLE?

_____

_____

_____

_____

_____

_____

_____

6.4 YOUR Quest FOR LOVE

We are all on a quest for love. We have a deep yearning to love and be loved. So what should you be looking for when it comes to love? How will you know if someone really loves you? What is the evidence of love?

The first thing we need to be clear about is that there are different types of love. There is the love we have for all men and women of goodwill. There is the love of friendship. There is romantic love. And there is agape, unconditional love.

During adolescence and early adult life, we tend to focus on romantic love. So, let's explore what it really means to love someone.

First, at the most basic and natural level, love desires what is best for the other person. You cannot want someone to do something that prevents her from becoming the-best-version-of-herself and at the same time claim that you love her. Love desires what is good for the other person. Along with this desire for what is best for the other person also comes the desire to share every good thing we have with that person.

Next, on a very human and practical level, love is a willingness to inconvenience yourself for another person. This does not mean that we should constantly inconvenience ourselves for those we love, but from time to time this is called for. Is this person willing to inconvenience himself for you? This could be something as simple as going to a Chinese restaurant when he really wanted to eat Mexican food, or as significant as caring for you when you are sick and cannot take care of yourself.

Then there is the love that Paul describes in Corinthians: "Love is patient; love is kind; love is not envious or boastful or arrogant or rude. It does not insist on its own way; it is not irritable or resentful; it does not rejoice in wrongdoing, but rejoices in the truth. It bears all things, believes all things, hopes all things, endures all things." (1 Corinthians 13:4–7) If you are looking for love, this is what you should be looking for. Ask yourself: Could I put this person into this passage?

Jose is patient; *Jose* is kind; *Jose* is not envious or boastful or arrogant or rude.

—or—

Samantha does not insist on her own way; *Samantha* is not irritable or resentful; *Samantha* does not rejoice in wrongdoing, but rejoices in the truth.

WHAT DOES THE BIBLE SAY ABOUT FRIENDSHIP?

LOOK IT UP!

- JOHN 15:12–15
- PROVERBS 13:20
- 1 CORINTHIANS 15:33
- LUKE 6:31
- ROMANS 12:10
- EPHESIANS 4:29–32
- PROVERBS 22:24–25

And even more important, can you place yourself in this passage? Replace every reference to love with your name. Does it ring true or do you have some work to do?

Finally, in your quest for romantic love, reflect on this line from the Scriptures: "Husbands, love your wives, just as Christ loved the church and gave himself up for her." (Ephesians 5:25)

Gentlemen, in marriage we are called to love our wives as Christ loved the Church. We are called to lay down our lives in sacrifice for them. Every day there are times in my marriage when I have to choose between being selfish and laying down my life for my wife and children.

Ladies, when it comes time to find a man to spend your life with, this is the caliber of man you should be looking for—one who loves you so much that he is willing to lay down his life for you the way Jesus did, one who is capable of selflessness.

Today's culture takes the trivial things and makes them important, and then takes the important things and makes them trivial. Start focusing on the important things. You are not too young to really start thinking about life's big questions. The sooner you do, the better. Most people don't start thinking about these questions until after they have made all of life's big decisions. Start exploring these big questions now, and allow the answers you find to direct the big decisions you will make in your life.

Love is important. You are right to make a big deal of it. *It* is a big deal. But we tend to focus on the wrong things in our quest for love. Allow God to guide you in your relationships. Pause from time to time to ask yourself: Are these people helping me become the-best-version-of-myself? Am I helping them to become the-best-version-of-themselves? If the answer is no, do something about it.

Anyone or anything that doesn't help you become the-best-version-of-yourself is too small for you. And anything you do that doesn't help other people become the-best-version-of-themselves is too small for you too.

LOVE
» → **BEARS** all things
» → *believes* all things
» → ENDURES all things

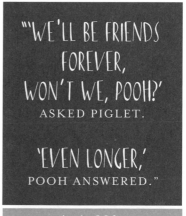

"'WE'LL BE FRIENDS FOREVER, WON'T WE, POOH?' ASKED PIGLET.

'EVEN LONGER,' POOH ANSWERED."

A. A. Milne, WINNIE-THE-POOH

What can we learn about love from Mary?

DISCUSSION QUESTIONS

1. IN WHAT WAYS HAVE YOU GONE LOOKING FOR LOVE IN THE WRONG PLACES?

2. WHO DO YOU KNOW WHO HAS A GREAT MARRIAGE? WHAT DO YOU ADMIRE ABOUT THEIR MARRIAGE?

3. WHAT VIRTUE DO YOU THINK IS MOST IMPORTANT TO HEALTHY RELATIONSHIPS?

6.5 DECISION point

When all is said and done, life is not about what street you live on or what school you went to or what type of car you drive; it's not about whether or not you made the football team or what position you played. Life is not about what grades you got in school or what job you had. It's not about how much money you have or how much money you make, or whether or not you vacation in all the right places and wear overpriced clothes with expensive labels on them. Life is about love. It's about whom you love and whom you hurt. It's about how you love yourself and hurt yourself. It's about how you love and hurt those people closest to you. It's about how you love or hurt the other pilgrims who cross your path as you make your journey through this life. Life is about love.

One day we will stand before God, and perhaps the questions he will ask us are: How well did you love? Who or what did you lay down your life for?

Love is a choice, not a feeling. Every day you make hundreds of choices—and every choice is a choice for love or against love. So choose wisely . . . because whom and what you choose to love will determine just about everything.

Love is a CHOICE [NOT A FEELING]

> "THE BEGINNING OF LOVE IS THE WILL TO LET THOSE WE LOVE BE PERFECTLY THEMSELVES, THE RESOLUTION NOT TO TWIST THEM TO FIT OUR OWN IMAGE. IF IN LOVING THEM WE DO NOT LOVE WHAT THEY ARE, BUT ONLY THEIR POTENTIAL LIKENESS TO OURSELVES, THEN WE DO NOT LOVE THEM: WE ONLY LOVE THE REFLECTION OF OURSELVES WE FIND IN THEM."

– THOMAS MERTON

Journal Questions

1. WHO OR WHAT ARE YOU WILLING TO LAY DOWN YOUR LIFE FOR?

_____

_____

_____

_____

_____

_____

2. WHO LOVES YOU IN THE WAY GOD ENVISIONS LOVE?

_____

_____

_____

_____

_____

_____

_____

3. HOW IS GOD CALLING YOU TO LOVE YOURSELF DIFFERENTLY SO THAT YOU CAN LOVE OTHERS MORE FULLY?

_____

_____

_____

_____

_____

_____

RELATIONSHIPS
CROSSWORD PUZZLE

ACROSS

1. The Creator of Heaven and earth

3. Mutual affection between two or more people

4. A commitment between a man and a woman by which they become husband and wife

6. The prosperity of plentiful and overflowing goodness

8. Like houses, relationships need to be built upon a solid _____.

11. Choose your friends _____.

13. God's vision of ____ is beautiful, selfless, and radical.

15. A group of people who share common attitudes, interests, and goals

DOWN

2. The reason for which something exists

5. Love is a _____, not a feeling.

7. Love rearranges our _____.

9. The only apostle recorded as being at the foot of the cross with Mary

10. There are two ___ in Palestine.

12. God gives us _____ so that we can help each other get to Heaven.

14. Relationships are not just about having ____.

16. Concerned more with the needs and wishes of others than with one's own

Answers on page 326

The EUCHARIST

My Lord and my God, I firmly believe that you are present in the Eucharist. Take the blindness from my eyes, so that I can see all people and things as you see them. Take the deafness from my ears, so that I can hear your truth and follow it. Take the hardness from my heart, so that I can live and love generously. Give me the grace to receive the Eucharist with humility, so that you can transform me a little more each day into the person you created me to be. Amen.

Matthew Kelly

7. THE EUCHARIST

For most of Jesus' public life people crowded around him. If he was teaching in the synagogue, they crowded around him. If he was walking in the street, they crowded around him. If he was having a meal in a home, they crowded around him.

But there were two times when people fled from Jesus.

The obvious one was after his arrest and crucifixion. Where were all the crowds that had followed him? Where were all those people who witnessed his miracles? Where were all the people he had cured and fed? Nowhere to be found.

The other time people fled from Jesus was when he spoke to them about the Eucharist. He said, "I am the bread of life. . . . Unless you eat the flesh of the Son of man and drink his blood, you have no life in you." (John 6:48, 53)

Immediately after this, we read in the Gospel: "When many of his disciples heard it, they said, 'This is a difficult teaching; who can accept it?'" (John 6:60) And a few lines later we read, "After this, many of his disciples turned back and no longer followed him." (John 6:66)

Notice Jesus didn't say, "Oh, come back. I was only kidding. Let's talk about it. Maybe I was wrong. Perhaps we can change this teaching. We can work something out." No, he turned to his disciples, just as he turns to you and me today, and said, "Do you also wish to leave me?"

Will you flee from Jesus or remain by his side?

The Eucharist is at the core of our faith. Let's explore what it is and what it means to you.

7.1 THE ONE THING

There are a lot of things I love about being Catholic, but at the top of the list is the Eucharist. Most people have never really stopped to think about it, but the Eucharist is amazing.

I was asked once: What would have to happen for you to leave the Catholic Church? I thought about the question for a long time. I combed through the lowest moments in Catholic history, testing each to see if one of them would have been the breaking point that made me leave. But after thinking it through I decided I could never leave the Catholic Church. The reason is because I believe that Jesus is truly

John 6:48–66

KNOW IT: Jesus says, "I am the bread of Life."

THINK ABOUT IT: In what ways do you need Jesus to feed you? What good things are you hungry for?

LIVE IT: Next time you receive the Eucharist ask Jesus to feed you in these ways.

"The longer you stay away from Communion, the more your soul will become weak, and in the end you will become dangerously indifferent."
—Saint John Bosco

present—body, blood, soul, and divinity—in the Eucharist. Where else can I get the Eucharist?

Sure, some other churches might have better music, but in the whole scheme of things music is trivial compared to the Eucharist. Other churches might have more engaging preachers, but these are trivial compared to the Eucharist. When we go to Mass on Sunday the danger is in thinking that the music and the homily are the most important things. Don't take the trivial and make it important. That's the way of the world. Get clear about what's really important, what matters most, and life will be a lot simpler and more joyful.

At Mass on Sunday, the homily could be in a language I don't understand, the music could be a complete train wreck, there could be kids running up and down the aisles screaming at the top of their lungs, throwing crayons and eating snacks (or eating crayons and throwing snacks), and that's OK—because the moment when I receive the Eucharist is a pivotal moment in my week. It's a moment of transformation, a moment when I get to receive who and what I wish to become. And I could never leave that. It doesn't matter how good the music or preaching is elsewhere; I cannot leave the Eucharist. I will not leave Jesus. I hope you won't either.

When I reflect on the gift of faith I have been given, I am led to the conclusion that once we believe in the Eucharist we are given the grace to look beyond a bad homily and the grace to look beyond a good homily; the grace to look beyond uninspiring music and the grace to look beyond music that elevates our hearts, minds, and souls. For it is beyond all of these things, way beyond all of these things, that we find Jesus in the Eucharist.

This sets the Catholic Church apart: Jesus truly present in the Eucharist. The Eucharist is uniquely Catholic.

Let me ask you a question. If you had to spend the rest of your life on a deserted island, and you could only take five people with you, whom would you take?

I can tell you a priest would be on my list of five people. No priest, no Mass. No Mass, no Eucharist. I can't live without the Eucharist. More important, I don't want to. And once you come to understand the power of the Eucharist, you won't want to either.

I was born Catholic and I will die Catholic. There are lots of reason for that, but none more compelling than the Eucharist.

JESUS · IS · TRULY present BODY, Blood, SOUL, & Divinity IN · THE · EUCHARIST

"IF I CAN GIVE YOU ANY ADVICE, I BEG YOU TO GET CLOSER TO THE EUCHARIST AND TO JESUS."

—MOTHER TERESA OF CALCUTTA

DISCUSSION QUESTIONS

1. WHAT IS YOUR FAVORITE THING ABOUT BEING CATHOLIC?

_____
_____
_____
_____
_____
_____

2. WHICH OF JESUS' TEACHINGS DO YOU FIND MOST DIFFICULT TO LIVE?

_____
_____
_____
_____
_____
_____
_____

3. IF YOU HAD TO SPEND THE REST OF YOUR LIFE ON A DESERTED ISLAND AND YOU COULD ONLY TAKE FIVE PEOPLE WITH YOU, WHOM WOULD YOU TAKE?

_____
_____
_____
_____
_____
_____
_____

GRACE IS THE ASSISTANCE GOD GIVES US TO DO WHAT IS GOOD, TRUE, NOBLE, AND RIGHT.

LUKE 22:19

KNOW IT: Jesus lays down his life for us, giving us his body.

THINK ABOUT IT: We are all called to make sacrifices throughout our lives. Are you willing to make sacrifices that benefit other people? If not, why not?

LIVE IT: How are you being called to lay down your life for others?

7.2 the TRUE presence

You might be thinking to yourself, "I'm not sure if I believe that Jesus is truly present in the host I receive at Mass on Sunday." You wouldn't be the first person to have doubts. Great faith and great doubt often go hand in hand. There was a priest who lived in Lanciano, Italy, around the year 700, who was plagued with doubts about the true presence . . . until one day. After that day he never again doubted that Jesus was truly present in the Eucharist.

What happened on that day? I'm glad you asked.

On that day, the priest was celebrating Mass in the small church, even though he was filled with doubts about the real presence of Jesus in the Eucharist. As he said the Words of Consecration ("Take this, all of you, and eat of it, for this is my body which will be given up for you.") the bread changed into living flesh and the wine changed into blood, before his eyes.

Today, you can go to Lanciano and see the flesh and blood that has remained there for more than thirteen hundred years. The flesh and blood have been studied by scientists on a number of occasions, and the following conclusions have been drawn: The flesh is real human flesh and the blood is real human blood, the flesh is muscular tissue from the heart, and there is no evidence of preservatives or any other chemical agents present.

This is one of thousands of Eucharistic miracles that have been documented throughout the life of the Church.

At the Last Supper Jesus "took the bread, and when he had given thanks, he broke it and gave it to them, saying, 'This is my body, which is given for you. Do this in remembrance of me.'" (Luke 22:19) We take Jesus at his word. At Mass on Sunday the priest extends his hands over simple bread and wine and asks the Holy Spirit to transform them into the body and blood of Jesus Christ.

If the Holy Spirit can do that to bread and wine, imagine what he can do with you if you open yourself up to the experience of Confirmation.

You are not just a body. You are a delicate composition of body and soul. If you haven't already, one day you will discover you need to feed your soul in order to live a full and happy life. And when that day comes I want you to remember today, because there is no better way to feed your soul than with the Eucharist.

The Eucharist is astonishing. God himself wants to nourish us. God himself wants to feed us spiritually. God wants to dwell in you.

Some people say that the bread and wine are just a symbol of Jesus' body and blood, but that is not what we believe as Catholics. And the evidence found in Divine Revelation suggests that it is not just a symbol. The Scriptures don't suggest the symbol. Jesus didn't say, "Unless you eat a symbol of my flesh and drink a symbol of my blood you will not have life." And remember there are two aspects of Divine Revelation: Scripture and Tradition. And from the earliest times, Christians have believed that the Eucharist was the body and blood of the Risen Jesus, and not just a symbol.

Can I prove it to you scientifically? No. Not everything can be explained or proven scientifically. If you could prove everything scientifically, there would be no need for faith. There is such a thing as mystery. We human beings don't know everything. If we did we would be God, and there is plenty of evidence in our daily lives that confirms that human beings are not God. Life is full of mystery, and mystery is a beautiful thing.

At the heart of the mystery that is the Catholic faith is the Eucharist. I hope with every passing year of your life you will explore and embrace the mystery of the Eucharist more.

The wiser you become, the closer you will want to be to God. And God wants to be close to us. Saint Francis de Sales wrote, "In the Eucharist we become one with God." To be one with God is a beautiful thing, and whether you are aware of it or not, it is your deepest yearning. You have an insatiable yearning to be one with God. I hope you will start listening to that yearning.

If you want to have a life-changing experience, find an Adoration Chapel in your area and visit it. Sit there in Jesus' presence for one hour. You will be amazed how powerful Jesus' presence is, and how much he will teach you about yourself and your life in one hour.

Who Was St. FRANCIS de SALES?

Saint Francis de Sales (1567–1622) was a priest and bishop and is regarded as one of the great spiritual writers of all time. During his era it was widely believed that holiness was only for monks and nuns, but he banished that idea. The central theme in his classic Introduction to the Devout Life is the idea that God calls every man and woman to live a holy life. Francis also spoke about the allure of money and things, pointing out that the danger of possessions is how easily they can possess us. Possessions increase our happiness only when we use them for our good and the good of others. Francis de Sales is the patron saint of writers and his feast day is January 24.

All the ANSWERS are in the TABERNACLE.

1. IS THERE A PERSON IN YOUR LIFE WHOSE PRESENCE JUST MAKES YOU FEEL
   CALM AND SAFE?

_____

_____

_____

_____

_____

2. WHEN DID YOU FIRST LEARN ABOUT JESUS BEING PRESENT IN THE EUCHARIST?

_____

_____

_____

_____

_____

_____

_____

3. HOW DO YOU THINK YOUR LIFE WOULD CHANGE IF YOU SPENT ONE HOUR EACH WEEK
   SITTING QUIETLY IN JESUS' PRESENCE?

_____

_____

_____

_____

_____

_____

"The holy Eucharist contains the whole spiritual treasure of the Church, that is, Christ himself. . . . He who is the living bread, whose flesh, vivified by the Holy Spirit and vivifying, gives life to men."

—VATICAN II

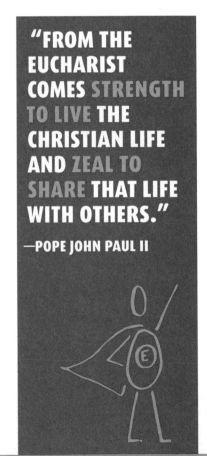

"FROM THE EUCHARIST COMES STRENGTH TO LIVE THE CHRISTIAN LIFE AND ZEAL TO SHARE THAT LIFE WITH OTHERS."

—POPE JOHN PAUL II

7.3 THE POWER OF THE EUCHARIST

When was the last time you did something that you knew wasn't good for you? Why did you do it? Think of reasons, come up with excuses, but at the end of the day it comes down to this: You have disordered desires that are very difficult to control.

Have you ever tried to quit a bad habit and failed? If you haven't already, the day will come when you will try to end a self-destructive habit and find yourself powerless over it. You will use all the willpower you can summon, but you will find yourself failing over and over again. These moments in life can be very humbling—and that's good, because they make us realize our need for God and his grace.

Grace is the assistance God gives us to do what is good, true, noble, and right. And there is no better way to receive God's grace than through the Eucharist.

There is a lot of talk these days about superfoods. Superfoods are high in nutrients and rich with antioxidants, and they keep your immune system strong to fight off disease. Some examples include pomegranate juice, salmon, alfalfa sprouts, sweet potatoes, kale, prunes, beets, apples, and beans.

The Eucharist is the ultimate superfood for the soul, loaded with grace to keep you spiritually healthy, give you the wisdom and strength to choose the right path, and fight off diseases like selfishness and other related vices and bad habits. And that is just a tiny fraction of the power the Eucharist holds.

When you go to Mass next Sunday, keep in mind, the Eucharist is not just a symbol. This is Jesus. The same Jesus who healed people with a touch. The same man who taught with more wisdom than any person who ever walked the earth. This is the guy who fed five thousand people with five loaves and two fishes. The same Jesus who rose from the dead.

We've all got problems. We all have struggles. But whatever you've got, he can handle. You need grace. You may not know it yet, but the sooner you realize it the better. And the Eucharist is the supreme source of the grace you need.

Isn't it time you allowed God to unleash the power of grace in your life?

discussion questions

1. WHEN WAS THE LAST TIME YOU DID SOMETHING THAT YOU KNEW WASN'T GOOD FOR YOU? WHY DID YOU DO IT IF YOU KNEW IT WASN'T GOOD FOR YOU?

2. HAVE YOU EVER TRIED TO QUIT A BAD HABIT AND FAILED?

3. WHEN YOU'RE IN A SITUATION AND YOU WANT TO DO WHAT IS GOOD AND RIGHT BUT ARE ATTRACTED TO THE WRONG CHOICE, DO YOU CALL ON GOD AND ASK FOR HIS HELP?

WHAT IS A MONSTRANCE?

A monstrance is an open or transparent receptacle in which the consecrated Host is exposed for veneration.

WHAT IS EUCHARISTIC ADORATION?

As Catholics we believe that Jesus Christ—body, blood, soul, and divinity—is truly present in the Eucharist, and as such, we believe that being in the presence of the Eucharist is powerful. Eucharistic adoration is the practice of praying in the presence of Jesus in the Eucharist. Simply to sit quietly before Jesus in the Eucharist can be incredibly powerful and has changed many people's lives. In the silence and in his presence great clarity begins to emerge about who we are, what we are here for, what matters most, and what matters least.

WHAT IS TRANSUBSTANTIATION?

Transubstantiation is the changing of simple bread and wine into the body and blood of Jesus Christ. This takes place at the consecration during Mass.

the • Eucharist
IS THE
Source & Summit
OF
Christian Life

CCC #1324

How many hours of her life do you think Mary spent in adoration of Jesus?

My Thoughts

The Sabbath is a day of religious observance and abstinence from work, kept by Jews from Friday evening to Saturday evening and by Christians on Sunday.

In what ways is God inviting you to honor the Sabbath?

God has declared Sunday—*the Lord's day*-as a day of rest.

Mark 1:35

KNOW IT: It seems that Jesus was always looking for quiet places to spend a few minutes in prayer.

THINK ABOUT IT: How hard is it for you to find a quiet place to pray each day? Is there one place that is most convenient?

LIVE IT: Renew your commitment to spending ten minutes each day in the classroom of silence with God.

7.4 GET CLOSE AND STAY CLOSE

What's the most beautiful church you have ever been in? How did it make you feel?

I began speaking and writing when I was nineteen. At the time I was in business school, and since then, I have been blessed to travel in more than fifty countries. Few things inspire me more than traveling. There is something about experiencing different people, places, and cultures that opens our hearts and minds.

I grew up Catholic and my experience of the Catholic Church was mostly limited to our parish, St. Martha's in suburban Sydney. But through travel I began to see how vast and impressive the Catholic Church is, in so many ways.

One thing that becomes abundantly clear when you start traveling is that the world is full of beautiful Catholic churches. Have you ever wondered why we build such beautiful churches? I can tell you this: It's not about the art or the architecture. It's because we believe that Jesus is truly present in the Eucharist.

Stand in St. Peter's Basilica in Rome, Notre Dame or Sacre Coeur in Paris, St. Mary's Cathedral in Sydney, Duomo Cathedral in Milan, Las Lajas Sanctuary in Colombia, St. Patrick's Cathedral in New York, the Basilica of the National Shrine of the Immaculate Conception in Washington DC, or any of a thousand other incredible Catholic churches around the world and you will feel awe and sense the sacred.

What do these beautiful churches really say to us? They say that there is something greater here than art and architecture, something more than history—and not just some*thing* . . . but some*one*. That someone is Jesus Christ, truly present in the Eucharist, present in all these churches, and present in the tabernacle in your local church.

That's why I love stopping by a church for a few quiet minutes.

We all have questions that we need answered, and we all need advice from time to time. But when we need advice we tend to ask people who know just about nothing about nothing, instead of going to the man who has all the answers.

All the answers are in the tabernacle. Jesus has all the answers and he patiently waits for us in the tabernacle, day and night, to share those answers with us. Next time you are grappling with a decision, stop by your church and ask Jesus for his advice. Receiving Jesus in the Eucharist is the ultimate spiritual experience, but there is also something powerful about just sitting in his presence.

In the Gospels we read time and time again about Jesus leaving his disciples and the crowds and going to a place set apart. In the first chapter of Mark's Gospel we read, "In the morning, while it was still very dark, he got up and went out to a deserted place, and there he prayed." (Mark 1:35) If Jesus needed this time in silence and solitude, how much more do you think we need it? The world is a busy and noisy place, and all of that tends to distract us from what matters most.

It is getting harder and harder to find a quiet place in this world, but one of the great gifts the Catholic Church gives to us all is places that are set apart for quiet reflection. Churches and chapels, retreat centers and monasteries—over the centuries the Church has established places in almost every community on earth for us to be still and quiet and reflect on what is happening within us and around us.

Once again, I want to encourage you to establish the habits of daily prayer in your life. This is a foundational habit that will serve you well for the rest of your life. The sooner you start taking your spiritual life seriously, the happier you will be.

Get close to God, and stay close to God.

Have you ever thought of Mary as the first tabernacle?

If you live until you are eighty-five years old, *how many Sundays* do you have left?

discussion questions

1. IF YOU COULD VISIT ONE OF THE BEAUTIFUL CHURCHES MENTIONED IN THIS SECTION, WHICH WOULD YOU CHOOSE?

_____
_____
_____
_____
_____
_____

2. AT THIS TIME IN YOUR LIFE, WHAT QUESTION WOULD YOU LIKE JESUS TO ANSWER FOR YOU? (YOUR QUESTION SHOULD BE ABOUT SOMETHING THAT APPLIES DIRECTLY TO YOU.)

_____
_____
_____
_____
_____
_____
_____

3. WHAT QUIET PLACES HAVE YOU FOUND TO SPEND A FEW MINUTES IN EACH DAY?

_____
_____
_____
_____
_____
_____
_____

VIRTUE IN FOCUS

Tem·per·ance
[tem-per-*uh* ns]

Controlling your thoughts, words, actions, and feelings.

Who do you know who exemplifies this virtue?

In what area of your life do you find it most difficult to practice temperance?

What is one way you can become more temperate this week?

What do you think Mary had planned for her life before the angel appeared to her?

7.5 DECISION point

Every Sunday morning you make a decision. It's the biggest decision of your week. To go or not to go, that is the question.

You might say that Mass is boring. I was bored at Mass for a long time, but then something happened. I started listening to what God was trying to say to me. I got myself a little journal and took it to Mass with me, and each week I wrote down the one thing that I felt God was saying to me. I have been doing this for fifteen years now. Each year I get a new journal. At home in my study, where I write, I have these fifteen journals on a shelf. When I get writer's block I pick one up and just start reading. Some days when I don't feel like praying I take one of these journals and just talk to God about some of the things he has said to me over the years. It is amazing the things God will say to us when we start listening.

I hope you go to Mass every Sunday for the rest of your lives so that God can nourish you with the Eucharist, but I also hope you will start to appreciate the bigger picture.

God has declared Sunday—the Sabbath day—as a day of rest. In Genesis 2:2 we read about God resting on the seventh day. Why? Why did God rest? Was he tired? No. God is a pure spirit and as such does not experience fatigue like we human beings do. So, why did he rest? He rested because he foresaw our need for rest. He wanted to show us how to live. He wanted to demonstrate that rest is a good thing, and something that we all need.

You have a legitimate need for rest. The Sabbath is God's response to your physical and spiritual need for rest and renewal. And nothing will renew you like receiving the Eucharist. It is literally food from Heaven.

On average you will live for another seventy years. That means you have 3,640 Sundays left. Don't waste a single one. It may seem like a lot, but you will be amazed at how quickly life passes. It feels like six months ago I was sitting where you are preparing for Confirmation . . . but that was twenty-five years ago.

You have a lot of decisions to make. Getting yourself to Mass on Sunday and receiving the Eucharist will help you make better decisions in every area of your life.

JOURNAL QUESTIONS

1. WHY DO YOU THINK OUR CULTURE HAS REJECTED THE SABBATH?

_____

_____

_____

_____

_____

_____

2. HOW CAN YOU HONOR THE SABBATH AS A DAY OF REST?

_____

_____

_____

_____

_____

_____

_____

3. HOW WOULD THE WORLD BE DIFFERENT IF EVERYONE TOOK ONE DAY EACH WEEK TO REST AND TURN THEIR ATTENTION TOWARD GOD?

_____

_____

_____

_____

_____

_____

_____

_____

Psalm 63

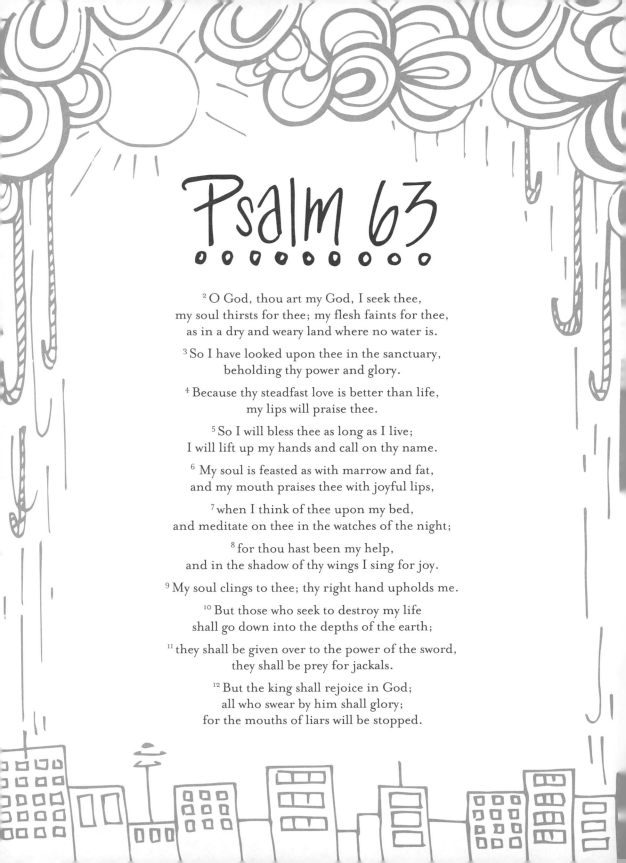

^{2} O God, thou art my God, I seek thee,
my soul thirsts for thee; my flesh faints for thee,
as in a dry and weary land where no water is.

^{3} So I have looked upon thee in the sanctuary,
beholding thy power and glory.

^{4} Because thy steadfast love is better than life,
my lips will praise thee.

^{5} So I will bless thee as long as I live;
I will lift up my hands and call on thy name.

^{6} My soul is feasted as with marrow and fat,
and my mouth praises thee with joyful lips,

^{7} when I think of thee upon my bed,
and meditate on thee in the watches of the night;

^{8} for thou hast been my help,
and in the shadow of thy wings I sing for joy.

^{9} My soul clings to thee; thy right hand upholds me.

^{10} But those who seek to destroy my life
shall go down into the depths of the earth;

^{11} they shall be given over to the power of the sword,
they shall be prey for jackals.

^{12} But the king shall rejoice in God;
all who swear by him shall glory;
for the mouths of liars will be stopped.

THE EUCHARIST
CROSSWORD PUZZLE

ACROSS

1. The changing of simple bread and wine into the body and blood of Jesus Christ

4. Uncertainty about something

5. A place that houses the Eucharist outside of Mass, where it can be kept for adoration

9. Trust and confidence in God and what he has revealed to us

11. What God has revealed about himself to humanity

12. The assistance God gives us to do what is good, true, noble, and right

15. The real presence of Jesus

DOWN

2. The ability to control oneself and direct one's actions

3. A town in Italy where a Eucharistic miracle took place around the year 700

6. One of the ways Catholics honor God and the Sabbath is by attending _____.

7. The seventh day of the week, observed as the day of rest and worship

8. Hard to do or accomplish

10. Worship with a profound love

13. An event that surpasses all human and natural powers

14. Something that is beyond human understanding

Answers on page 327

SESSION EIGHT

The

HOLY SPIRIT

Come, Holy Spirit, I invite you into the very depths of my being.
Lead me, guide me, coach me, encourage me, and challenge me.
Direct me in all things. Teach me to become a great decision maker,
so that in every moment of every day I can choose what is good,
right, noble, and just. Amen.

Matthew Kelly

8. THE HOLY SPIRIT

Have you ever noticed the difference between a person who is inspired and one who is not? Sometimes when you watch two teams compete in sports, you can tell one team is inspired and the other isn't. Inspiration makes a huge difference.

For twenty years I have been working with people of all ages and from all walks of life, and one thing that I have noticed over and over again is that people don't do anything until they are inspired, but once they are inspired there is almost nothing they cannot do.

The disciples are a perfect example. Before Pentecost they were full of fear. After Pentecost they were full of courage. What changed? They got inspired. They got filled with the Holy Spirit. Just like you are going to at Confirmation.

Think about those times in your life when you have felt inspired to do something really great. Where does that inspiration come from? The Holy Spirit. God inspires us to do great things with our lives.

Jesus didn't leave us to face the world alone. He promised he would be with us and that he would send the Holy Spirit to guide, inspire, and encourage us. Jesus made that promise not just to the disciples, and not just to other people; it was a promise he made to you. And in Confirmation Jesus is going to make good on his promise.

So let's take a look at who the Holy Spirit is and what he means to your life.

8.1 WHO IS THE HOLY SPIRIT?

One of the shortest Christian prayers is the Sign of the Cross. Sixteen words. (In the name of the Father, and of the Son, and of the Holy Spirit. Amen.) It's not just the way we begin and end prayer; it is a prayer unto itself. And it contains one of the most sublime mysteries of our faith: the Trinity.

The Trinity is three Persons in one God. We don't worship three different gods, but one single being who is threefold and yet remains one. Confusing? It should be a little confusing if we really think about it.

But to get us started, think about water. Water can take different forms: liquid, ice, or steam. It is still H_2O; it is just taking different forms. Now, God does not change from one form to another at different times; God is always three and always one. Still confused? That's OK.

You see, you cannot come to the conclusion of the Trinity by reason alone. It would not matter how much you thought about it; you would

H2O.

Imagine a world without water. Without water, life would not exist. Water is essential, and 780 million people don't have access to clean water today. As a result they are in a constant struggle for survival.

never arrive at the Trinity through reason alone. And science cannot prove or disprove the Trinity. We know about the Trinity through Revelation. If God had not chosen to reveal himself to us we would not know about the Trinity. This is one of the beautiful mysteries of our faith.

You cannot know everything through reason and science, some things we only know because God has revealed them to us. And if there were no mystery there would be no need for faith, because without mystery religion would be simply an intellectual pursuit . . . and it is so much more than that.

In the Scriptures God is revealed as the Father who creates us (Genesis 1), his Son who redeems us (Matthew 1), and the Holy Spirit who inspires us (Acts 1). The whole history we find in the Bible is the story of God's ongoing concern for the human family, and for each of us individually as his children.

The Holy Spirit is the Third Person of the Trinity. He is the one whom Jesus promised the Father would send to guide and encourage us. When you think of it, the Holy Spirit is incredibly practical. How often in your life do you need guidance and encouragement? Whether you are aware of it or not, you need these things every day, and the Holy Spirit is within you to provide them.

But it would be a mistake to think that the Holy Spirit just came into being after Jesus died and rose from the dead. The Spirit has always been with the Father and the Son. Open your Bibles to the very beginning and you will discover the Holy Spirit in the second verse. Genesis 1:2 reads, "In the beginning when God created the heavens and the earth, the earth was a formless void and darkness covered the face of the deep, while the Spirit of God was moving over the face of the waters." ⟶

Genesis 1:2

KNOW IT: God created the heavens and the earth. Creation is not an accident. You are not an accident. God intended to create you and the whole universe.

THINK ABOUT IT: Not only did God create you, but he created you in his image. You are therefore creative in your own ways.

LIVE IT: How is God inviting you to be creative?

But what does all this mean to you? Why should you care about the Holy Spirit?

Think about it like this. In the previous session we talked about the power of Jesus' presence. Well, listen to what Jesus says in John 16:7: "I tell you the truth, it is to your advantage that I go away." Now, why would it be to our advantage for Jesus to go away? Jesus continues, "For if I do not go away the Spirit will not come to you."

How powerful must the Spirit be? Are you ready to have that power unleashed in your life? What will unleashing the Holy Spirit in your life mean to you?

The Holy Spirit will help you find and understand truth, and you will never have more happiness in your life than you have truth. The more truth you allow into your heart, mind, and soul, the happier you will be. But if you allow the truth to be crowded out with lies and deceit, you

John 16:13

"This is a prayer we need to pray every day, every day: Holy Spirit may my heart be open to the Word of God, may my heart be open to good, may my heart be open to the beauty of God, every day."

—Pope Francis

will find yourself miserable. The Holy Spirit wants to help you build a throne for truth in your heart.

The Spirit of God is within you. This is good news. It means that you have a power within you that you have not even begun to comprehend.

The Holy Spirit will give you the courage to face difficult situations.

The Holy Spirit means that you are never alone. He is always with you, ready to guide you, encourage you, comfort you, and challenge you.

The Holy Spirit is a true friend who always wants what is best for you.

The Holy Spirit gives you the wisdom to know what is right and what is wrong, and leads you in the path of what is good and right.

The Holy Spirit empowers you to do things you would not otherwise be able to do.

The Holy Spirit is transformational. Think about Peter, who denied Jesus three times before his death out of selfish fear. But after Pentecost he literally risked his life just to let people know about Jesus.

The Holy Spirit doesn't change us into someone else; he just brings the best and the most out of us.

The Holy Spirit will help you know and do God's will.

But here is my favorite: The Holy Spirit will allow you to maintain joy even in the midst of suffering. Suffering is an inevitable part of life. It is easy to be joyful when things are going well, but the Holy Spirit brings us joy in times of suffering, and that is a thing of beauty.

Saint Paul is a perfect example here. Ephesians, Philippians, Colossians, and Philemon are called the "prison" epistles because they were written during Paul's first imprisonment, mentioned in Acts 28. Throughout these writings he talks about his joy and all the things he rejoices about. When you think about the fact that he was in prison for being Christian and you consider the filthy conditions of prisons at the time, you have to ask yourself: What did he have to be joyful about?

He was joyful even in the midst of suffering because he was filled with the Holy Spirit.

All this is what the Holy Spirit wants to do for you.

I don't know how seriously you are taking this whole Confirmation thing, but trust me, it is worth taking a little more seriously. You will never regret it. But if you don't take it seriously, I can guarantee you there will come a time when you will regret that.

This is important stuff. I want to encourage you to take it seriously. You'll be glad you did.

Discussion Questions

1. IN YOUR OWN WORDS, WHO IS THE HOLY SPIRIT?

_____
_____
_____
_____
_____
_____

2. DESCRIBE A TIME IN YOUR LIFE WHEN YOU FELT INSPIRED BY THE HOLY SPIRIT.

_____
_____
_____
_____
_____
_____
_____

3. WOULD YOU LIKE TO LEARN HOW TO EXPERIENCE JOY EVEN IN THE MIDST OF GREAT SUFFERING LIKE SAINT PAUL? WHAT DO YOU THINK HIS SECRET WAS?

_____
_____
_____
_____
_____
_____
_____

THE GOAL OF OUR LIFE IS TO LIVE WITH GOD FOREVER.
God, who loves us, gave us life.
OUR OWN RESPONSE OF LOVE ALLOWS GOD'S LIFE
to flow into us WITHOUT LIMIT.

All the things in this world are **GIFTS FROM GOD**,
Presented to us so that WE CAN KNOW GOD MORE EASILY
AND MAKE *a return of love* MORE READILY.
As a result, we appreciate and use all these gifts of God
Insofar as they help us TO DEVELOP AS LOVING PERSONS.
But if any of these gifts become the *center of our lives,*
THEY DISPLACE GOD
And so hinder our growth toward our goal.

In everyday life, then, we must hold ourselves in balance
Before all of these created gifts
insofar as **WE HAVE A CHOICE**
And are not bound by some obligation.
WE SHOULD NOT FIX OUR DESIRES on health or sickness,
Wealth or poverty, success or failure, a long life or a short one.
For everything has the potential of *calling forth* in us
A DEEPER RESPONSE TO OUR LIFE IN GOD.

Our only desire and our **ONE CHOICE** should be this:
I WANT AND I CHOOSE WHAT BETTER LEADS
TO GOD'S *deepening* HIS LIFE IN ME.

———

St. Ignatius of Loyola

Matthew 6:33

KNOW IT: Seek first the things of God.

THINK ABOUT IT: What are your priorities? Are they worldly priorities or godly priorities?

LIVE IT: Make God's priorities your own today.

Solomon was the son of David and King of Israel from c. 970 to 931 BC. The Bible credits Solomon with building the first temple in Jerusalem and portrays him as the wisest man of his time. This wisdom was a gift from God; the first book of Kings recounts how Solomon prayed for wisdom. During his reign he became incredibly wealthy and powerful, but ultimately his sins, which included turning away from God and to idolatry, led to the kingdom being torn in two. The story of Solomon teaches us how seductive and disorienting power, fame, and money can be.

8.2 UNOPENED GIFTS

If God appeared to you in a vision and said, "Ask me for anything and I will give it to you," what would you ask him for? Think about it for a moment. Would you ask for money, a long life, success in a career, victory for your favorite sports team?

This is exactly what happened to Solomon, the son of King David. Biblical scholars believe that Solomon was probably only around twelve years old when he became king. In 1 Kings 3:5–15 we read about God appearing to Solomon in a dream and asking what he would like God to give him. Solomon asked for wisdom. In particular, he wanted the wisdom to discern right from wrong, good from evil. This pleased God so much that he granted Solomon wisdom in abundance, but he also granted him riches, honor, and a long life.

Here we find a connection between how God treated Solomon and Jesus' teachings. In Matthew 6:33 we read, "Seek first the kingdom of God and his righteousness, and all these other things will be given to you in addition." This is what Solomon did, and God responded lavishly.

God is a giver of gifts.

One Christmas when I was a child, I half-unwrapped gifts to see what they were, and if the gift was not the one thing I was looking for, I wouldn't even finish unwrapping it; I would just move on to the next parcel. I remember opening one of those half-unwrapped gifts a few days later and realizing that I had misjudged the importance and value of the gift.

At Baptism you received the seven gifts of the Holy Spirit, but you may not have fully unwrapped them yet. At Confirmation these gifts will be strengthened in you; the question is, how will you respond to them?

I could put a million dollars in a bank account for you, but if you ignored it and never used it, it wouldn't do you any good. The gifts of the Holy Spirit are worth more than many millions of dollars, but if you don't engage them and nurture them, you will not experience all that they have to offer.

How was Mary different from Solomon?

So, what are the seven gifts of the Holy Spirit?

1. Wisdom: The ability to discern what is true, right, and lasting. Wisdom enables us to see life from God's perspective. It helps you to establish the right priorities in your life, and leads you to think and act in mature ways.

2. Understanding: Allows you to look beyond the shallowness of the world and see the lasting truth in every situation, by recognizing how God is working in our lives.

3. Counsel: The right judgment that allows us to see what is right and what is wrong, and the prudence to act accordingly.

4. Fortitude: The courage and strength of will to do what you know you should, even if that means personal loss or suffering.

5. Knowledge: The ability to see things from a supernatural viewpoint. In particular, to know what God is asking of you.

6. Piety: A loyalty to God that manifests as generous love and affectionate obedience. This is the gift that allows you to love and worship God as he deserves to be loved and worshipped.

7. Fear of the Lord (Reverence): Helps us to grasp God's greatness and our dependence on him. As a result, we are filled with enormous respect for God and we dread above all offending him or being separated from him. Our Jewish ancestors believed that fear of the Lord was the beginning of wisdom. Of course, it is not a fear like we usually think of fear today. It is more like an overwhelming sense of not wanting to disappoint the One who has done (and continues to do) so much for us.

These are the seven gifts of the Holy Spirit. When the bishop prays over you at your Confirmation, he will be praying that you are filled with them. Each of these gifts helps you to become the-best-version-of-yourself and live the life God created you to live.

Every day you face situations that require these gifts. We have taken a few minutes to explore them, but I want to encourage you to delve into them more. If you don't know what they are, you won't use them. Knowing them is essential if you are going to activate them in your daily life.

WHAT YOU **CHOOSE** TO **THINK ABOUT** IS A **REALLY IMPORTANT CHOICE** YOU MAKE **EVERY DAY.**

· GIFTS · OF · THE · SPIRIT ·

WISDOM
Understanding
COUNSEL
FORTITUDE
KNOWLEDGE
Piety
FEAR OF THE LORD (REVERENCE)

GET THE APP!

Discussion QUESTIONS

1. HAVE YOU EVER GIVEN SOMEONE A GIFT AND HE OR SHE WAS UNGRATEFUL? HOW DID THAT MAKE YOU FEEL?

2. WHICH OF THE SEVEN GIFTS OF THE HOLY SPIRIT DO YOU FEEL MOST IN NEED OF AT THIS TIME IN YOUR LIFE?

3. HOW WOULD YOUR LIFE BE BETTER IF YOU REALLY OPENED YOURSELF UP TO THE GIFTS OF THE HOLY SPIRIT?

MY THOUGHTS

8.3 The Fruits of the Holy Spirit

How do we know if we are filled with the Holy Spirit? How will you know if you are seeking God's loving plan for your life and responding to it? Jesus advises us that we can judge a tree by its fruits. "A good tree cannot bear bad fruit, nor can a bad tree bear good fruit." (Matthew 7:18) What fruit is your life bearing today? What fruit do you want your life to bear in the future? What fruit do you think God wants you to bear?

If we are really allowing the Holy Spirit to flourish within us, the fruits should be bubbling forth in our lives. Those fruits are: love, joy, peace, patience, kindness, goodness, generosity, gentleness, faithfulness, modesty, self-control, and chastity.

You might not know it yet, but these are the things you want. You want these fruits more than anything else you have ever wanted. In fact, every yearning you have is for these things. We try to substitute other things for them, but it never works.

Embracing and engaging the gifts of the Holy Spirit that we spoke about earlier—wisdom, understanding, counsel, fortitude, knowledge, piety, and fear of the Lord—is the path that leads to the fruit of the Holy Spirit.

Let's take a look at the twelve fruits of the Holy Spirit.

Love: To love God above all things and to love others as God calls us to.

Joy: This is more than just being happy. It is a feeling awakened by the possession or expectation of something good. And this joy can be present deep within us even when things don't go our way.

Peace: The serenity and tranquility that flows from order. The world can make our lives disordered and chaotic. God wants to bring order to our lives—and with that order comes a deep and abiding peace.

Patience: Enables us to endure inconvenience, difficulties, and hardship without complaint.

Kindness: Concern for others who are in trouble or in need.

Goodness: Doing what is good and right in every circumstance.

Generosity: To give freely of our time, talent, and treasure beyond what justice requires.

Gentleness: To be submissive to God and considerate of others.

Faithfulness: To be reliable and trustworthy.

Modesty: The moderation of our speech, dress, and behavior.

Self-control: The control of our desires so that we can focus them on what is good and right.

Chastity: The moderation of desire for sexual pleasure according to right reason, faith, and state in life.

If you really take the time to consider what you want from life, you will discover that a life filled with the fruit of the Holy Spirit is what you are yearning for. If you consider the opposite of each of the fruits, you will discover that they lead to a life of slavery and misery.

When we reject the fruit of the Holy Spirit we fall into a life of sin. Sin rejects God's design for who we are and the way we should live our lives. In doing so, sin rejects order and embraces the chaos of disorder. This disorder robs us of the tranquility and peace that God desires for us. When your room is tidy and things are in the places they belong, there is a certain peace and tranquility that comes from that. If your room is a mess, with things scattered all around, the chaos of that environment robs you of peace and tranquility and creates anxiousness.

The way of God is one of peace and order. The way of sin is one of chaos and anxiousness. Which will you choose?

VIRTUE IN FOCUS

Gen·tle·ness
[jen-tl-*ness*]

mildness of speech, temperament, and behavior; kindness and tenderness

Who do you know who exemplifies the virtue of gentleness?

In what ways is God calling you to be gentle with others?

How is God inviting you to be gentle with yourself?

"DO NOT BE AFRAID. DO NOT BE SATISFIED WITH MEDIOCRITY. PUT OUT INTO THE DEEP AND LET DOWN YOUR NETS FOR A CATCH."

—JOHN PAUL II

DISCUSSION QUESTIONS

1. WHICH PERSON IN YOUR LIFE WOULD YOU LIKE TO FILL WITH JOY?

2. HOW WOULD A LACK OF SELF-CONTROL MAKE IT HARDER TO EXPERIENCE THE OTHER ELEVEN FRUITS OF THE HOLY SPIRIT?

3. CAN YOU SEE HOW GOD'S WAYS ARE DESIGNED TO BRING ORDER TO OUR LIVES AND LIBERATE US FROM WORLDLY CHAOS?

MY THOUGHTS

8.4 PROMPTED

When I was a teenager I thought I could make every decision on my own. As I got older I came to the realization that so many people have gathered so much wisdom from their successes and their failures—and most people are more than happy to share that wisdom if you ask them to. Since then I have learned many things from many people. But every day I call on the Holy Spirit to guide me.

Do you remember in Session 4 when I talked about walking the Camino? While I was walking that path across northern Spain, at every fork in the road I was looking for the sign that showed me which way to go. Life is a long journey. Every day we come to many forks in the road and we have to decide which path we will walk. The signs are there to guide us, but they tend to be less visible. Our conscience sometimes nudges us in a particular direction; at other times it alerts us to danger ahead. This is the Holy Spirit prompting us to act in ways that are good and noble.

What does it mean to be prompted? To prompt means to encourage, inspire, or remind someone to act. Sometimes we need the Holy Spirit to encourage us. We know what we should do, but it seems difficult and we need the Holy Spirit to give us courage. At other times we need the Holy Spirit to inspire us. We don't know what to do and we need him to fill our minds with the right ideas. And then there are times when we get carried away or distracted and simply need the Holy Spirit to remind us.

Learning to listen to the promptings of the Holy Spirit is one of the most important skills you can develop. As with most things, we get good at recognizing the promptings of the Holy Spirit by practicing. The Holy Spirit is always prompting us toward truth and away from lies. He is always encouraging us toward the-best-version-of-ourselves and away from a-lesser-version-of-ourselves. The Holy Spirit is always prompting us toward what is good for us, and away from what is not.

So, how do we learn to recognize the promptings of the Holy Spirit?

A great place to start is with a few minutes of prayer each day. Prayer creates a stronger connection between you and God. The stronger the connection, the clearer the message. We have all been on phone calls when the connection is horrible and you either can't hear the other person at all, or you only get every second or third word. How is your connection with God? Is it a good, strong, clear connection? Or is it a weak and jumbled connection? How can you increase the number of bars you have in your connection with God?

PEOPLE DON'T DO ANYTHING UNTIL THEY ARE *Inspired* BUT ONCE THEY ARE INSPIRED THERE IS ALMOST *Nothing* THEY CAN'T DO.

Daily prayer is an opportunity to strengthen our connection with God. The stronger the connection, the more clearly we will hear the promptings of the Holy Spirit. The more we follow those promptings, the happier we will be.

In Session 4 we practiced The Prayer Process. Have you been using it each day in your daily prayer? I hope so. It is a game changer.

The reason I bring it up again now is because it is perfectly suited to teach us to listen to the promptings of the Holy Spirit. Let's walk through it again quickly and I will explain.

You will remember there are seven parts to the Prayer Process. The first part is Gratitude.

1. GRATITUDE: Begin by thanking God in a personal dialogue for whatever you are most grateful for today.

Here we are asking the Holy Spirit to remind us of all the people, things, experiences, and opportunities we have to be grateful for today.

2. AWARENESS: Revisit the times in the past twenty-four hours when you were and were not the-best-version-of-yourself. Talk to God about these situations and what you learned from them.

Now we are asking the Holy Spirit to inspire us to learn from the events of the past twenty-four hours.

3. SIGNIFICANT MOMENTS: Identify something you experienced in the past twenty-four hours and explore what God might be trying to say to you through that event (or person).

We don't always recognize the signs God places in our path at the time. Here we ask the Holy Spirit to let us know if we missed any significant signs today.

4. PEACE: Ask God to forgive you for any wrong you have committed (against yourself, another person, or him) and to fill you with a deep and abiding peace.

Here the Holy Spirit enlightens us to the mistakes we have made along the way, so that we can avoid them in the future.

5. FREEDOM: Speak with God about how he is inviting you to change your life, so that you can experience the freedom to be the-best-version-of-yourself.

Now the Holy Spirit challenges us and encourages us to change.

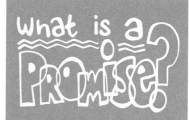

A promise is a statement telling someone that you will definitely do something or that something will definitely happen in the future.

Jesus made many promises. One of those promises was that he would send us the Holy Spirit. What other promises did Jesus make? Do you believe him? Do you take him at his word? Do you trust Jesus?

"EVERY TRUE PRAYER IS A PRAYER OF THE CHURCH; BY MEANS OF THAT PRAYER THE CHURCH PRAYS, SINCE IT IS THE HOLY SPIRIT LIVING IN THE CHURCH, WHO IN EVERY SINGLE SOUL 'PRAYS IN US WITH UNSPEAKABLE GROANINGS.'"
—EDITH STEIN

"LET'S ASK OURSELVES: ARE WE OPEN TO THE HOLY SPIRIT?"

—POPE FRANCIS

6. OTHERS: Lift up to God anyone you feel called to pray for today, asking God to bless and guide them.

Here the Holy Spirit reminds us of all those who need our love, support, and encouragement.

7. Pray the Our Father.

Allowing the gifts and fruit of the Holy Spirit to animate us is an everyday job. With every choice you either embrace or reject the Holy Spirit—and the fruits and gifts he wants to fill you with.

Take a few minutes out of each day to connect with God in prayer. This will strengthen your connection with him and allow you to hear the promptings of the Holy Spirit more clearly. Listen to those promptings and you will discover something I have learned over the years: Every regret in life comes from not listening to the voice of God in our lives. You will never regret following your conscience and the promptings of the Holy Spirit. All of life's regrets come when we ignore our conscience and the promptings of the Holy Spirit.

Pentecost is the feast commemorating the descent of the Holy Spirit upon the Apostles of Jesus as described in Acts of the Apostles 2:1–31. For this reason Pentecost is referred to as the Birthday of the Church.

DISCUSSION

1. IF YOU WERE GOING TO GO ON A PILGRIMAGE AND WALK THE CAMINO, WHOM WOULD YOU TAKE WITH YOU? WHY?

2. WHEN WAS THE LAST TIME YOU FELT THE HOLY SPIRIT PROMPTING YOU TO DO SOMETHING? OR NOT TO DO SOMETHING?

3. WHAT IS YOUR FAVORITE PART OF THE PRAYER PROCESS? WHY?

Psalm 139

O LORD, thou hast searched me
and known me!

2 Thou knowest when I sit down
and when I rise up; thou discernest
my thoughts from afar.

3 Thou searchest out my path and my lying down,
and art acquainted with all my ways.

4 Even before a word is on my tongue,
lo, O LORD, thou knowest it altogether.

5 Thou dost beset me behind and before,
and layest thy hand upon me.

6 Such knowledge is too wonderful for me;
it is high, I cannot attain it.

7 Whither shall I go from thy Spirit?
Or whither shall I flee from thy presence?

8 If I ascend to heaven, thou art there!
If I make my bed in Sheol, thou art there!

9 If I take the wings of the morning
and dwell in the uttermost parts of the sea,

10 even there thy hand shall lead me,
and thy right hand shall hold me.

11 If I say, "Let only darkness cover me,
and the light about me be night,"

12 even the darkness is not dark to thee,
the night is bright as the day;
for darkness is as light with thee.

13 For thou didst form my inward parts,
thou didst knit me together in
my mother's womb.

14 I praise thee, for thou art fearful and
wonderful. Wonderful are thy works!

Thou knowest me right well;
15 my frame was not hidden from thee,
when I was being made in secret, intricately
wrought in the depths of the earth.

16 Thy eyes beheld my unformed substance;
in thy book were written, every one of them,
the days that were formed for me,
when as yet there was none of them.

17 How precious to me are thy thoughts,
O God! How vast is the sum of them!

18 If I would count them, they are
more than the sand.
When I awake, I am still with thee.

19 O that thou wouldst slay the wicked,
O God, and that men of blood would
depart from me, 20 men who maliciously
defy thee, who lift themselves up
against thee for evil!

21 Do I not hate them that hate thee,
O LORD? And do I not loathe them
that rise up against thee?

22 I hate them with perfect hatred;
I count them my enemies.

23 Search me, O God, and know my heart!
Try me and know my thoughts!

24 And see if there be any wicked way in me,
and lead me in the way everlasting!

8.5 DECISION point

1 Corinthians 6:19

KNOW IT:
You are a temple of the Holy Spirit.

THINK ABOUT IT:
Are you honoring your body as a temple of the Holy Spirit?

LIVE IT: What changes do you need to make to make your body a better home for God?

You have another decision to make. Are you going to welcome the Holy Spirit into your life or ignore and reject him?

If you are going to welcome the Holy Spirit, then prepare yourself to receive him. If you had an important visitor coming to your home, you would tidy up and make special preparations.

In the previous session we talked about the beautiful churches all around the world and why we build such beautiful churches. The reason is because they are Jesus' home. But visit a great cathedral in any major city in the world and you will find two types of people. The first type is there to pray. The second is just there to look around. The first recognizes that Jesus is present. The second does not. Pilgrims and tourists. Don't be a tourist!

The Scriptures teach us that you are a temple of the Holy Spirit (1 Corinthians 6:19). The Holy Spirit is always present within us. Embrace that. Celebrate that. The Holy Spirit is the ultimate adviser.

You are of course free to ignore or reject the Holy Spirit. But keep in mind that there are consequences if you do. The consequences of embracing the Holy Spirit are peace, joy, order, and purpose. The consequences of rejecting the Holy Spirit and his direction in your life are anxiety, chaos, and the despair of purposelessness.

If you do choose to welcome the Holy Spirit into your life, he will invite you to join in his work. The Holy Spirit is the great encourager. Life is not easy and everyone needs daily encouragement, because the world is full of discouragement and bullying.

I hope you will live an inspired life. I hope you will live in the Spirit. If you do, I know you too will become a great encourager.

What do you think was the best conversation Mary ever had with the Holy Spirit?

JOURNAL questions

1. ARE YOU GOING TO WELCOME THE HOLY SPIRIT INTO YOUR LIFE?

2. HOW WILL HAVING THE HOLY SPIRIT AS YOUR CONSTANT COMPANION MAKE LIFE BETTER?

3. WHOM DO YOU FEEL CALLED TO ENCOURAGE TODAY?

THE HOLY SPIRIT
CROSSWORD PUZZLE

ACROSS

1. Mildness of speech, temperament, and behavior; kindness and tenderness

3. Virtue; moral excellence

7. Something that is in accordance with fact or reality

9. Three persons in one God: Father, Son, Holy Spirit

11. When the Holy Spirit descended on the disciples after the Ascension of Jesus

12. Filled with a desire to do something that is good

14. Friendliness, generosity, and considerateness

DOWN

2. Behavior, manner, or appearance intended to avoid impropriety or indecency

4. The third person in the Trinity, sent by God to guide and encourage us

5. What God has allowed us to know about him that cannot be discovered by reason alone

6. Giving more of something than is strictly necessary or expected

8. Followers and students of Jesus

10. The capacity to accept or tolerate delay, trouble, or suffering without getting angry or upset

13. Loyalty, constancy, and steadfastness

Answers on page 327

The

CHURCH

Lord Jesus, you prayed that your people would be one; forgive us Lord and take away the pride and arrogance which divides your Church. Break down the walls which separate us; unite us with your bonds of love and accomplish your will. I pray that by the power of your Spirit your healing would work in the body of your Church and through me, to bring about the purpose of your will. Amen.

Author Unknown

WHEN YOU DON'T SHOW UP, SOMETHING IS MISSING.

Romans 12:5

KNOW IT: We are one body.

THINK ABOUT IT:
We are all in this together. It is not every man and every woman for him- or herself.

LIVE IT: What gifts has God given you to contribute to the rest of the body? How do you need the rest of the Church to help you grow?

What would it have been like to be at Mary's side during those first days of the Church?

9. THE CHURCH

What is your image of the Church? When you think about the Church, what comes to mind? The building. The Pope. St. Peter's Basilica in Rome. Your parish. A place to pray. A place of healing. A community.

I like to think of the Catholic Church as a big family—a family of faith; the biggest family in the world. There are more than 1.2 billion Catholics in the world, and more than eighty million Catholics in the United States alone. That's a big family!

This family—the Church—is made up of people like you and me. We are pilgrims on a journey together. When we are at our best, we form dynamic communities. People need community. We need people to do life with, others who can encourage and challenge us. We need others to live for so we don't get swallowed up by our own selfishness.

Paul tells us in Romans 12:5 that we are all one body. The right hand cannot leave the body. It needs the body and the body needs it. Without the body, it is useless. In the same way, we need each other.

We need the Church—and the Church needs us.

We are the Church. So when you don't show up, something is missing. When you don't show up, the Church can't fulfill its mission. So I hope you will continue to show up or start showing up. And more than just showing up, I hope you will get involved by sharing your talents, your energy, and your compassion with your spiritual family—the Church.

9.1 THE FIRST CHRISTIANS & THE EARLY CHURCH

On any Sunday you can just wander into your local church for Mass, but the first Christians didn't have it so easy. The early Christians were persecuted by both the Jews and the Roman Empire. From the earliest times, Christians have been discriminated against, tortured, and murdered for their faith. You may be tempted to think that this is all behind us now, but that would be a mistake. This is still happening in many parts of the world today. Google "persecution of Christians today" and what you discover will surprise and sadden you.

That's right. More than two thousand years later, Christians are still being beaten and murdered because of their faith. And in modern nations, like America, that are becoming increasingly secular, public policy is being used to discriminate against Christians more with every passing day.

Life for the first Christians was not easy, so why were so many people attracted to their way of life?

The ancient world was brutal, cold, and impersonal. By contrast, Christianity was warm, caring, and deeply personal. The first Christians modeled a more humane, compassionate, noble, and loving way of life—and it was phenomenally attractive. This is why people were joining them a thousand at a time, even though joining meant risking their lives.

In the first century the Church was organized around agape love. What is agape love?

Agape love is a choice we make to love another person regardless of whether he loves us back or not. It means that you choose to love someone even if he is your enemy. Agape love is not based on emotion in any way. In fact, it may at times be contrary to every emotion you have. It is a choice, an act of the will. Agape love is unconditional love. It is the love that sets aside self-interest. It is the love that Jesus modeled for us and calls us to.

This kind of love was profound, revolutionary, countercultural, and attractive two thousand years ago, and it is profound, revolutionary, countercultural, and attractive today. In some way the Church has lost this, and we need to get this agape love back at the center of our communities. The Church needs your help to do that.

Life for the early Christians was not easy, and life for a modern Christian is not easy. It's difficult to love people who ridicule or hurt you. It's difficult to be discriminated against because of your beliefs. It's difficult to stand up for objective truth in a society that thinks truth is whatever the majority decides.

It's difficult to be a good Christian. But that shouldn't be a surprise. Jesus didn't say, "Follow me and you will have a comfortable life." He didn't teach, "Follow me and I will make things easy for you so you never have to worry about anything." No, he didn't mince his words; he made it very clear from the very beginning: "If any want to become my followers, let them deny themselves and take up their cross and follow me." (Matthew 6:24) He did, however, offer this path as a way to fullness of life now and for eternity—and promise to send us the Holy Spirit to guide, encourage, and inspire us.

The world needs more agape love. This is the love Jesus calls us to. Just as the ancient world of the first Christians was brutal, cold, distant, impersonal, and ruled by self-interest, so too is the modern world. As modern society abandons Christianity, the world becomes more and more like it was before the birth of Christianity. All around us there

---

Matthew 6:24

KNOW IT: Deny yourself. Take up your cross. Follow Jesus.

THINK ABOUT IT: Believe it or not, this is the path to the happiness you have been seeking your whole life.

LIVE IT: Find three small ways to deny yourself today.

//////// What is ////////
CHRISTIAN
PERSECUTION?

The act of harassing, annoying, bullying, torturing, excluding, or killing someone because he or she is Christian.

is plenty of evidence that the harsh, impersonal, cold brutality of the pagan world is taking hold of modern society.

The rise of Christianity changed the world with agape love. When Christianity is truly lived it is warm, inviting, caring, deeply personal, and phenomenally attractive, and it sets self-interest aside. The world needs a new and massive wave of agape love. Are you willing to be part of that? We are at another decision point.

Agape love was profound and revolutionary two thousand years ago and remains so today. How many of your peers are walking the halls lonely and depressed? How many don't feel loved? Where is their hope? What gets them through the day?

Agape love is not just a concept. It's a revolutionary invitation for you to reach out to others and share with them the love of God.

"GOD MADE ME TO KNOW HIM, TO LOVE HIM, AND TO SERVE HIM IN THIS WORLD, AND TO BE HAPPY WITH HIM FOREVER IN THE NEXT."

BALTIMORE CATECHISM, LESSON ONE, QUESTION 150.

discussion questions

1. WHEN YOU THINK OF CHURCH, WHAT COMES TO MIND?

_____
_____
_____
_____
_____
_____
_____

2. IF YOU COULD ASK A GROUP OF EARLY CHRISTIANS ONE QUESTION, WHAT WOULD YOU ASK?

_____
_____
_____
_____
_____
_____
_____
_____

3. WHY IS IT DIFFICULT TO PRACTICE AGAPE LOVE?

_____
_____
_____
_____
_____
_____
_____

I AM THE *daughter*
OF A GREAT **KING.**
He is my father
AND MY GOD.
THE WORLD MAY PRAISE ME
OR CRITICIZE ME.

IT MATTERS NOT.

HE IS WITH ME,
always at my side,
GUIDING AND PROTECTING ME.
I DO NOT FEAR
because
I AM HIS.

9.2 : One, Holy, Catholic, & Apostolic

At Mass on Sunday when we pray the Creed, we say, "I believe in one, holy, catholic, and apostolic Church." What does that mean? These are known as the four marks of the Catholic Church and can be traced back to early Christian times. Let's take a look at them one at a time, and explore what they mean for you.

What does it mean that the Church is "one"?

Jesus only started one Church. When we talk about the oneness of the Church we are talking about the unity of God's people. The Church is often referred to as the Body of Christ. Paul speaks about this beautifully in 1 Corinthians 12. He speaks about how we are all given different gifts, but these gifts are given to us not for our own gratification but for "the common good." And he speaks about how we are all part of one body, but each part of the body plays a unique and vital role.

What are your gifts? How is God calling you to use them for the common good? What unique and vital role is God calling you to play in the Church?

God's vision for the Church is that all men and women be united in belief, agape love, and mission. God's vision for the Church is that it be one. This is what Jesus prayed for right before he was arrested and crucified. He prayed for his disciples—and he prayed for you and me. We read about this in chapter seventeen of John's Gospel. It is a beautiful prayer for unity, but Jesus also explains why he is praying for unity. In verse 13, he prays his reason: "so that they may have my joy made complete in themselves." He wants our joy to be complete. He wants your joy to be complete.

Then he prays to God the Father, "I ask not only on behalf of these, but also on behalf of those who will believe in me through their word that they may be one." (John 17:20-21) Let's take one more look. Jesus prays, "I ask not only on behalf of these [the disciples], but also on behalf of those who will believe in me through their word [that's you and me] that they may be one." He wants there to be unity among every Christian—from the first disciples to the last believer at the end of the world.

This is one of the most beautiful passages in the Bible, and perhaps the greatest prayer in the New Testament. It is God praying to God. Jesus asks the Father to give us each perseverance, holiness, joy, and unity.

Over the centuries the oneness of the Church has been attacked,

On Average YOU WILL LIVE FOR ANOTHER 70 YEARS. THAT MEANS YOU HAVE 3,640 SUNDAYS LEFT. Don't WASTE a single ONE.

questioned, and undermined. As a result Christianity is massively divided today—but the Catholic Church remains one. It is the one church that Jesus started.

People sometimes ask me, "Why should I stay in the Catholic Church?" There are lots of reasons you should stay Catholic and grow in your faith every day, but what is more compelling than to say, "You should stay because Jesus prayed you would"? There in the garden of Gethsemane two thousand years ago Jesus agonized over every person who would think about leaving his Church, and he prayed that they would remain one.

The Church is one—this is the first mark.

The second mark of the Church is "holy." What does it this mean that the Church is "holy"?

One definition of the word *holy* is, "set apart for a special purpose by God and for God."

When we speak about the Church being holy, it does not imply that the members of the Church are free from sin and selfishness. This is a common misconception. The holiness of the Church is not derived from the holiness of its members, but rather from the holiness of Jesus.

God created the Church for a reason. So, what is the purpose of the Church? Jesus founded his Church to continue his redemptive and sanctifying work in the world. You might be wondering what this means.

Jesus' redemptive work liberates us from sin, puts us back in right relationship with God, and leads us to Heaven. His sanctifying work helps us to grow in holiness and become the-best-version-of-ourselves by playing the unique role he calls us to play in his divine plan.

The Church is holy because Christ is holy—this is the second mark.

The third mark is "catholic." Not big *C* Catholic, but little *c* catholic. What does it mean that the Church is "catholic"?

The word *catholic* with a small c means "universal." In this sense the Church is for everyone, just as Christ died on the cross and rose from the dead for us all. The Church is also catholic (or universal) in the sense that she has been sent out by Jesus on a mission to the whole of the human race. This small c catholic is what we are speaking of in the Creed, and the third mark of the Church.

When we speak of someone being Catholic with a big C we are speaking of a baptized Christian who accepts and believes the teachings of

What is Baptism?

God rescues us from death through baptism and invites us to a new and vibrant life in him. Baptism is the first sacrament and a prerequisite for all other sacraments. In baptism we become members of the Church, members of the one body of Christ. Through baptism we are liberated from sin and invited to live in the joy God created us for.

OUR HEARTS ARE **RESTLESS** UNTIL THEY *Rest in you.*

SAINT AUGUSTINE

CATHOLICS HAVE BEEN MAKING INCREDIBLE CONTRIBUTIONS TO THE WORLD FOR 2,000 YEARS. WHAT WILL YOUR CONTRIBUTION BE?

Matthew 16: 16–19

KNOW IT: Peter was the first pope, and the papacy is the rock that Jesus chose to build his Church upon.

THINK ABOUT IT: We can trace our spiritual heritage back through 265 popes. That is a beautiful thing.

LIVE IT: Being pope is difficult. Pray for the pope today.

the Church, strives to live in communion with the Church through the Sacraments and her teachings, and embraces the life Christ calls them to. We are all called to catholic unity as God's children, but not everyone responds to this call. The call is small c catholic; the response is big C Catholic.

The fourth and final mark of the Church is "apostolic." What does it mean that the Church is "apostolic"?

On the day of your Confirmation the bishop will extend his hands over you, pray that you receive the Holy Spirit, and anoint you with the sacred oil (chrism) and the Sign of the Cross.

Why? What gives him the right? Who gives him the authority to do that?

This is one of the great questions of Christian history. If you can develop a clear understanding of this, a lot of other things will fall into place. Let's turn to the Scriptures for some insight.

Jesus was walking down the road one day, talking with his disciples, answering questions, and asking questions. Toward the end of these discussions he asks the disciples who they think he is. Peter replies, "You are the Christ, the son of .the living God." (Matthew 16:16) What seemed like a very spontaneous conversation then turned into something very formal when Jesus said, "You are Peter and on this rock I will build my Church." Jesus goes on to say, "I will give you the keys to the Kingdom of Heaven, whatever you bind on earth will be bound in heaven and whatever you loose on earth will be loosed in heaven." (Matthew 16:18–19)

Jesus gave Peter the authority to lead the Church, and through Peter he gave the other apostles authority. As Catholics we can trace a direct line from your bishop back two thousand years to Peter. Pope Francis is the 265th successor of Peter.

This is what we mean when we say the Church is "apostolic." The apostles were the foundation that Jesus chose to build his Church upon. They were the witnesses whom Jesus chose to send out on a mission to the whole world. The Church celebrates and defends the teachings passed on by the apostles, continues to be guided by the apostles, and carries on the mission entrusted first to the apostles.

Your bishop is a successor to the apostles. That's profound and beautiful.

So at Mass next Sunday you will probably hear some people mindlessly mumbling the Creed. Don't be one of them. Say it loud and proud: "I believe in one, holy, catholic, and apostolic Church."

DISCUSSION QUESTIONS

1. IF JESUS WANTED THE CHURCH TO BE ONE, WHY DO YOU THINK THERE ARE SO MANY DIFFERENT CHURCHES TODAY?

_____
_____
_____
_____
_____
_____

2. HOW MANY POPES HAVE THERE BEEN DURING YOUR LIFETIME? WHO WERE THEY? WHAT DO YOU REMEMBER ABOUT THEM?

_____
_____
_____
_____
_____
_____
_____

3. WHAT DO YOU THINK WAS JESUS' MAIN MESSAGE?

_____
_____
_____
_____
_____
_____
_____
_____

Psalm 16

Preserve me, O God, for in thee I take refuge.
² I say to the Lord, "Thou art my Lord;
I have no good apart from thee."

³ As for the saints in the land, they are the noble,
in whom is all my delight.

⁴ Those who choose another god multiply their sorrows;
their libations of blood I will not pour out
or take their names upon my lips.
⁵ The Lord is my chosen portion and my cup;
thou holdest my lot.
⁶ The lines have fallen for me in pleasant places;
yea, I have a goodly heritage.

⁷ I bless the Lord who gives me counsel;
in the night also my heart instructs me.

⁸ I keep the Lord always before me;
because he is at my right hand, I shall not be moved.

⁹ Therefore my heart is glad, and my soul rejoices;
my body also dwells secure.

¹⁰ For thou dost not give me up to Sheol,
or let thy godly one see the Pit.

¹¹ Thou dost show me the path of life;
in thy presence there is fulness of joy,
in thy right hand are pleasures for evermore.

> "When we honestly ask ourselves which person in our lives means the most to us, we often find that it is those who, instead of giving advice, solutions, or cures, have chosen rather to share our pain and touch our wounds with a warm and tender hand. The friend who can be silent with us in a moment of despair or confusion, who can stay with us in an hour of grief and bereavement, who can tolerate not knowing, not curing, not healing and face with us the reality of our powerlessness, that is a friend who cares."
>
> –Henri J. M. Nouwen

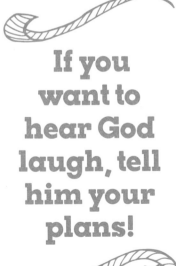

If you want to hear God laugh, tell him your plans!

9.3 THE Good, THE BAD, THE Ugly & THE Lies

The Good

For two thousand years wherever you find Catholics you find a group of people making phenomenal contributions to their local, national, and international communities. Every single day the Catholic Church feeds more people, houses more people, clothes more people, visits more imprisoned, cares for more sick people, and educates more people than any other institution on the planet.

The Church gave birth to scientific method, which has been at the center of scientific discovery for hundreds of years. The Church gave birth to the first university. The early Church was the first to institutionalize the care of widows, orphans, and the sick. The Church has also made incredible contributions in music, art, medicine, architecture, language, and law. In the area of law, equality before the law, trial by jury, and proof beyond a reasonable doubt are all the fruit of Catholic thought.

And no other organization or institution has done more than the Catholic Church in defending human rights around the world. The Catholic idea of charity—that we help those in need, without the expectation of anything in return, whether they are Catholic or not, and even if they despise us—is the idea of charity that even our secular society today strives to achieve.

In fact, all of these Catholic contributions spring from the notion of agape love. For two thousand years the Catholic Church has been a force for tremendous good in the world.

The Bad

There have also been some dark moments in our story. Our past is not perfect. Pope John Paul II made more than one hundred public apologies during his papacy on behalf of Catholics for events reaching back as far as one thousand years.

He apologized to women, Jews, minorities, people convicted by the Inquisition, Muslims killed by the Crusaders, and almost everyone who had suffered at the hands of the Catholic Church throughout history. He apologized for Catholics' involvement in the African slave trade, the Church's role in religious wars and burnings at the stake, and the legal process Galileo suffered. He apologized for injustices committed against women and the inactivity and silence of many Catholics during the Holocaust.

Our past is not without blemish. There have been some horrible moments in Catholic history. But it is important to recognize that these moments are the result of individuals wandering away from the teachings of Christ and his Church.

Here we find one of the central mysteries of God's plan: The Church is made up of human beings like you and me, who are in many ways weak and imperfect.

Some people look at the failings of the Church and use them as an excuse to leave. I see it very differently. All of the lowest moments in Church history are examples of what happens when we don't live the Catholic faith authentically. I have studied these low moments, and what I've found is immorality and personal weakness, selfishness and abuse of power. I've found Christ's teachings misunderstood and misrepresented. But the scandals that stain our history do not exist because we lived our Catholicism, but rather, because we *failed* to live it. And what I find most of all in the Church's history is a reflection of my own fragile and broken humanity.

When we behave as second-rate-versions-of-ourselves bad things happen. That's true for us as individuals and it's true for the Church.

The Ugly

One of the ugliest scandals surrounding the Catholic Church is also one of the most recent: the sexual abuse scandal among priests. There is never any excuse for the abuse of a child. It is not only immoral and unchristian, but it is criminal in every civilized society. The abuse and the scandal were also mishandled in some cases by Church officials.

Scandals like this rock people's faith. When the Church fails to live up to her mission and the values she invites others to live by, the faith of millions of ordinary people is affected. Why? The Church is supposed to help people get closer to God. But when she gets caught up in a scandal it can stand as an obstacle between God and the people.

The first e-mail Pope John Paul II sent was an apology to everyone who had been abused by a priest or religious. Benedict XVI also apologized to the victims.

There have been some truly ugly moments in Catholic history. They are inexcusable. We should pray for the victims of these parts of our history.

WHO WAS John Paul II?

Saint John Paul II (1920–2005) was born in Poland. In 1978 he was elected the 264th Bishop of Rome. For the next twenty years he traveled the world tirelessly, bringing the hope, peace, and joy of the Gospel to everyone who would listen. He had a deep love for young people and out of love instituted World Youth Day. In 1981, Pope John Paul II was shot in St. Peter's Square. He survived the assassination attempt and visited his shooter in prison on Christmas in 1983. He is one of the modern giants of our faith. His story cannot be contained in a thousand pages. If you want to have a life-changing experience, read George Weigel's biography of Pope John Paul II, *Witness to Hope.*

Sometimes we have to suffer for the Church, just as Mary suffered watching her son being ridiculed and tortured.

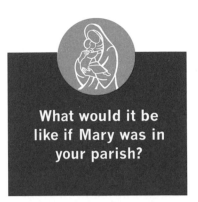

What would it be like if Mary was in your parish?

Faith·ful·ness

[**feyth**-*fuh*l-ness]

loyalty, constancy, and steadfastness

What are you faithful to?

Who is the most faithful person you know?

What can you do to increase your faith?

The Lies

History is also full of lies about the Catholic Church. These lies are often perpetuated by modern popular culture. Let's take a look at some.

One lie is the idea that the Church is against science and wants to keep everyone ignorant so they can be controlled. This is nonsense. Many of the great scientific discoveries were made by Catholic priests. And if the Church wanted to keep everyone ignorant why did it develop universities and become the champion of education for the common man?

Another lie that is perpetuated about the Church is that it is opposed to progress and is an obstacle to progress. This is also an absurd lie. The Church has been a champion of progress from the very beginning, and this is a tradition that has continued throughout our rich history of contribution. The Catholic Church has nurtured and encouraged progress in education, law, art, music, architecture, science, philosophy, theology, language, and human rights. In fact, many of the best minds of our times believe that Western civilization is almost completely indebted to the Catholic Church.

Today one of the biggest lies surrounds the priesthood. The media would have you believe that every priest sexually abuses children. In a recent poll, when asked what percentage of priests were pedophiles, respondents said between 33 and 50 percent. In fact, 1.8 percent of priests were involved in the scandal. The great majority of priests are good men who have given their lives to help you and me grow spiritually, become the-best-version-of-ourselves, and get to Heaven.

The world tends to ignore the goodness of the Church and blow our mistakes out of proportion to make them all-encompassing. At the beginning of this section we talked about some of the Church's great contributions—how many of those did you already know about? I've met many Catholics who didn't know any of those things.

The last lie I want to explore briefly with you is the idea that the Church is always behind the times. Not so. It is easy to present the Church as being old-fashioned and out of date, but this is a lie. The Church is a prophet and as such is ahead of the times.

One modern example of this can be found in the papal encyclical "Humanae Vitae." In it Pope Paul VI explained what would happen if artificial contraceptives became widely used in society. It was written in 1968, before you and I were born. It was written in a time very different from the world we live in today. But it is full of prophecy, and what Paul VI predicted would happen is exactly what has happened.

Pope Paul VI predicted artificial contraception would be bad for marriage, bad for families, and in particular, that it would lead to the objectification of women.

He was an unwelcome prophet of his times, and remains an unwelcome prophet in our times—but he is modern proof that the Church is ahead of the times, not behind the times.

The bottom line is this: Don't believe everything you hear about the Church. When someone criticizes the Church, ask them to prove it. If you have doubts about something, delve into the issue yourself so that you can really understand the great history of the Catholic Church. It is not a perfect history, but the Church has always been a force for incredible good in the world.

There have been some regrettable moments in the life of the Catholic Church, but a fair look at history demonstrates that violence and abuse are not the overarching story of Catholicism. Our story is primarily one of agape love, incredible contribution, and the relief of human suffering.

I'm proud to be Catholic, and the more I learn about our history, the prouder I become.

WHO WAS
FREDERIC · OZANAM?

FREDERIC OZANAM (1813-1853) WAS TWENTY YEARS OLD AND STUDYING IN PARIS WHEN HE HE FELT CALLED TO HELP THE POOR. HE GOT SOME FRIENDS TOGETHER AND BEGAN TO SERVE THE POOR. THEY CALLED THEM-SELVES "THE CONFERENCE OF CHARITY." THEY WERE SERVANTS AND ADVOCATES FOR THE POOR. LATER THEY BECAME KNOWN AS THE SOCIETY OF SAINT VINCENT DE PAUL. TODAY THE SOCIETY EX-ISTS IN DOZENS OF COUNTRIES AROUND THE WORLD. TENS OF THOUSANDS OF PARISHES HAVE A SAINT VINCENT DE PAUL GROUP. THEY FEED, CLOTHE, HOUSE, AND PROVIDE HEALING MEDICAL HELP FOR MILLIONS OF MEN, WOMEN, AND CHILDREN EVERY DAY. THE SOCIETY OF SAINT VINCENT DE PAUL IS JUST ONE OF HUNDREDS OF CATHOLIC ORGANIZATIONS THAT SERVE THE POOR AND MAR-GINALIZED OF THE WORLD. CATH-OLICS HAVE A GREAT HISTORY OF CONTRIBUTION. FREDERIC WASN'T THAT MUCH OLDER THAN YOU WHEN HE BEGAN THIS GREAT WORK. HE COULD NOT HAVE EN-VISIONED WHERE IT WOULD LEAD. BUT THAT'S HOW GOD WORKS.

how will you serve the church?

D·I·S·C·U·S·S·I·O·N
QUESTIONS

1. WHAT MAKES YOU PROUDEST TO BE CATHOLIC?

_____

_____

_____

_____

_____

_____

2. IN WHAT WAYS HAS THE CHURCH DISAPPOINTED YOU?

_____

_____

_____

_____

_____

_____

3. WE ALL MAKE MISTAKES, AND WE ALL SIN AGAINST GOD. DO YOUR OWN FAILINGS
HELP YOU TO UNDERSTAND WHY THERE HAVE BEEN SCANDALS AT DIFFERENT
TIMES IN THE HISTORY OF THE CHURCH?

_____

_____

_____

_____

_____

_____

_____

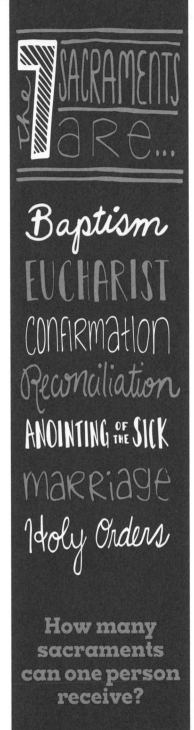

The 7 SACRAMENTS are...

Baptism

EUCHARIST

confirmation

Reconciliation

ANOINTING OF THE SICK

marriage

Holy Orders

How many sacraments can one person receive?

9.4 Ten GREAT Reasons to be Catholic

I love being Catholic, and there are an infinite number of great reasons to be Catholic, but let's take a look at ten of them.

You can't put these things in order, and we could argue about the order until the end of the world. Be here they are:

10. This is the Church that Jesus Christ started and sent the Holy Spirit to guide. It is unique and original.

9. The Catholic Church has relieved more suffering than any other group of people in the history of the world. We care for the sick, the hungry, the lonely, the homeless, the uneducated, and the imprisoned. I love being part of that.

8. We have history and mystery. To really understand Christianity you need a historical perspective, and the history of Christianity is Catholic. For more than fifteen hundred years there were no Baptists, Methodists, Presbyterians, Anglicans, Pentecostal Christians, Lutherans, Mormons, Evangelical Christians, Non-Denominational Christians. Today, there are more than twenty-five thousand different Christian denominations, but they all lack the rich and beautiful history we have as Catholics. We have history, and we have mystery. We know it's all right not to have the answer to everything. Some things are a mystery, and that's OK.

7. We have the Saints. These are the great heroes and heroines of Christianity. They are the most diverse group of people in history. Some were rich and some were poor; some were very well educated and some had no formal education; some were young and others were old. They have lived in every century, on every continent, in every country—and they all tried to be the-best-version-of-themselves. Now they are in Heaven, cheering you on.

6. We believe in the power of prayer. At every moment of every day Mass is being prayed in thousands of places around the world. That's our family praying for the whole world. We don't just pray for Catholics; we pray for everyone. Imagine how different the history of the world would have been if the Catholic Church had never offered a single prayer.

5. It's the same all around the world. I took a group on a pilgrimage a few years ago and we all went to Mass in Florence. That night I asked the group about the experience of attending Mass in Italian. They said, "Even though I don't speak Italian, I still knew what was going on." Catholicism is the same everywhere, and that's a beautiful thing.

4. The Catholic Church is the premier defender of human rights.

3. You need to be part of something bigger than yourself. Life is not about you. It's about laying down your life in the service of others out of love for God. You could lay down your life for a sport, a career, money, things . . . and people do. But what a waste! The Catholic Church has the most important mission in the world—and you are invited to get involved and be a part of that great mission!

2. The Eucharist. Jesus Christ is truly present in the Eucharist.

1. You don't say no to God when he invites you. There are some invitations we don't turn down.

I can come up with great reasons to be Catholic all day long, but ultimately you need to come up with your own. I can't give you my love of the Church. I wish I could. In the end you have to make Catholicism your own.

GOD HAS A BETTER PLAN THAN ANY YOU CAN PUT TOGETHER FOR YOURSELF.

The **SACRAMENTS** *are at the* **CENTER** *of the* **LIFE OF THE CHURCH.**

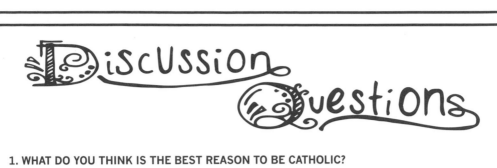

Discussion Questions

1. WHAT DO YOU THINK IS THE BEST REASON TO BE CATHOLIC?

_____

_____

_____

_____

_____

_____

2. WHAT DID YOU LEARN IN THIS SESSION THAT REALLY MADE YOU STOP AND THINK?

_____

_____

_____

_____

_____

_____

_____

3. HOW DID THE TOP TEN REASONS TO BE CATHOLIC CHANGE THE WAY YOU VIEW CATHOLICISM?

_____

_____

_____

_____

_____

_____

_____

9.5 DECISION point

There are a lot of people who turn their backs on Catholicism simply because it is old. Catholicism is old; I admit it. But let me ask you a question: If you found an ancient treasure map, would you throw it away just because it was old? No. I don't think you would. You would go looking for the treasure. The age of a map doesn't determine the value of the map. It doesn't matter how old the map is. What matters is whether or not the map leads to treasure.

Catholicism is a treasure map. It may be old, but it still leads to treasure. I hope you have the courage and the wisdom to seek out the treasure that is Catholicism. And once you find it, I hope you spend the rest of your life marveling at its beauty and applying it to your life.

Do that and you will live an uncommon life filled with purpose and happiness.

If you could invite Mary to give a lecture at your school, what would you ask her to speak about?

YOU DON'T THROW AWAY A Treasure MAP JUST BECAUSE IT'S OLD.

JOURNAL QUESTIONS

1. HOW DO YOU THINK YOUR LIFE MIGHT BE BETTER IF YOU FOLLOWED THE MAP
   THE CHURCH INVITES US TO FOLLOW?

2. IN WHAT WAYS IS GOD CALLING YOU TO BE COUNTERCULTURAL LIKE THE
   FIRST CHRISTIANS WERE?

3. HOW PURPOSEFULLY ARE YOU LIVING YOUR LIFE? GIVE YOURSELF A SCORE
   BETWEEN ONE AND TEN.

THE CHURCH
CROSSWORD PUZZLE

ACROSS

2. The rich story of how our faith has been lived and passed along

4. The improper treatment of another human being

5. Liberation from sin that puts us back in right relationship with God

7. Successor of the Apostles

9 The killing of more than six million Jews and others by the Nazis during World War II

12. Of or relating to the succession of spiritual authority of the original Twelve Apostles

15. A man or woman of heroic virtue

DOWN

1. The celebration of the Eucharist

3. The act of harassing, annoying, and bullying someone because he/she is Christian

6. A group of people who support each other in living out their faith

8. A truth that can only be known by revelation and cannot be fully understood

10. The process of improving something

11. Set apart for a special purpose by God and for God

13. The Bishop of Rome

14. Not exclusive or elitist, but for everyone

Answers on page 327

MY

THOUGHTS

CONFIRMATION

Lord, make me an instrument of your peace; where there is hatred, let me sow love; where there is injury, pardon; where there is error, truth; where there is doubt, faith; where there is despair, hope; where there is darkness, light; and where there is sadness, joy.

O Divine Master, grant that I may not so much seek to be consoled as to console; to be understood as to understand; to be loved as to love. For it is in giving that we receive; it is in pardoning that we are pardoned; and it is in dying that we are born to eternal life. Amen.

St. Francis of Assisi

10. CONFIRMATION

Over and over throughout the Bible we read about God choosing people and calling them to a new life. God called Noah, Abraham, Moses, Gideon, Joshua, David, Jeremiah, Jonah, Mary, John the Baptist, Peter, James, John, Matthew, Zechariah, the rich young man, and now God is calling you.

You are called and chosen.

God has a plan for you and your life. We read in Jeremiah 29:11, " 'I know the plans I have for you,' says the Lord, 'plans for your welfare and not for harm, to give you a future with hope.' "

God is deeply interested in every aspect of your life—and that's why he does everything he can to encourage you to develop a powerful spiritual life.

You are called and chosen. God has chosen you and now he is calling you to a new life.

10.1 WHAT IS CONFIRMATION?

Confirmation is a great opportunity to start taking your spiritual self seriously. So much is going to happen in your life that you will have little or no control over. We can plan and dream, and we should. But life is not easy and often delivers unwelcome experiences that test us in ways unexpected. Education can prepare you for a career, and exercise can prepare you to compete athletically, but developing your spiritual self is the real preparation for life, and Confirmation is part of that preparation.

What is Confirmation? Confirmation is a sacrament. What is a sacrament? Good question. A sacrament is an encounter with Jesus Christ. Jesus gave us the Sacraments to transform us spiritually. There are seven sacraments, and through them we receive the grace necessary to live the life God invites us to. And all seven are deeply rooted in the Scriptures and Tradition.

The seven sacraments are: Baptism, Eucharist, Confirmation, Reconciliation, Anointing of the Sick, Marriage, and Holy Orders.

Baptism, Eucharist, and Confirmation are all sacraments of initiation. At your baptism you became a new creation spiritually. The Eucharist

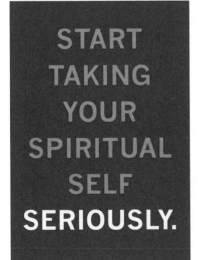

feeds you spiritually. In Confirmation you will be strengthened for your spiritual journey throughout the rest of life.

Confirmation will unleash the Holy Spirit in your life, just as it did in the lives of the disciples at Pentecost. In this way Confirmation perpetuates Pentecost in the Church, so that the work of Jesus can be continued in every age.

How long has Confirmation been a part of the Christian experience? From the beginning. In chapter 8 of Acts we read about Peter and John traveling to Samaria to confirm those who had only been baptized: "Now when the Apostles at Jerusalem heard that Samaria had accepted the word of God, they sent Peter and John to them. The two went down and prayed for them that they might receive the Holy Spirit. . . . Then Peter and John laid their hands on them and they received the Holy Spirit." (Acts 8:14–17).

Just as Peter and John went to Samaria, their successor (your bishop) is coming to confirm you. He will do just as Peter and John did in Samaria: pray for you and lay his hands on you that you might receive the Holy Spirit.

God chose you from the beginning. At baptism your parents responded to God and stood up for you. Now you have to make a choice for yourself, and stand up for yourself.

Just as Jesus chose the first twelve disciples, he is choosing you today. Just as God chose Jeremiah and Joshua, Moses and Abraham, he is choosing you today.

Will you accept God's blessing on your life? Will you allow God to anoint you and become a disciple?

Acts 8:14–17

KNOW IT: Our Church leaders have been praying for us to receive the Holy Spirit from the beginning.

THINK ABOUT IT: There is a direct, unbroken connection between the bishop who will confirm you and the first Apostles.

LIVE IT: Study the history of our great faith.

THE LORD'S PRAYER, ALSO COMMONLY KNOWN AS THE OUR FATHER, AND AS PATER NOSTER IN LATIN, IS A CENTRAL PRAYER OF CHRISTIANITY. IT IS FOUND IN THE GOSPEL OF MATTHEW (6:9–13).

If Mary was your sponsor for Confirmation, what would you ask her to pray for as you prepare to be confirmed?

discussion questions

1. DO YOU BELIEVE THAT GOD HAS GOOD PLANS FOR YOU?

_____
_____
_____
_____
_____
_____

2. WHAT CAN YOU DO TO FIND OUT THE PLANS GOD HAS FOR YOUR FUTURE?

_____
_____
_____
_____
_____
_____
_____

3. HOW HAS YOUR IDEA OF CONFIRMATION CHANGED SINCE WE BEGAN OUR TIME TOGETHER?

_____
_____
_____
_____
_____
_____
_____
_____

My Thoughts

10.2 THE POWER OF PREPARATION

For months now you have been preparing for Confirmation. Some of the preparation has probably been fun, and some of it has probably just been hard work. Winning an Olympic gold medal is fun; preparing to win it is mostly hard work.

We prepare for everything we consider important. You wouldn't show up to play a soccer game and expect to win if you hadn't been training. We don't expect to excel in exams if we haven't studied. And people in the business world wouldn't show up unprepared to give a presentation and expect to get the contract. Preparation is essential for any great experience.

This preparation for Confirmation has not been just to ready you for a single day, but to prepare you for life. Now, as we draw closer to the actual day, I want to encourage you to prepare yourself in these two ways:

1) Receive the Sacrament of Reconciliation. We all need a fresh start from time to time, and Confirmation is a perfect opportunity to have a fresh start with God. I do things every day that are incongruent with the-best-version-of-myself. In doing so I betray my true self and God. These are things I have to work on. If I don't work on them they will become habits. And bad habits drag us down. I've got sins and you've got sins. And the thing about sins is they are heavy. Do you want to carry them around? I don't. The good news is God wants to lighten your load.

I love watching the Olympics. It's amazing how disciplined and dedicated the athletes are. Many of them spend four, eight, or even twelve years preparing for a single event—and sometimes that event only lasts ten seconds.

The one thing that really struck me during the most recent Olympics was that all the athletes had coaches. Some of them had three, four, or even five different coaches. These athletes are the best in the world at what they do and still they value coaching.

So here's my question for you. Whom are you getting your spiritual coaching from? You see, nobody achieves excellence at anything without coaching. So if we really want to cast off the mediocrity of the world and grow in spiritual excellence we need coaching.

Our Lives CHANGE — WHEN OUR — HABITS CHANGE

"We are to love God for Himself, because of a twofold reason: nothing is more reasonable, nothing more profitable."

SAINT BERNARD OF CLAIRVAUX

My wife and I try to go to Reconciliation once a month. We realize we need the spiritual coaching. And no surprise, I am a better husband, a better father, a better son and brother, a better boss and colleague when I make a habit of going to Reconciliation regularly.

The other thing I notice about world-class athletes is that they want to know what their faults, defects, and weaknesses are. This is a sign of excellence.

Too often in the spiritual life we don't want to know our faults, defects, and weaknesses. This is a classic sign of mediocrity. And it's sad, because the truth is, it is by facing and wrestling with our weaknesses that we are transformed by God into the person he created us to be, and prepared for the mission he has designed just for us.

So before your Confirmation, get to Reconciliation. Allow God to unburden you of your sins and give you a fresh start. And more than that, think about making reconciliation a regular part of your life. Seek the spiritual coaching you need to thrive spiritually. Don't settle for mediocrity. Seek excellence in the spiritual life.

2) Pray every day. You need a few minutes each day to connect with yourself and to connect with God. Without this you won't work out who you are and what you are here for . . . and then you will just end up living a life of "quiet desperation."

Have you been using The Prayer Process? How has it changed the way you look at yourself and the world?

The older I get, the more I value prayer. When I was young I used to pray for my will; as I have gotten older I have learned to pray for God's will. When I was young I saw getting what I wanted as the path to happiness, but as I have gotten older I see getting what God wants as the path to happiness. I want to encourage you and challenge you to make a place for prayer in your daily routine. Set a time for it. Build it into a habit. Lots of days you are not going to feel like doing it, just like Olympic athletes don't feel like getting up for training on lots of days. Develop the discipline of daily prayer and I promise you great things will come from it.

I know you are busy, and I know how hard it is to sit down for a few minutes in silence. I get it. But I'm not sure you understand how much this can change your life. So, I'll say it again. Take a few minutes each day to pray. Not just leading up to Confirmation, but every day for the rest of your life. This is the ultimate good habit.

What is IDOLATRY?

Idolatry is the worship of a physical object as a god, or a disordered attachment or devotion to something.

WHO ARE YOU GETTING YOUR SPIRITUAL COACHING FROM?

What does it mean to be anointed?

To be anointed is to be set apart for God, to be chosen by God for a special mission.

GOD CHOSE YOU FROM THE BEGINNING.

JUST AS GOD CHOSE JEREMIAH AND JOSHUA, MOSES AND ABRAHAM,

HE IS CHOOSING YOU AGAIN TODAY.

Our lives change when our habits change. If you make daily prayer and regular Reconciliation habits in your life, I know you will grow in ways you never imagined, which in turn will open you up to opportunities you never dreamed about. Great spiritual habits connect you with the dreams God has for you, and God always has better dreams for us than we have for ourselves. I wonder what God is dreaming for you?

When I started working on this Confirmation program I made a commitment to pray every day for the people who will experience it. So I want you to know that I am praying for you.

Confirmation is getting close. Whether you are aware of it or not, the Holy Spirit is going to change you through Confirmation. But the more you prepare yourself and cooperate with God throughout this experience, the more powerful it will be. Allow the Holy Spirit to unleash his power in your life and you will be amazed by what happens.

What date were you BAPTIZED

[   ]

What date did you receive *First Holy Communion*

[   ]

What advice do you think Mary would give you about preparing for Confirmation?

DISCUSSION

1. WHAT EVENT IN YOUR LIFE HAVE YOU PREPARED FOR MORE THAN ANY OTHER?

2. WHO HAVE BEEN YOUR SPIRITUAL COACHES AND MENTORS THROUGHOUT YOUR LIFE?

3. HOW HAS THE WAY YOU PRAY AND WHAT YOU PRAY FOR CHANGED OVER THE PAST FEW MONTHS?

OUR FATHER ═══════════

WHO ART IN *heaven*

HALLOWED BE THY NAME;

THY **KINGDOM** COME;

THY WILL BE DONE ON EARTH
AS IT IS IN HEAVEN.

→ GIVE US THIS DAY ←

OUR **DAILY BREAD;**

AND **FORGIVE US** OUR **TRESPASSES**

AS WE FORGIVE THOSE WHO TRESPASS AGAINST US;

And lead us **NOT** *into* **TEMPTATION,**

BUT **DELIVER** US FROM **EVIL.**

═══════════ AMEN.

Jeremiah 29:11

"For I know the plans I have for you, says the Lord, plans for welfare and not for evil, to give you a future and a hope."

KNOW IT: God has an incredible plan for you.

THINK ABOUT IT: How open are you to God's plan for you?

LIVE IT: Ask God during your prayer time today to start revealing to you his plan.

WE PREPARE FOR *Everything* WE CONSIDER IMPORTANT.

10.3 HOW WILL CONFIRMATION CHANGE YOU?

How will Confirmation change you? That depends a lot upon you. Open yourself up to the Holy Spirit. Respond to the grace God is pouring out upon you at this time in your life, and something wonderful will happen.

When the bishop traces the sign of the cross on your forehead and prays, "Be sealed with the gift of the Holy Spirit," something very powerful is going to happen to you. At that moment an indelible and permanent mark will be placed on your soul. Throughout your life that moment will influence you in a thousand ways. Some of them you will be aware of and others you will be completely oblivious to.

My daughter, Isabel, has absolutely no fear of anything. This is a problem. She is two years old and she will stand up on the couch, start walking across it, and then walk straight off the edge of it. But I am there to catch her and put her safely on the floor. This is just one of a dozen ways my wife and I protect her every day from things that she is completely oblivious to.

God does the same thing for us. We are mostly oblivious to his workings in our lives. But one day, in this life or the next, we will look back and see that all along his hand has been guiding us.

Confirmation is going to change you in wonderful ways. Here are just a few examples of how it will profoundly influence you if you open yourself up to it:

1. Better relationships. Confirmation is going to help you have better relationships by increasing your emotional intelligence, self-knowledge, and spiritual intelligence.

2. A sense of mission. Confirmation is going to fill you with a sense of mission by revealing the true meaning of life.

3. The perfect career path. Confirmation will help you choose a career that is perfectly suited to you by encouraging you to explore your God-given talents and abilities.

4. Inner peace. Confirmation will fill you with a sense of inner peace, even when the world around you is crazy, by teaching you to make time for quiet prayer and reflection each day.

5. Great decision making. And as we have been discussing all along, Confirmation will help you to make better decisions as you open yourself up to the gifts of the Holy Spirit.

6. Discipleship. Confirmation will affirm that you are a disciple of Jesus Christ, and send you out to bring the love of God to the world.

How will all this come about? As God releases the gifts of the Holy Spirit into your life and you cooperate with them.

This might be a good time to revisit the Seven Gifts of the Holy Spirit. These gifts will change your life—if you let them. God is a perfect gentleman, and so he will not force even these good things on you. He offers them to you freely for you to embrace or reject.

1. Wisdom: The ability to discern what is true, right, and lasting. Wisdom enables you to see life from God's perspective. It helps you to establish the right priorities in your life, and leads you to think and act in mature ways.

2. Understanding: Allows you to look beyond the shallowness of the world and see the lasting truth in every situation, by recognizing how God is working in your life.

3. Counsel: The right judgment that allows you to see what is right and what is wrong, and the prudence to act accordingly.

4. Fortitude: The courage and strength of will to do what you know you should do, even if that means personal loss or suffering.

5. Knowledge: The ability to see things from a supernatural viewpoint. In particular, to know what God is asking of you.

6. Piety: A loyalty to God that manifests as generous love and affectionate obedience. This is the gift that allows you to love and worship God as he deserves to be loved and worshipped.

7. Fear of the Lord (Reverence): Helps you to grasp God's greatness and your dependence on him. As a result, you are filled with enormous respect for God and you dread above all offending him or being separated from him. Our Jewish ancestors believed that fear of the Lord was the beginning of wisdom. Of course, it is not a fear like we usually think of fear today. It is more like an overwhelming reverence that we allow to direct our words and actions.

Confirmation is going to change your life in wonderful ways. I'm excited for you. You are so fortunate that someone loves you enough that they want you to have this experience. I'd like to encourage you to thank that person sometime this week. Whoever it is that loves you enough that they want you to be confirmed, take a moment to show your appreciation for all they do for you.

> ➤➤ **"LOVE,** ◄ ◄◄
> AND DO WHAT YOU WILL.
> IF YOU KEEP SILENCE,
> *do it out of love.*
> IF YOU CRY OUT,
> *do it out of love.*
> ────IF YOU────
> REFRAIN FROM PUNISHING,
> *do it out of love."*
>
> AUGUSTINE OF HIPPO

WHEN I WAS YOUNG I USED TO PRAY FOR MY WILL; AS I HAVE GOTTEN OLDER I HAVE LEARNED TO PRAY FOR GOD'S WILL.

WHEN I WAS YOUNG I SAW GETTING WHAT I WANTED AS THE PATH TO HAPPINESS, BUT AS I HAVE GOTTEN OLDER I SEE GETTING WHAT GOD WANTS AS THE PATH TO HAPPINESS.

Discussion QUESTIONS

1. IN WHAT PRACTICAL WAYS DO YOU THINK CONFIRMATION WILL CHANGE YOU?

2. WHICH OF THE SEVEN GIFTS OF THE HOLY SPIRIT COULD YOU MOST USE AT THIS TIME IN YOUR LIFE?

3. WHEN DID YOU LAST PRAY TO THE HOLY SPIRIT, ASKING FOR HELP TO MAKE A DECISION?

MY · THOUGHTS

"CHARITY IS CERTAINLY GREATER THAN ANY RULE. MOREOVER, ALL RULES MUST LEAD TO CHARITY."

–SAINT VINCENT DE PAUL

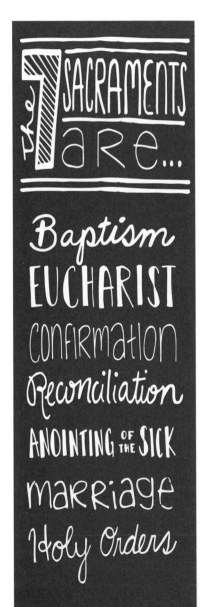

The 7 SACRAMENTS are...

Baptism
EUCHARIST
Confirmation
Reconciliation
ANOINTING OF THE SICK
Marriage
Holy Orders

10.4 On the DAY

With many of the most important events in our lives, we don't realize their importance until they are over, and sometimes not until many years later. And even when we know an event is important and we really try to be present and absorb it for all it is, it still passes us by so quickly.

Before I got married, so many people told me that their wedding day was a blur because there was so much happening. So on my wedding day I really tried to be present, to fully grasp the moment, but still I found it slipping away so quickly.

Sometimes I will hold my boy, Walter, or my daughter, Isabel, or baby Harry, and it will be a perfect moment . . . and I will try to completely absorb that moment. But as hard as I try, the moment slips through my fingers.

The day of your Confirmation will pass very quickly. Try to be present. On the day of your Confirmation, find ten minutes before the ceremony to reflect on what is about to happen.

It also helps to understand what will happen on that day so that when it is happening you can be present to it. Let's go step by step through the Confirmation experience.

The Rite of Confirmation has five parts, which will take place at different times during the Mass:

• the presentation of candidates

• homily

• renewal of baptismal promises

• laying on of hands and anointing with chrism

• general intercessions

The Mass will begin, as always, with the **Sign of the Cross**, which is itself one of the shortest and most powerful prayers of all time.

The bishop will then lead us in the **Opening Prayer.** Here is an example:

"Lord, fulfill the promise given by your Son and send the Holy Spirit to enlighten our minds and lead us to all truth."

We will then listen to the **Word of God** in the readings. The Holy Spirit helps us to understand the readings and teaches us to discern what God is saying to us through them.

You will then be **presented to the bishop for Confirmation.** You will be called as a group or by name. By standing before the bishop you are expressing your desire to be Christian and to live the life God invites us to.

This is followed by the **homily.** Now the bishop will speak to you about the Scripture readings, the Sacrament of Confirmation, and the incredible life God is inviting you to.

You will then be invited to **renew your baptismal promises.** Each question is an invitation to which you respond, "I do."

V: Do you reject Satan?

R: I do.

V: And all his works?

R: I do.

V: And all his empty promises?

R: I do.

V: Do you believe in God, the Father Almighty, creator of heaven and earth?

R: I do.

V: Do you believe in Jesus Christ, his only Son, our Lord, who was born of the Virgin Mary, was crucified, died, and was buried, rose from the dead, and is now seated at the right hand of the Father?

R: I do.

V: Do you believe in the Holy Spirit, the holy Catholic Church, the communion of saints, the forgiveness of sins, the resurrection of the body, and life everlasting?

R: I do.

V: God, the all-powerful Father of our Lord Jesus Christ, has given us a new birth by water and the Holy Spirit, and forgiven all our sins. May he also keep us faithful to our Lord Jesus Christ forever and ever.

R: Amen.

Mod·es·ty
[**mod**-*uh*-stee]

behavior, speech, manner, and appearance that avoids impropriety or indecency

In what ways is modesty counter cultural?

In what ways do you practice modesty?

How is God inviting you to be more modest?

WHAT IS emotional INTELLIGENCE?

Emotional intelligence is the ability to observe, assess, control, and express our own emotions; the ability to identify, understand, and respond to the emotions of others; and the self-awareness to know how what we are doing or saying is affecting the people around us.

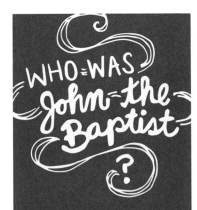

John the Baptist was an itinerant preacher and one of the great religious figures of all time. Jesus and John the Baptist were cousins, through their mothers, Mary and Elizabeth. John was the child who danced for joy in Elizabeth's womb when Mary visited, which we remember in the Second Joyful Mystery of the Rosary (Luke 1:39–56). John challenged people to repent, to turn away from their sinful and selfish ways and turn back to God (Matthew 3:1–17). John's mission was to prepare the way for Jesus. What's your mission? We celebrate John the Baptist with two feast days: June 24 (birth) and August 29 (death).

After a short prayer the bishop will invite you and your sponsor to come before him for the **Laying on of hands and Anointing with chrism.** Your sponsor will place his or her hand on your right shoulder, you or your sponsor will tell the bishop your Confirmation name, then the bishop will trace the sign of the cross on your forehead with the sacred oil chrism and say, "Be sealed with the Gift of the Holy Spirit." You respond, "Amen." Then the bishop will extend to you a sign of peace, saying, "Peace be with you." You respond, "And with your spirit."

After all the candidates have stood before the bishop, the Mass continues with the **General Intercessions.** This is that time in the Mass when we pray for all the needs of every member of the community, and for the whole world.

You will experience a special unity as we pray together the **Lord's Prayer,** offer each other a **Sign of Peace,** and receive **Holy Communion.**

The bishop will then bring the Mass to a close with a **Solemn Blessing** and send you into the world to witness to God's love by living out the mission he has entrusted to you.

I want to encourage you in a special way to be mindful of that moment when the bishop lays his hands on you and anoints you with the chrism. That is going to be one of the most powerful moments of your life. Focus in that moment and ask God to open your heart, mind, and soul to every good thing he wants to bestow upon you.

How would you act differently if Mary was sitting next to you in class this week?

DISCUSSION QUESTIONS

1. IF YOU COULD ASK THE BISHOP ONE QUESTION, WHAT WOULD YOU ASK?

_____

_____

_____

_____

_____

_____

2. ARE YOU NERVOUS ABOUT YOUR CONFIRMATION?

_____

_____

_____

_____

_____

_____

_____

3. HOW ARE YOU PREPARING FOR CONFIRMATION?

_____

_____

_____

_____

_____

_____

_____

Psalm 117

¹ Praise the Lord, all you nations!
Extol him, all you peoples!

² For great is his steadfast love
toward us, and the faithfulness
of the Lord endures forever.
Praise the Lord!

OPEN *yourself* UP TO THE HOLY SPIRIT.

Joshua 24:15

KNOW IT: We all serve something or someone with our lives.

THINK ABOUT IT: Are you serving God with your life? If not, whom or what are you serving?

LIVE IT: Look for one way to serve God better today than you did yesterday.

What would you like Mary to teach you?

10.5 DECISION point

Once the actual day has come and gone, this is the first decision you will be faced with: Is Confirmation a beginning or an end? Clearly God intends it to be an incredible new beginning for you, but will you accept his invitation to that new beginning?

After Moses confronted Pharaoh and led the Israelites out of Egypt, but before they reached the Promised Land, he died. Joshua (who is the central figure of the book of Joshua) then became the leader of the Israelites and led them into the Promised Land.

Like Moses, Joshua had to confront the people about their lives. Their priorities had become all mixed up again, and they were once again serving false gods. In chapter 24, Joshua calls together the twelve tribes of Israel and gives them a short history lesson. He reminds them how good God has been to them, that they were slaves in Egypt but God liberated them, protected them, guided them, and gave them the Promised Land. Then he confronts them for abandoning the one true God and worshipping other gods just like their ancestors did. Finally, he invites them to renew their covenant with God.

In Joshua 24:15 there are two great lines. In the first Joshua says to the people, "If you are unwilling to serve the Lord, choose this day whom you will serve." What is he saying? He is saying, don't be cowards. If you are not going to serve the one true God, at least declare yourself in your wickedness and deceit. Don't pretend. We all serve something or someone with our lives. Choose.

Joshua then goes on to say, "But as for me and my household, we will serve the Lord." That's the second great line. He is saying to the people: You have to decide for yourself, but my decision is made—my family and I will serve the Lord.

You probably won't be tempted to worship golden calves like the ancient Israelites, but it would be a mistake to think that idolatry is a thing of the past. There is a lot more idolatry today than there was back then. You will be tempted to worship at altars of individualism, hedonism, minimalism, egotism, materialism, careerism, and many others.

On the day of your Confirmation the bishop is going to confront you just as Joshua confronted the people of his time. The bishop is going to invite you to turn away from everything that is false in your life and renew your covenant with God, just as Joshua did for the Israelites. What will you choose?

You get to decide for yourself, but as for me and my household, we will serve the Lord. I have worshiped at these other altars. They left me empty and unfulfilled, but serving God fills me with joy and purpose.

Congratulations on making this journey toward Confirmation. I know it can be the beginning of incredible things for you.

WHO OR WHAT ARE YOU GOING TO SERVE?

CHILD OF GOD
-OR-
SLAVE TO THE WORLD?

1. HOW WILL THIS EXPERIENCE INFLUENCE YOU TEN YEARS FROM NOW?

_____

_____

_____

_____

_____

_____

2. IN WHAT WAYS DO YOU SENSE PREPARING FOR CONFIRMATION IS CHANGING YOU?

_____

_____

_____

_____

_____

_____

3. HOW IS THIS EXPERIENCE HELPING YOU TO CLARIFY YOUR VALUES?

_____

_____

_____

_____

_____

_____

_____

CONFIRMATION
CROSSWORD PUZZLE

ACROSS

1. Helps you to grasp God's greatness and your dependence on him

4. The ability to see things from a supernatural viewpoint—in particular, to know what God is asking of you

6. The right judgment, which allows you to see what is right and what is wrong, and the prudence to act accordingly

8. To trace the Sign of the Cross with holy oil on the forehead

11. Our lives change when our _____ change.

12. During the Confirmation ceremony, the bishop will trace the sign of the cross on each candidate's forehead, anointing them with this holy oil.

14. An encounter with Jesus Christ

DOWN

2. Loyalty to God that manifests as a generous love and affectionate obedience

3. A sacrament in which God unburdens you of your sins and gives you a fresh start

5. The short talk given by a priest during Mass after the Gospel reading

7. The courage and strength of will to do what you know you should do, even if it means personal loss or suffering

9. Allows you to look beyond the shallowness of the world and see the lasting truth in every situation

10. The ability to discern what is true, right, and lasting

13. A prayer to God on behalf of someone else

15. Confirmation is a great opportunity to start taking your _____ self seriously.

16. Someone preparing to receive the sacrament of Confirmation

Answers on page 327

Made for

MISSION

Lord, teach me to be generous. Teach me to serve you as you deserve; to give and not to count the cost, to fight and not to heed the wounds, to toil and not to seek for rest, to labor and not to ask for reward, save that of knowing that I do your will. Amen.

St. Ignatius

11. MADE FOR MISSION

I got a new iPhone the other day and on the back it says, "Designed by Apple." The phone came with an instruction manual. The sensible thing to do would be to study the instruction manual so that I will know exactly how the device works. But because I have a rough sense of how it works, I just start using it. Over time I will learn more and more features, but unless I study that instruction manual I will never use it exactly as it was intended . . . and I will miss out on many features that I don't even know exist.

Sometimes we forget that as human beings we have been masterfully designed by God. Sure, you can fumble your way through life and you will learn many of the features of the human being. But if you really want to understand exactly what God had in mind when he created you, if you really want to understand what you were designed for, you need to study the instruction manual.

God has given us his moral law, his son Jesus, the Bible, the Ten Commandments, the teachings of the Church, and the Sacraments all to help us understand that we have been masterfully designed for a purpose. And every Sunday God holds a seminar at your parish to explain features that you didn't even know you had—it's called the Mass.

Designed by God. You don't have a sticker on you that says it, but it's true. Nobody knows what an iPhone is capable of like Apple does. And nobody knows what you are capable of like God does.

If you use an iPhone in ways it was not intended for, it will most likely break down and stop working. In the same way, if you live in ways counter to what God designed you for, over time you will break down.

Everything has its purpose. Use things for what they were intended, and all will be well. Start using things for something they were not intended, and they will break down.

You have been designed by God with a purpose. Ignore how he has designed you and you will be inviting every type of misery into your life. Embrace how God has designed you and you will experience unimaginable joy, even when things don't go your way.

Part of God's design is mission. You have been designed for mission, created for mission. You have been placed on this earth at this time to fulfill a specific mission. If you don't embrace and fulfill your mission, it will be left undone. Nobody else has been assigned that mission. Just you.

You were made for mission.

YOU WERE MADE FOR MISSION.

You have a unique blend of talents and abilities that are perfectly suited to carry out whatever mission God has assigned to you on this earth.

11.1 THE WORLD IS A MESS

The world is incredible in many ways. But in lots of other ways, it is a mess, and the mess causes a lot of suffering for a lot of people.

This is one thing everyone can agree on. Nobody thinks, "The world is in great shape, all is well, we just need to keep it moving in the direction it's going!" No. There is a universal sense that all is not well, and that the world needs changing.

The mess manifests in lots of ways: Poverty. Starvation. Hatred. Pollution. Greed. Crime. War. Human trafficking. Divorce. Violence. Lying. Cheating. Stealing. Prejudice. Sexual abuse. Conflict. Unemployment. Loneliness.

And these problems are not in some far-off corner of the world. They're right here, in our cities and suburbs, and in our homes. But I don't need to tell you that. You are more aware of these things than I was at your age. That's because in many cases, sadly, you have been exposed to them.

The world needs changing. But the real question is: What are you going to do about it?

Don't say, "I am too young to do anything about it." Young people are capable of incredible things. And if you hide behind that excuse you will end up being one of those people who spend the first half of their lives saying, "I am too young" and the second half saying, "I am too old."

Now is the time to start thinking about how you can make a difference. Now is the perfect time to start thinking about your mission in life.

The first step is to recognize that most of the mess—and most of the suffering—in this world is caused by sin. When we reject God's plan and pursue our own selfish agenda, we leave behind us a trail of heartache and suffering. Sin makes us unhappy, and it brings misery to others. We saw this earlier in the program when we explored the Ten Commandments and asked the question: How much suffering would be avoided if everyone lived in alignment with the Ten Commandments?

The first step in living a purposeful life is to align ourselves with God and his plans for us and the world. The more I am aligned with God, the less mess, heartache, and suffering I cause.

There is a great story about the boy Samuel in the Bible. When he was about thirteen years old he worked for Eli in the temple. One night Samuel heard a voice calling his name. He thought it was Eli, so he

1 Samuel 3:1-21

KNOW IT: God kept calling Samuel until he responded.

THINK ABOUT IT: What is God calling you to?

LIVE IT: From time to time, use some of your prayer time to ask God what he is calling you to now.

went to him and asked what he needed. But Eli said he had not called Samuel and sent him back to bed. This happened three times, and then Eli realized it was the voice of God that was calling Samuel. Eli instructed Samuel, "Go, lie down, and if he calls you again say, 'Speak, Lord, your servant is listening.'" (1 Samuel 3:1–21). The Lord called Samuel again and told him he was going to do great things through him. Samuel went on to become one of the great prophets, guiding the people of Israel with courage and wisdom.

If you listen carefully, I think you will discover that God is calling you to do something about the mess in the world. How will you respond? "Not now God, I'm busy"? or "Speak, Lord, your servant is listening."

The world is a mess in many ways, but the beautiful thing is, you and I can do something about it. Deep down you know the world is not as it should be. So let's get busy doing something about that.

Luceat LUX vestra

Let your LIGHT Shine

What did Mary teach us about letting our light shine?

GET THE
APP!

Discussion Questions

1. IN WHAT WAYS DO YOU THINK THE WORLD IS A MESS?

_____
_____
_____
_____
_____
_____

2. HOW DO YOU SENSE GOD IS CALLING YOU TO MAKE THE WORLD A BETTER PLACE?

_____
_____
_____
_____
_____
_____

3. WHAT'S ONE THING YOU CAN DO TODAY THAT WILL MAKE THE WORLD A BETTER PLACE?

_____
_____
_____
_____
_____
_____

FOR THOUSANDS OF YEARS God has been using ORDINARY PEOPLE to do **EXTRAORDINARY THINGS.** God delights in dynamic collaboration with humanity. He doesn't necessarily choose the people who are the **BEST-EDUCATED** or those who are *good-looking;* he doesn't choose people because they are in POSITIONS OF POWER AND AUTHORITY; and he doesn't always choose the most *eloquent* and *persuasive.* There is **ONE TYPE OF PERSON** that God has used **POWERFULLY** over and over again *throughout history.* It is the *prerequisite* **FOR MISSION.** God does **INCREDIBLE THINGS** with the people who MAKE THEMSELVES **AVAILABLE** TO HIM.

HOW *Available* ARE YOU TO GOD?

11.2 A WORLD WITHOUT NEIGHBORS

If your next-door neighbor had a child who was starving, what would you do? Would you help? Give the child some of your extra food? Find a way to get the child some food? Go without food yourself so that the child could be fed?

There is another great story, in Luke's Gospel. A man came to Jesus and asked him what he needed to do to get to Heaven. Jesus replied by asking a question himself: What is written in the law? (The Jewish people strove to live by "the law," which is found in the Torah, the first five books of the Bible.) The man replied, "You shall love the Lord your God with all your heart, and with all your soul, and with all your strength, and with all your mind; and your neighbor as yourself." To this Jesus said, "You have given the right answer, do this, and you will live." (Luke 10:25–28) But the man pressed Jesus for clarification, asking, "And who is my neighbor?" Jesus replied, "A man was going down from Jerusalem to Jericho, and fell into the hands of robbers, who stripped him, beat him, and went away, leaving him half dead. Now by chance a priest was going down that road; and when he saw him, he passed by on the other side. So likewise a Levite, when he came to the place and saw him, passed by on the other side. But a Samaritan while traveling came near him; and when he saw him, he was moved with pity. He went to him and bandaged his wounds, having poured oil and wine on them. Then he put him on his own animal, brought him to an inn, and took care of him. The next day he took out two denarii, gave them to the innkeeper, and said, 'Take care of him; and when I come back, I will repay you whatever more you spend.' Which of these three, do you think, was a neighbor to the man who fell into the hands of the robbers?" The man said, "The one who showed him mercy." Jesus said to him, "Go and do likewise." (Luke 10:29–37)

In many ways we live in a world without neighbors today. Many people don't even know who their next-door neighbors are, and too often if a child were starving next door we wouldn't even know.

So, who is my neighbor?

Lately, I have been thinking a lot about this. My wife and I have three beautiful children and we do all we can to see to it that they have all they need physically, emotionally, intellectually, and spiritually. We are blessed materially and financially. But 22 percent of children in America live in poverty—that's more than sixteen million children. And while they may not live next door, they are my neighbors—and more than that, they are my brothers and sisters in Christ. And this is just America.

There are 2.2 billion children in the world, and one billion of them live in poverty.

WHO IS YOUR NEIGHBOR?

Luke 10:25-37

KNOW IT: The Samaritans were looked down on in Jesus' time.

THINK ABOUT IT: Whom do you exclude, ignore, or look down upon?

LIVE IT: Go out of your way this week to include someone you would usually exclude.

Twenty-one thousand children die from poverty around the world every day. That's one child every four seconds, fourteen children dying every minute . . . and thirty-one children who have died since we began talking about it just over two minutes ago.

"They die quietly in some of the poorest villages on earth, far removed from the scrutiny and the conscience of the world. Being meek and weak in life makes these dying multitudes even more invisible in death." Unicef

They are our neighbors, yes, but more than that they are our family, our brothers and sisters. They are God's children.

What's the difference if the starving child lives next door or across the ocean? They are still God's children. And as always, God has a plan for his children. But he needs your help to fulfill his plan.

Will you set your plan aside and embrace his? If enough people do that, the world will become more just and much kinder, and be rid of so much unnecessary suffering.

"THEY DIE QUIETLY IN SOME OF THE POOREST VILLAGES ON EARTH, FAR REMOVED FROM THE SCRUTINY AND THE CONSCIENCE OF THE WORLD. BEING MEEK AND WEAK IN LIFE MAKES THESE DYING MULTITUDES EVEN MORE INVISIBLE IN DEATH."

—UNICEF

1. JESUS CALLS US TO LOVE OUR NEIGHBOR AS WE LOVE OURSELVES.
   WHOM DO YOU CONSIDER TO BE YOUR NEIGHBOR?

_____
_____
_____
_____
_____
_____

2. WHY DO YOU THINK SO MANY CHILDREN DIE FROM LACK OF FOOD?

_____
_____
_____
_____
_____
_____

3. ARE YOU WILLING TO MAKE SACRIFICES TO REDUCE THE AMOUNT
   OF SUFFERING IN THE WORLD?

_____
_____
_____
_____
_____
_____

my Thoughts

11.3 Finding Your MISSION

Have you ever been told, "You can do anything you set your mind to," or "You can be whatever you want to be as long as you work harder than anyone else," or "You can have anything you want as long as you want it bad enough"? Lies. It's not true. They are nice ideas, but they are not true.

It wouldn't have mattered how hard Mother Teresa had worked at it or wanted it, she was never going to play basketball in the NBA. She lacked a number of abilities necessary to make that happen. And what a waste it would have been if instead of pursuing her God-given mission, Mother Teresa had been a basketball player.

Once again we discover the huge gulf between the ways of the world and the vision God has for your life. The world says life is about doing what you want, and that doing what you want will make you happy. God says he has the ultimate plan for your life, and following that plan is what will make you happy.

The thing is, God knows you better than anyone else. He knows you better than you know yourself. He designed you, and he designed you with a specific mission in mind. You were designed on purpose and for a purpose.

Albert Einstein wrote, "Everybody is a genius. But if you judge a fish by its ability to climb a tree, it will live its whole life believing that it is stupid." If you are going to discover your mission, we first need to discover your genius. What are you uniquely designed to contribute?

If you bought a car and you wanted to discover how to bring the best out of it and achieve optimum performance, whom would you talk to about that? You could go online and read Internet articles. You could go down to the dealership and speak to the mechanic who specializes in that particular car. But the best person to speak to would be the person who designed and built the car.

In the same way, if you want to discover your mission, your genius, and how to bring the best out of yourself, the person to talk to is the one who designed and built you: *God.*

God speaks to us in lots of ways, but there are three ordinary voices that he uses to speak to us every day.

The first ordinary voice of God is: legitimate needs.

If you don't eat, you will die. Who created you with this need to eat? God.

If you don't breathe you will die even quicker. God has created you with legitimate needs. You have these legitimate needs in all four aspects of the human being: physical, emotional, intellectual, and spiritual. Physically you have legitimate needs for food, sleep, exercise, clothing, shelter, and many other things. Emotionally you have legitimate needs for opportunities to love and be loved. Intellectually you have legitimate needs to learn new things and stimulate and expand your thinking. Spiritually you have legitimate needs for silence, solitude, Scriptures, and sacraments.

The world says you will be most fully alive when you get what you want, but it's not true. In your lifetime you will encounter hundreds of people who are obsessed with getting what they want, but getting what they want won't make them happy. The reason is profoundly simple: You never can get enough of what you don't really need.

God has given you these legitimate needs. They are clues about how to live life to the fullest.

The second ordinary voice of God is: talents and abilities.

You have a unique blend of talents and abilities that are perfectly suited to carry out whatever mission God has assigned to you on this earth. There are two types: universal and unique. Universal talents are those that we all have. For example, we all have the ability to make a difference in other people's lives. Unique talents are those that everyone does not have. For example, the ability to paint like Van Gogh, write a symphony like Mozart, or be the best basketball player in the world.

The world is obsessed with unique talent, but when you consider the ability to make a difference in other people's lives alongside the ability to throw a great fastball, the baseball thing seems trivial. The reason it seems trivial is because it is. The world takes the trivial and makes it important, and takes the important and makes it trivial.

God has given you a unique blend of talents and abilities, and your talents and abilities are vocational. What does that mean? Well, they hold clues about your mission, your genius, your vocation, and the best way for you to live.

The third ordinary voice of God is: deepest desire.

Deep in your heart you have desires for good things, and God has placed those desires in your heart to guide you to the life he envisioned for you.

At lunchtime I often have a desire for chocolate doughnuts. But the desire for doughnuts is not a deep desire; in fact it is a fairly shallow

WHAT IS YOUR RELATIONSHIP with the POOR?

YOU CAN NEVER get enough OF WHAT YOU DON'T really NEED

You have a unique blend of talents & abilities that are PERFECTLY SUITED to carry out whatever MISSION GOD HAS ASSIGNED TO YOU on this earth.

desire. God wants us to get beyond our shallow desires, which are often selfish or pointless, and uncover the deepest desires of our hearts.

When I am the-best-version-of-myself, I say no to the doughnuts and I have a salad for lunch instead. To the world this is a simple choice between doughnuts and a salad. But as we grow spiritually, God shows us that there are many layers and dimensions to every decision.

On one level, yes, it's just a choice between doughnuts and a salad. On another level it's a choice between doughnuts and being healthy. That's a different perspective. On another level it's a choice between doughnuts and being alive and healthy enough to walk my daughter down the aisle when she gets married . . . to be alive to see her life unfold . . . and meet the person she will spend her life with . . . and meet my grandchildren. . . .

When we embrace God and his way of life, he reveals many dimensions of everyday life that we have never seen or thought about before. God is speaking to you through your deepest desires. Seek out your deepest desires for good things and have the courage to pursue them.

The most common preface to any sentence in the Bible is "God said . . ." God said to Adam, Noah, Moses, and Abraham. God spoke to everyone. It isn't that he has stopped speaking, but that humanity has stopped listening. God speaks to us in so many ways—through prayer, the Scriptures, the sacraments; through the life, teachings, and history of the Church; through other people, events, and circumstances.

You have been designed by God for a specific mission. This is what John Henry Newman wrote, "God has created me to do him some definite service. He has committed some work to me, which he has not committed to another. I have my mission." God has assigned a mission to you. If you don't fulfill your mission it will go undone. The world is a mess because too many people have abandoned their God-given mission.

Find your mission. It will change your life in the most wonderful ways . . . forever!

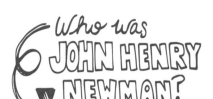

Who was JOHN HENRY NEWMAN?

JOHN HENRY NEWMAN (1801–1890) was one of the central religious figures in England in the nineteenth century. A respected academic, he was originally a priest in the Church of England and a leader in the Oxford Movement. This was an influential group of Anglicans who wanted to return the Church of England to many Catholic beliefs and practices. In 1845 Newman left the Church of England and was received in the Roman Catholic Church, where he was eventually appointed as cardinal by Pope Leo XIII. Unlike most saints, his feast day is not the day of his death, but rather the day of his conversion to Catholicism, September 19.

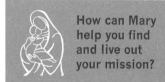

How can Mary help you find and live out your mission?

DISCUSSION?

1. WHO DO YOU KNOW WHO HAS FOUND AND FOLLOWED HIS/HER MISSION IN LIFE?

_____

_____

_____

_____

_____

_____

2. HAVE YOU EVER ASKED GOD WHAT MISSION HE HAS FOR YOU?

_____

_____

_____

_____

_____

_____

_____

3. HOW DO YOU THINK WHAT YOU WANT FOR YOURSELF IS DIFFERENT
   FROM WHAT GOD WANTS FOR YOU?

_____

_____

_____

_____

_____

_____

_____

PSALM 141

I call upon thee, O Lord; make haste to me!
Give ear to my voice, when I call to thee!

2 Let my prayer be counted as incense before thee,
and the lifting up of my hands as an evening sacrifice!

3 Set a guard over my mouth, O Lord,
keep watch over the door of my lips!

4 Incline not my heart to any evil,
to busy myself with wicked deeds
in company with men who work iniquity;
and let me not eat of their dainties!

5 Let a good man strike or rebuke me in kindness,
but let the oil of the wicked never anoint my head;
for my prayer is continually against their wicked deeds.

6 When they are given over to those who shall condemn them,
then they shall learn that the word of the Lord is true.

7 As a rock which one cleaves and shatters on the land,
so shall their bones be strewn at the mouth of Sheol.

8 But my eyes are toward thee, O Lord God;
in thee I seek refuge; leave me not defenseless!

9 Keep me from the trap which they have laid for me,
and from the snares of evildoers!

10 Let the wicked together fall
into their own nets, while I escape.

11.4 YOUR UNTAPPED GREATNESS

Two months to the day before he died, Martin Luther King Jr. gave a speech in Atlanta, in which he said, "Everybody can be great, because everybody can serve. You don't have to have a college degree to serve. You don't have to make your subject and your verb agree to serve. You don't have to know about Plato and Aristotle to serve. You don't have to know Einstein's theory of relativity to serve. You don't have to know the second law of thermodynamics in physics to serve. You only need a heart full of grace, a soul generated by love."

The world says greatness is reserved for a few. God says everyone can be great. The world says if you are great everyone will serve you. God says if you are great you will serve everyone.

One of the greatest lessons I have learned in life is that getting outside myself is the starting point for good things to happen. When we get beyond ourselves and serve others we start down a sure path to happiness.

You can search the whole world for happiness, but it will elude you until you realize that it is only by bringing happiness to others that we ever find happiness for ourselves. Serving others is the surest path to happiness in this world, to discovering who you are and what you are here for. Serving others is at the core of the mission God has designed just for you.

But it is so easy to get caught up in ourselves, our plans, and our selfish desires. And when we are all caught up in ourselves, it is easy to ignore the suffering that is going on all around us.

There is a story in Luke's Gospel that makes me very uneasy every time I hear or read it. It is the story of Lazarus and the rich man. It goes like this:

There was a rich man who was dressed in purple and fine linen and who feasted sumptuously every day. And at his gate lay a poor man named Lazarus, covered with sores, who longed to satisfy his hunger with what fell from the rich man's table; even the dogs would come and lick his sores. The poor man died and was carried away by the angels to be with Abraham. The rich man also died and was buried. In Hades, where he was being tormented, he looked up and saw Abraham far away with Lazarus by his side. He called out, "Father Abraham, have mercy on me, and send Lazarus to dip the tip of his finger in water and cool my tongue; for I am in agony in these flames." But Abraham said, "Child, remember that during your lifetime you received your good things, and

Lazarus in like manner evil things; but now he is comforted here, and you are in agony. Besides all this, between you and us a great chasm has been fixed, so that those who might want to pass from here to you cannot do so, and no one can cross from there to us." (Luke 16:19-26)

This parable makes me uncomfortable because like the rich man I have nice clothes and plenty of them, and I have plenty to eat every day, and there are a lot of people suffering in this world. They might not be on my doorstep, but they are not far away. It makes me uncomfortable because this is Jesus speaking. This story is straight from the mouth of God. And from what Jesus describes of the afterlife, I know where I want to end up.

Our Christianity is constantly challenging us to assess our relationship with the poor. For a long time I would give money to the poor. I would donate to organizations that help the poor and I would give people on the street a few dollars. These things are good, but they don't give us personal contact with the poor. Our relationship with the poor can become very transactional if we are not careful. God calls us to more than that.

When it comes to helping the poor—and more than that, when it comes to being with the poor—our family, the Catholic Church, has an incredible track record. I have spoken often about the genius of Catholicism, and here we find it expressed in one of its most beautiful and practical ways.

Have you ever heard of the **Works of Mercy**? As Christians we bring the love and mercy of God to others by performing these works. That's a thing of beauty. Think about it: You get to bring the love and mercy of God to other people.

So, what are these works of mercy? They are divided into two categories: the Corporal Works of Mercy, which concern the material needs of others, and the Spiritual Works of Mercy, which concern the spiritual needs of others.

The Corporal Works of Mercy are:

- To feed the hungry
- To give drink to the thirsty
- To clothe the naked
- To shelter the homeless
- To visit the sick
- To visit the imprisoned
- To bury the dead

> "JEALOUSY IS THE TRIBUTE MEDIOCRITY PAYS TO GENIUS."
> —FULTON SHEEN

IS TECHNOLOGY GOOD OR BAD?

Like many things in this world, including material possessions and money, technology is morally neutral. It is neither good nor bad. What makes it good or bad is how we use it. Are you using technology in ways that are good or bad? Are you using it to help you become a-better-version-of-yourself?

Vocation means "call." It's an invitation from God. There are many ways to live your life, but God has given you a unique blend of talents, abilities, and personality to carry out a mission that he has not assigned to anybody else. God may call you to the vocation of marriage, he may call you to live a single life, or he may call you to live as a priest or religious. Finding your vocation is like coming home after a long journey. It brings with it an indescribable joy.

The Spiritual Works of Mercy are:

• To instruct the ignorant

• To counsel the doubtful

• To correct sinners

• To bear wrongs patiently

• To forgive offenses willingly

• To comfort the afflicted

• To pray for the living and the dead

How would the world be different if everyone practiced just one work of mercy each day? How would the world be different if these works of mercy defined the way we live our lives? There is genius in Catholicism, but sadly it is little known and little practiced.

So here is my challenge for you. Each day for the next thirty days I want to encourage you to intentionally practice one of these works of mercy. You will be amazed how this thirty-day challenge can change you, the way you see the world, and your life.

You are so young and your lives are before you, so I want to beg you not to waste your single years waiting for life to happen. You will never have a better opportunity to serve than while you are young and single. Too many people spend their single years trying to wish them away. Singleness, like everything else, has a purpose. It is a time to discover who you are, what you are here for, what matters most, and what matters least. Nothing will help you develop this kind of personal clarity like service.

So, get outside yourself. Stop thinking that it is all about you. Find meaningful ways to serve. You will be so glad you did.

Discussion Questions

1. WHO DO YOU KNOW WHO IS GREAT AT SERVING OTHER PEOPLE?

_____
_____
_____
_____
_____

2. WHAT DOES THE STORY ABOUT THE RICH MAN AND LAZARUS MAKE YOU THINK ABOUT?

_____
_____
_____
_____
_____
_____

3. DO YOU THINK YOU WILL BE HAPPIER IF YOU FIND AND FOLLOW YOUR MISSION?

_____
_____
_____
_____
_____
_____

The Road Not Taken
by Robert Frost

Two roads diverged in a yellow wood,
And sorry I could not travel both
And be one traveler, long I stood
And looked down one as far as I could
To where it bent in the undergrowth;

Then took the other, as just as fair,
And having perhaps the better claim,
Because it was grassy and wanted wear;
Though as for that the passing there
Had worn them really about the same,

And both that morning equally lay
In leaves no step had trodden black.
Oh, I kept the first for another day!
Yet knowing how way leads on to way,
I doubted if I should ever come back.

I shall be telling this with a sigh
Somewhere ages and ages hence:
Two roads diverged in a wood, and I—
I took the one less traveled by,
And that has made all the difference.

MOTHER TERESA

Gen·er·os·i·ty

[jen-*uh*-**ros**-i-tee]

Going beyond your own selfishness to give of your time, talent, and treasure to benefit others

Who is the most generous person you know?

Are generous people happier?

How can you be more generous?

11.5 DECISION point

I cannot tell you what you should do with your life. I wish I could. Your parents, teachers, and friends cannot tell you either. We can all advise you, but ultimately God has created a unique journey for you, and it is only by listening to his voice that you will discover the indescribable joy that comes to us when we finally discover our mission in life.

I have experienced this joy. It is not just an idea. There are two very concrete examples of it in my life. The first is with my work as an author and a speaker. There are many things I could be doing, but I know this is the thing that God wants me to be doing—that he created me for. How do I know? It's hard to describe. When you find your thing, you just know. There is a joy and a timelessness that you experience. You love doing it, even though it isn't always fun; you lose track of time when you are hard at work; and you have a deep peace within you, which comes from the sense that this is the thing for you to dedicate your life to. I want you to discover and experience that.

The other area of my life where I experience this joy is in my marriage. I have lived away from Australia for almost twenty years now. But every time I fly into Sydney, and see the Harbour Bridge and the Opera House, I still get the same feeling. It is the feeling of arriving home. I travel a lot for work, and there is something wonderful about coming home. When I met Meggie I had that feeling. When I married her I had that feeling, the feeling that I was finally home. Whatever vocation God calls you to, I want you to experience that same feeling of arriving home after a long journey.

I can't tell you what your mission in life is, but I can tell you two things that will flawlessly help you to discover it.

1) While you may not know the specifics of your mission, you do know your mission in a broad sense, because it is the same for us all. Your mission is to make the love of God known to the world. In your own place and time, in your own ways, you are here to bring the love of God to every person who crosses your path.

2) Do the next right thing. The surest way to discover your mission is to do what you know to be the right thing, right now. If you do the next right thing often enough for long enough, you will live your way into the incredible life that God has designed just for you.

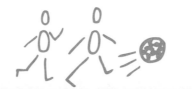

JOURNAL QUESTIONS

1. WHAT ARE YOU AFRAID OF?

_____
_____
_____
_____
_____
_____
_____

2. ONE DAY, WHEN YOU ARE DYING, WHAT DO YOU WANT TO SEE WHEN YOU LOOK BACK ON YOUR LIFE?

_____
_____
_____
_____
_____
_____
_____
_____

3. HOW AVAILABLE ARE YOU TO GOD?

_____
_____
_____
_____
_____
_____

MADE FOR MISSION
CROSSWORD PUZZLE

ACROSS

2. Done with purpose; deliberate
4. A native or inhabitant of Samaria
6. A disorderly or dirty accumulation, heap, or jumble
7. Everybody is a _____ in their own way.
8. A necessity
11. To feed the_____ is a corporal work of mercy.
14. To willingly _____ someone who has wronged you is a spiritual work of mercy.

DOWN

1. A short story that uses familiar events to illustrate a point
3. Abilities you have been given to help fulfill your God-given mission
5. To go out of your way to be of assistance to someone else
9. Something that is desired but not necessarily needed
10. You have been masterfully designed for a _____.
12. To be kind, caring, compassionate, and forgiving is to show _____.
13. The law of God as revealed to Moses and recorded in the first five books of the Hebrew Scriptures
15. God made you for a _____.

Answers on page 327

My Thoughts

HOLINESS
is possible

We thank you for this day and for all your blessings. Help us to remain always grateful for all you do for us and in us. Watch over in a special way today anyone who is hungry, lonely, depressed, addicted, unemployed, or just in need of the human touch, and inspire us to realize that we are your partners in the work you wish to do in the world. Help us to remain ever mindful of the great love you have for each and every one of us, and give us the courage to respond with the bold enthusiasm of a little child. We ask all this in Jesus' name. Amen.

Matthew Kelly

12. HOLINESS IS POSSIBLE

We are almost at the end of our time together, and now it's time for us to put all the pieces together.

When we play football, we know the goal is to score as many points as possible. In business the goal is to produce high-quality goods and services and produce a profit. The goal of golf is to finish with the lowest score. We approach almost everything we do with a goal or a desired outcome in mind.

So, what is the goal of the Christian life? It's amazing how many people have no idea. Henry David Thoreau wrote, "In the long run, men hit only what they aim at. Therefore, they had better aim at something high." What are we aiming at? What is the goal we are moving toward?

Holiness is the goal of the Christian life. I know. Huge concept. Serious stuff. But I want you to keep three things in mind:

First, what you think holiness is and what it actually is might very well be two quite different things. Second, you want holiness. You may not realize it yet, but you do. Finally, it may be a big concept and serious stuff, but a little bit of seriousness is highly agreeable to the soul. As I have said to you time and time again throughout this series, you are not too young to start thinking about life's big questions. You are not too young for a little bit of seriousness. In fact, the sooner you embrace some seriousness, the more fruitful and fulfilling your life will be.

12.1 THE holy MOMENT

So, what is holiness? Our culture makes holiness seem boring. Nothing could be further from the truth. The culture pretends that anything religious encroaches on our freedom, when in fact authentic spirituality sets us free. Some people think that if you are to be holy you can never have any fun. Another lie. Nobody lived more fully than the saints. The truth is, there is nothing more attractive than holiness. And perhaps the biggest surprise of all is that you want to live a holy life more than you want anything else.

You have an enormous yearning for happiness. Almost every decision you make is based on this yearning. The reality is the more you grow in holiness, the happier you will be. Happiness and holiness are linked. God wants you to be happy and he wants you to live a holy life; the two cannot be separated.

> "WHAT REALLY MATTERS IN LIFE IS THAT WE ARE LOVED BY CHRIST AND THAT WE LOVE HIM IN RETURN. IN COMPARISON TO THE LOVE OF JESUS, EVERYTHING ELSE IS SECONDARY. AND, WITHOUT THE LOVE OF JESUS, EVERYTHING IS USELESS."
>
> POPE JOHN PAUL II

You also have an enormous desire for relationships. But what kind of relationships do you want? Do you want relationships that are filled with lying, cheating, and gossip, in which you always have to have your guard up? That stuff is exhausting, because we can never relax in relationships like those.

Life has taught me that in great relationships we can relax because we know our friends want what is good for us. They are helping us to become the-best-version-of-ourselves, and no matter what happens, we know that they have our best interests at heart.

Do you want to be in relationships with people who are patient or impatient? Humble or prideful? Generous or stingy? Thoughtful or careless? Faithful or unfaithful? Whether you are aware of it or not, you want holiness—and you want to be around other people who are striving to live holy lives.

The problem is, most Christians have never considered holiness as a possibility. Most Christians don't actually believe that holiness is possible. That's the lie. It's the most devastating lie in the history of Christianity. The tragic thing is, this is not a lie that gets told about Christians, it's a lie we tell ourselves. It is subtle, deceptive, and disorienting.

We might believe that holiness is possible for someone else, like Mother Teresa or our grandma, but not for us. We know our faults and failings and weaknesses, we know the horrible thoughts we have at times, and we know what we are capable of because we know the dark things we have done.

But I am here to let you in on a life-changing secret: Holiness is possible. It's possible for you to live a holy life. This changes everything. This opens up incredible possibilities.

It's easy to say, but let me prove it to you.

If I said to you, "I want you to create one holy moment today," you would probably ask me, "What is a holy moment?"

A holy moment happens when you are being the person God created you to be and doing what he wants you to do in that moment. Examples of holy moments include being patient with your little brother or sister, helping someone in need, being a good friend, welcoming someone who has been rejected by others, and avoiding gossip.

Anyone can create a single holy moment. If you really set your mind to it, you could create a holy moment today. And if you can create one holy moment today, you can create two tomorrow, and four the next day. Once you know how to create a single holy moment, you can duplicate the process.

1 Thessalonians 4:3

"For this is the will of God, your sanctification: that you abstain from immorality..."

KNOW IT: God wants you to live a holy life.

THINK ABOUT IT: How many holy moments can you create today?

LIVE IT: Make it a point to create one holy moment each hour.

The Little Way: DO small THINGS with GREAT LOVE

The saints were not born saints, and they weren't perfect. They were men and women like you and me who realized that the world's vision for them was bankrupt, so they turned to God and his vision for their lives. They created one holy moment at a time, and over the course of their lives they strung together thousands of holy moments to create a holy life. You can do that too.

Holiness is possible, and once we come to that realization everything changes and possibilities we never considered before open up before us.

DISCUSSION·QUESTIONS

1. WHO IS THE HOLIEST PERSON YOU KNOW? WHAT MAKES THAT PERSON HOLY?

2. WHO IS YOUR FAVORITE SAINT? WHY?

3. WHAT'S ONE THING YOU HAVE LEARNED THROUGHOUT THE DECISION POINT EXPERIENCE THAT SURPRISED YOU?

"IT IS JESUS THAT YOU SEEK *when you dream of happiness;* He is waiting for you when nothing else you find satisfies you; HE IS THE *beauty* TO WHICH *you are so attracted;* it is He who provoked you with that *thirst for fullness* that will not let you SETTLE FOR COMPROMISE; it is He who urges you to shed the masks of a false life; IT IS HE WHO READS *in your heart* YOUR MOST GENUINE CHOICES, THE CHOICES THAT OTHERS TRY TO STIFLE. IT IS JESUS WHO STIRS IN YOU THE DESIRE TO DO SOMETHING GREAT WITH YOUR LIVES, *the will to follow an ideal,* the refusal to allow yourselves TO BE GROUND DOWN BY MEDIOCRITY, the courage to *commit yourselves humbly* AND PATIENTLY TO IMPROVING YOURSELVES AND SOCIETY, making the world *more human* and more fraternal."

[POPE JOHN PAUL II]

my Thoughts

12.2 Everything IS AN Opportunity

Sometimes people fall into the trap of thinking that holiness is about doing something extraordinary. But most of the time holiness is just about doing the ordinary things of everyday life really well.

People used to ask Mother Teresa for advice, asking her what they should do with their lives, and she would tell them, "Do something beautiful for God!"

When she became a nun Mother Teresa chose her name because she had been influenced and inspired by Saint Therese of Lisieux, a nineteenth-century Carmelite nun. Saint Therese was famous for what she called "the little way."

The Little Way suggests that we can grow in holiness just by doing the ordinary things of everyday life well. For example, Therese wrote that simply picking something up off the ground when it is inconvenient or when you would rather not and offering that small action to God could help you grow in holiness. In the same way, giving your full attention to the person you are with (rather than texting someone else) is a way you can grow in holiness, as is doing your chores without being asked, or doing your brother's or sister's chores because you know they are having a tough day. The little way is everywhere.

Holiness doesn't necessarily mean doing extraordinary things. God invites us to do the little things of everyday life with great love. When is the last time you did something with great love? And even when holiness does involve something extraordinary, that extraordinary thing usually comes as a culmination of a thousand small things done with great love.

Once we discover the little way, we begin to recognize that opportunities to grow in holiness are everywhere. Everything that happens every day is an opportunity for holiness. The way we interact with people, the way we work or study, and how we use our free time are all opportunities to grow in holiness.

Have you ever known someone who was holy? Who is the holiest person you have ever met? The man who encouraged me to pray for ten minutes a day was a holy man. When I first met him I was about fifteen years old, and I have never forgotten what he taught me about life. He gave me dozens of insights, but what he taught me about work and study I have used every day.

"When you study," he said to me, "put the initials of someone at the top of each page of notes, or at the top of each page you read in a book. Then, in a very short prayer, offer the work on that page to God

EVERYTHING IS AN OPPORTUNITY TO Grow IN HOLINESS

as a prayer for that person. Perhaps your dad is having a hard time at work or your grandmother is sick, or maybe you have a friend or a sibling who needs your prayers. Place their initials at the top of a page, and offer that work to God as a prayer for that person. In this way, we can transform every hour of study into an hour of prayer."

At the time I had a job after school working at a pharmacy, riding around delivering packages to the elderly. He taught me the same thing about my work. Back then I had a watch that would chime on the hour. He said to me, "Each time your watch chimes, offer the next hour of your work to God for a particular person or intention. In this way we transform every hour of work into prayer" (1 Thessalonians 5:17).

Saint Paul wrote, "Pray without ceasing." But we cannot all just go to church all day long and pray, so what did Paul mean? He was encouraging us to transform everything we do into prayer.

Everything is an opportunity to grow in holiness. One thing that is beautifully unique about Christianity is our belief that suffering has value. Life is difficult. Life is wonderful and beautiful, but it is also difficult. And suffering is an inevitable part of life. The question is, how are you going to respond to suffering?

Even suffering is an opportunity to grow in holiness. Jesus said, "If anyone wishes to come after me, he must deny himself, and take up his cross and follow me." (Matthew 16:24) I visited with a good friend of mine last week, an old priest who has been in horrific pain for months with back problems. When I visited he told me he had been sitting in the chair he was in for twenty-three hours a day for more than a week while he was waiting to have an operation. He smiled a huge smile and said, "But I'm not wasting any of my suffering. I am offering it up to God as a prayer for all the young people who will experience the Confirmation program." How cool is that? He is offering his suffering as a prayer for you!

We all have our crosses to carry. What cross are you carrying right now? Are you trying to carry it alone or are you letting Jesus help you? He wants to help. And as you carry your cross are you offering your suffering up to God as a prayer?

Each Sunday at Mass as the offertory gifts are being brought up I place any sufferings or challenges I have in my life on the altar. I give them to God. I offer them up. I also place my marriage on the altar, and my children, and my health, my money and work, my things. I place everything on the altar, my whole life and my whole self. I offer it all to God.

Everything is an opportunity to grow in holiness. I hope this session will help you to recognize the opportunities each day. The Church needs a whole new generation of people committed to living holy lives.

discussion questions

1. WHO DO YOU KNOW WHO DOES LITTLE THINGS WITH GREAT LOVE?

_____
_____
_____
_____
_____
_____

2. WHAT LITTLE THINGS CAN YOU DO WITH GREAT LOVE TODAY?

_____
_____
_____
_____
_____
_____

3. WHAT DOES TODAY'S CULTURE THINK ABOUT DOING LITTLE THINGS WITH GREAT LOVE?

_____
_____
_____
_____
_____
_____
_____

12.3 your YES can change the WORLD

Throughout your life there are going to be times when you feel like there must be more to life or that something is missing. We all have the same kind of empty feeling from time to time. You see, we all have a hole in us that needs to be filled.

We try to fill that hole in lots of different ways. When I was a child I thought the hole would be filled if Santa brought me just what I wanted or if I won enough soccer games and golf matches. As I grew older I tried to fill that hole with other things.

We try to fill the hole with pleasure, but that doesn't work. We tell ourselves, "Maybe I can fill it with stuff!" So we get a car, a house, clothes, a watch, handbags, jewelry, shoes—everything the material world has to offer. But that doesn't fill the hole either, and the empty feeling remains. So we go off to see the world and find ourselves, but that doesn't fill the hole. Next we chase accomplishment. "If I can just achieve enough, perhaps that will fill the hole." We achieve great things, but the emptiness continues to reign. The hole is still there.

We are slow learners, so we usually cycle through several rounds of each of these attempts at filling the hole. More pleasure, more travel, more stuff, more accomplishments, the right friends, sex, drugs, fame, status . . . but time and time again the emptiness continues. In fact, the more you try to fill the hole with these things, the bigger the hole seems to be.

We all experience the same kind of emptiness. Why? The reason is profoundly simple. We each have a God-sized hole in us. Only God can fill the hole. Try anything else you want, but it won't work. It never has and it never will.

My favorite line in the Catechism is the opening line in Chapter One, which reads: "The desire for God is written in the human heart, because man is created by God and for God; and God never ceases to draw man to himself. Only in God will he find the truth and the happiness he never stops searching for."

You have a God-sized hole in you. What are you trying to fill it with? Are you ready to let God take away that emptiness once and for all? Life is choices. You get to decide.

It's amazing how a simple yes or no can change your life.

One of the most practical things about growing spiritually is that we get really good at saying no. Most people are bad at saying no. Every day we find ourselves saying yes to things that we know we should be

---

WHAT ARE YOU *trying to* FILL YOUR EMPTINESS —*with?*—

1 Thessalonians 5:17

"pray constantly"

KNOW IT: We are called to transform every moment into a prayer.

THINK ABOUT IT: How can you transform your daily activity into prayer? For whom can you offer these prayers to God?

LIVE IT: Offer each hour of work or study to God as a prayer for a specific intention.

saying no to. We do this because of peer pressure, fear of missing out on something, a false feeling of obligation, or just to stay busy so we can distract ourselves from really thinking about life and what God is calling us to. But here's the thing: When we say yes to stuff we know is not for us, we miss out on the stuff that is uniquely ours.

Let me give you an example. I was talking to a friend of mine the other day and I asked him how his girlfriend, Julie, was. He said she was great, so I asked him if he thought she was the one for him. He said no. So I asked him when they were going to break up. He said they weren't going to break up. I asked why and he said that he really liked her and they had fun together.

"What are you doing Friday night?" I asked.

"Taking Julie to that new movie."

On Friday night, when he was out at the movies with Julie, that might have been the night when he was going to meet the woman that God had created just for him. When we say yes to stuff that is not for us, we miss out on the stuff that God created just for us.

Get really good at saying no to anything that you know is not for you. And the only way to say no to anything, is to have a deeper yes. As we grow spiritually—through prayer, the Scriptures, and the Sacraments - we get really clear about: who we are, what we are here for, what matters most, and what matters least. This personal clarity allows us to be really good at saying yes to the right things and no to the stuff that just isn't part of God's plan for us.

If you have been practicing The Prayer Process each day I'm sure you are already getting a clearer sense of who you are, what you're here for, what matters most, and what matters least. And that personal clarity is a beautiful thing.

From the beginning it has been my hope that this program will help you become a great decision maker, because decision making is so central to our experience of life. Learning to say yes to the right things and no to the wrong things is essential.

Now it's time to face the decision at hand. At baptism your parents and godparents made a choice for you. Now you have to decide for yourself—and make no mistake, it is one of the biggest decisions of your life. God has chosen you. The question is: How will you respond?

We have been making this journey toward Confirmation, and now we are almost there. It's time to commit. Say yes to Confirmation, but much more than that, decide today to say yes to Jesus and his Church. Choose them, for they have chosen you. Open your workbooks and sign

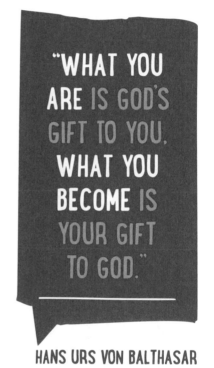

"WHAT YOU ARE IS GOD'S GIFT TO YOU, WHAT YOU BECOME IS YOUR GIFT TO GOD."

HANS URS VON BALTHASAR

100% AVAILABLE

WHO WAS DAVID?

David was an ancestor of Jesus (c. 1040 BC–970 BC) and perhaps the most brilliant leader of ancient Israel. He had the mind and charisma to inspire a great nation. In other ways he was a very ordinary man who struggled with destructive passion and was motivated at times by political gain. Yet through it all he had a deep love of God. The Bible describes David as a man after God's own heart (Acts 13:22).

When David was just a boy he was summoned to play music for King Saul in order to cure his melancholy. David also gained fame in his youth when he killed the Philistine Goliath with his slingshot. After Saul died, David rose to power and became King of Israel, uniting the twelve tribes.

the pledge. Read it slowly, pray about it, and sign it. Say yes to God and his Church, and say yes enthusiastically. Not just a whimpering, passive yes, but a wholehearted and enthusiastic YES.

Your Catholic faith will always be a part of you. You get to decide if it is going to be something powerful and positive, or something negative and misunderstood.

God has a plan. When we don't play our part, the whole thing falls apart. It's all connected. Imagine if Mary had said no. Her yes has touched every person who has lived for two thousand years. You see, every decision made by every person echoes down through history.

Sometimes I wonder if the reason we don't have a cure for cancer, AIDS, and Alzheimer's is because the people who were going to find those cures were among the fifty-five million children who have been aborted in the United States since *Roe v. Wade*. God had a plan for every one of those children, just as he has a plan for you. You have a part to play in God's plan for the world.

You might be tempted to think, "Oh, I'm nobody special; God doesn't have any special plans for me." But that would be a mistake. Read Chapter 17 of the first book of Samuel for a great example. David's father sent him to take food to his brothers, who were in the army. When he got there Goliath, the enormous and much feared Philistine, was daring the Israelites to fight him, but they were all too afraid. David said to king Saul, "I'll fight him." Saul told him he could not because David, who was little more than a child, was too young. David and Saul went back and forth and finally the king agreed. The rest is history. David slew Goliath, and in time God made this lowly shepherd boy the king of his people.

David made himself available.

God uses the most unlikely people to do his greatest work. As you read the Bible, you'll discover that he almost never uses those in positions of power and authority; he doesn't necessarily use the most educated, or the best looking, or even the most qualified. Whom does God use to do his most powerful work here on earth? He uses the people who make themselves available to him. How available are you to God? Ten percent, 50 percent, 95 percent? Or are you 100 percent available for whatever God calls you to today?

Want to see something truly incredible? Make yourself available to God.

DISCUSSION QUESTIONS

1. ARE YOU READY TO LET GOD COME AND FILL YOU UP IN ALL THE WAYS YOU NEED AND WANT TO BE FILLED?

2. WHAT HAVE YOU SAID YES TO IN THE PAST THAT YOU KNEW WAS NOT FOR YOU?

3. WHAT'S PREVENTING YOU FROM MAKING YOURSELF MORE AVAILABLE TO GOD?

The Pledge

God, the Father of infinite love and mercy,
I pledge to walk with you.

Thank you for the gift of life;
I pledge to live it to the fullest.

Thank you for sending your Son Jesus to redeem us;
I pledge to be his disciple.

Thank you for sending your Spirit to lead and direct us;
I pledge to follow his guidance.

Thank you for the gift of the Catholic Church;
I pledge to allow her to teach
and inspire me to live life to the fullest.

Help me to be patient with anything that I don't understand
about our incredible faith.

Fill me with joy so that I can always be a good witness
to your love and mercy in the world.

Give me wisdom, grace, and courage to live up
to this pledge I make to you today.

Amen.

_____

Sign Here

DECISION
point

Catholicism is like a really old treasure map.

Your **YES** can change the **WORLD**

ITS **OLD.** BUT IT **STILL** LEADS TO

Treasure

GOD WANTS YOU TO BECOME

the **BEST** VERSION OF **YOURSELF**

12.4 REVIEW

We have covered tons of material throughout this program. Many of the ideas we have talked about with you are going to be part of your daily experience for the rest of your lives. I suspect you will spend the rest of your lives unpacking what we have discussed here in our short time together. So, I hope you will keep your workbook and that it will become a touchstone for your life. There will be times when you come to a decision point, and at those times I hope you will take out your workbook and review some of the key principles we have shared together as you have been preparing for Confirmation. I hope our paths cross somewhere along the way . . . and whether it is five, ten, or twenty years from now, I hope you will take out that workbook and show it to me. And as I flip through the pages I hope to find it dog-eared and worn out, with notes and highlighting everywhere. That will tell me that you have found that book to be a worthy companion for your journey.

Now let's take a look at some key messages from each of the sessions we have already experienced.

GOD WANTS YOU TO BECOME A GREAT DECISION MAKER.

YOU WERE MADE FOR **MISSION**

Sin makes us unhappy.

LIFE IS *choices*

YOU ARE CALLED & Chosen by GOD.

HOW WILL YOU RESPOND?

THE **WORLD** IS A MESS BECAUSE OF SELFISHNESS.

Holiness IS POSSIBLE

God gives us *relationships* to help us become **the-best-version-of-ourselves.** He gives us relationships so that we can *help each other get to Heaven.*

What's HOLDING you back?

Anyone or anything that doesn't help you become the-best-version-of-yourself is too small for you.

PRAY everyday

JESUS · IS · TRULY *present* IN · THE · EUCHARIST

THE CATHOLIC CHURCH is the biggest family in the WORLD

HAPPINESS IS THE RESULT OF RIGHT LIVING.

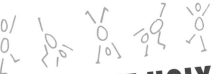

ALLOW THE HOLY SPIRIT TO LEAD AND GUIDE YOU.

I HAVE NEVER MET ANYONE WHO RELIED TOO MUCH ON THE HOLY SPIRIT.

THE GUIDE to a HAPPY life

THE BIBLE has the POWER to transform your life.

GREAT DECISION

JESUS WANTS TO TURN **YOUR LIFE** UPSIDE DOWN, AND THEN IT WILL BE RIGHT SIDE UP.

Place **JESUS** at the center of your life!

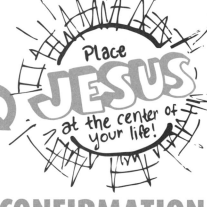

REBEL AGAINST THE CULTURE

CONFIRMATION is a great opportunity to start taking your spirituality seriously. **You'll be glad you did.**

There is a such thing as UNIVERSAL TRUTH

What do you think Mary did each day to stay focused on what matters most?

HOW DID MOSES PRAY?

Moses teaches us that to pray means to have intimate conversation with God. The Bible tells us that Moses went up the mountain, that God appeared to him in the burning bush, and that God and Moses had a real conversation. God gave Moses an assignment. Moses had questions. God talked Moses through his questions, and then sent him on his mission. Throughout his life as the leader of his people, Moses would withdraw to the mountain to pray before a big decision. How did he pray? He had intimate and personal conversation with God. (Exodus 33:11)

Wow, we have covered a lifetime of ideas. Now it's time to draw it all together.

Our lives change when our habits change. Throughout our time together I have been encouraging you to develop strong positive habits in your life. We spoke about using the Prayer Process to establish the habit of daily prayer. We explored dedicating a few minutes each day to reading the Bible. We spoke about getting to Mass each Sunday and honoring the Sabbath as a day of rest. We also explored how powerful frequenting the sacrament of Reconciliation can be. And we discussed how good friendships are one of the most powerful habits we can develop. Every habit we discussed was chosen because it will help you develop a dynamic relationship with God and become the-best-version-of-yourself.

Many years ago I was in Austria, and one night there was a huge storm. The next day I took a walk and there were trees down everywhere, and huge limbs ripped from other trees. But not far from where I was staying there was a park with soccer fields, and in the middle of the park there was a huge tree that looked like the storm hadn't even touched it. I stood there looking at it for a while.

That tree taught me this powerful lesson: A tree with strong roots can weather any storm.

There are going to be storms in your life. I don't know when, and you don't know when. They come mostly unannounced and unexpected. If we knew when they were coming we would prepare for them. But the storms of life don't announce themselves in advance. They rush upon the shores of our lives when we least expect them.

The habits we have discussed throughout this series are like strong roots. Sink them deep into your life and you will weather any storm. Don't wait for the storms to arrive, because by then it will be too late to sink the roots. On that day you either have strong roots or you don't.

These habits will also help you to become a great decision maker. You will discover that there are few life skills more practical than this one. We have discovered many decision points in our time together, and you will discover many more in the years ahead. I hope you are better equipped to make those decisions now.

Whatever habits you choose to make your own, whatever decisions you make along the way, they will determine the type of life you live.

Don't live a small life. That doesn't mean you need to do extraordinary things. To do the ordinary things extraordinarily well and with great love is to live the full measure of life. To live a small life is to be mean, fearful, greedy, distrustful of God and humanity, unhappy, and selfish. Don't live a small life. Live a life large enough to match your birthright as a son or daughter of God. Live joyfully and generously, with the kindness of the saints, trusting always in God, who loves you and wants good things for you.

a TREE with Strong Roots can weather any STORM

D·I·S·C·U·S·S·I·O·N
QUESTIONS

1. WHAT NEW HABIT HAVE YOU DEVELOPED SINCE YOU STARTED THIS PROGRAM?

_____
_____
_____
_____
_____
_____
_____

2. WHAT IS THE BEST IDEA YOU HEARD DURING THE ENTIRE EXPERIENCE?

_____
_____
_____
_____
_____
_____
_____

3. WHAT IS ONE THING YOU CAN DO THIS WEEK TO BETTER PREPARE YOURSELF FOR CONFIRMATION?

_____
_____
_____
_____
_____
_____
_____
_____

WHAT DREAMS HAS GOD PLACED IN YOUR HEART?

Chas·ti·ty
[chas-ti-tee]

sexual purity and self-control in thought, intention, and conduct

Why is chastity important?

What does the culture try to tell you about chastity?

What can you do to rebel against what the culture says about chastity?

12.5 DREAM!

As human beings we have many fabulous abilities, but God has bestowed on us two truly incredible gifts. The first is free will. We each have the ability to choose. The second is the ability to dream. Unlike any of the other creatures that God created, we can look into the future, imagine something better in the future, and then come back to the present and work in the present to bring about the future we have envisioned. Our ability to dream is an astounding gift.

So, what are your dreams? What dreams has God placed in your heart? You see, your dreams are your dreams for a reason. God has given us the ability to dream and placed certain dreams for good things in each of our hearts. What are your dreams? And what are you doing about them?

When I was a teenager I had a great soccer coach, but he was really tough on us. One day I got up in his face and screamed at him, "What do you want from me?" He looked at me calmly and said, "What do you want for yourself?"

Throughout your life there will be many people who want something from you. There will be relatively few who want absolutely nothing from you.

I don't want anything from you, but there are some things I want *for* you. I want you to experience the love of God in ways so powerful that you cannot resist embracing him with your whole heart, mind, and soul. I want you to become all he created you to be—the-very-best-version-of-yourself. I want you to experience the incredible joy that comes from saying yes to God and placing Jesus at the center of your life. I want you to be astounded by the genius of Catholicism. And after a long, full, and happy life filled with love, laughter, and dreams come true, I want you to die well and spend all of eternity with God in Heaven.

For four years I have been praying for you every day. And I am going to keep praying for you each day for the rest of my life. I pray that you have the courage and the wisdom to make these things we have discussed part of your life, and I pray that in your own way you will bring the love of God to others as they cross your path.

This time with you has been an honor. Thank you for allowing me to make this journey with you. I hope our paths cross again soon.

When I got married I was thirty-five years old, and for fifteen years I had been on the road, traveling from one city to the next. One of the things that I love about being married is that I have someone to pray with. There is something wonderful and powerful about praying with other people. Jesus said, "Wherever two or more are gathered in my name, I am there among them."(Matthew 18:20) Here we are, gathered in Jesus' name. If it weren't for him, we wouldn't be here right now. So let us close our eyes, and end our time together with prayer:

Loving Father,

We thank you for this day and for all your blessings.

Help us to remain always grateful for all you do for us and in us,

watch over in a special way today anyone who is hungry, lonely, depressed, addicted, unemployed, or just in need of the human touch,

and inspire us to realize that we are your partners in the work you wish to do in the world.

Help us to remain ever mindful of the great love you have for each and every one of us, and give us the courage to respond with the bold enthusiasm of a little child.

We ask all this in Jesus' name as we pray as he taught us to.

Our Father . . .

On behalf of everyone at Dynamic Catholic, I want to thank you for participating in this journey toward Confirmation. We hope we can serve you in powerful ways throughout your life. Don't let this be the end. Make a commitment to do something every day for the rest of your life that will help you grow spiritually. And I look forward to meeting you somewhere along the way as our pilgrimage continues...

DON'T LIVE ~a~ SMALL LIFE.

JOURNAL QUESTIONS

1. WHAT ARE YOUR DREAMS?

_____
_____
_____
_____
_____
_____
_____

2. WHAT CROSS ARE YOU CARRYING AT THIS TIME IN YOUR LIFE?

_____
_____
_____
_____
_____
_____
_____

3. WHAT DO YOU HOPE YOUR LIFE WILL BE LIKE FIVE YEARS FROM NOW?

_____
_____
_____
_____
_____
_____
_____
_____
_____

M-Y- -T-H-O-U-G-H-T-S

Psalm 27

The Lord is my light and my salvation;
whom shall I fear?

The Lord is the stronghold of my life;
of whom shall I be afraid?

²When evildoers assail me,
uttering slanders against me,
my adversaries and foes,
they shall stumble and fall.

³Though a host encamp against me,
my heart shall not fear;
though war arise against me,
yet I will be confident.

⁴One thing have I asked of the Lord,
that will I seek after;
that I may dwell in the house
of the Lord all the days of my life,
to behold the beauty of the Lord,
and to inquire in his temple.

⁵For he will hide me in his shelter
in the day of trouble;
he will conceal me under the
cover of his tent, he will set me
high upon a rock.

⁶And now my head shall be lifted up
above my enemies round about me;
and I will offer in his tent
sacrifices with shouts of joy;
I will sing and make melody
to the Lord.

⁷Hear, O Lord, when I cry aloud,
be gracious to me and answer me!

⁸Thou hast said, "Seek ye my face."
My heart says to thee,
"Thy face, Lord, do I seek."

⁹Hide not thy face from me.
Turn not thy servant away in anger,
thou who hast been my help.
Cast me not off, forsake me not,

O God of my salvation!

¹⁰For my father and my mother have
forsaken me, but the Lord
will take me up.

¹¹Teach me thy way, O Lord;
and lead me on a level path
because of my enemies.

¹²Give me not up to the will
of my adversaries; for false witnesses
have risen against me,
and they breathe out violence.

¹³I believe that I shall see the
goodness of the Lord in the land
of the living!

¹⁴Wait for the Lord; be strong,
and let your heart take courage;
yea, wait for the Lord!

HOLINESS IS POSSIBLE
CROSSWORD PUZZLE

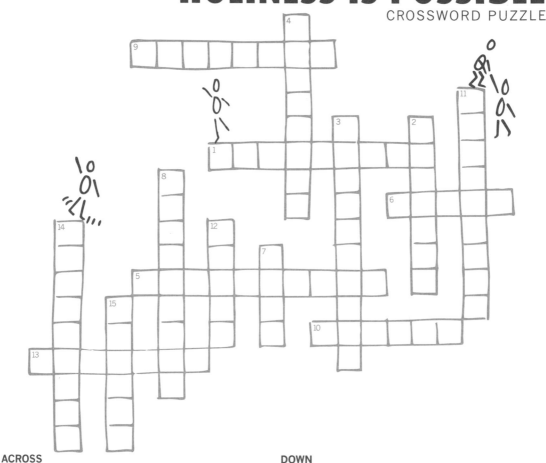

ACROSS

1. Contains answers about the teachings of the Catholic Church

5. Going beyond your own selfishness to give of your time, talent, and treasure to benefit others

6. We all have a _____ to carry.

9. A conclusion or resolution reached after consideration

10. Showing modesty of one's self-importance

13. Able to accept or tolerate delays, problems, or suffering without becoming annoyed or anxious

DOWN

2. To accept or support willingly and enthusiastically

3. Showing consideration for the needs of other people

4. _____ is possible, and once we come to that realization everything changes and possibilities we never considered before open up before us.

7. Anyone can create a single _____ moment.

8. Experiencing pain, distress, or hardship

11. Someone who believes that Jesus is the Messiah, that he walked the earth, was brutally murdered, and rose from the dead. Someone devoted to living as Jesus invites us to live.

12. Our ability to _____ is an astounding gift.

14. God uses the people who make themselves _____ to him.

15. Nobody lived more fully than the _____.

Answers on page 327

SESSION ONE
p. 28

SESSION TWO
p. 55

SESSION THREE
p. 84

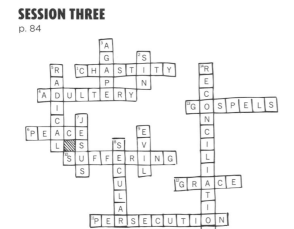

SESSION FOUR
p. 109

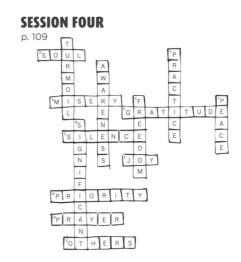

SESSION FIVE
p. 138

SESSION SIX
p. 164

SESSION SEVEN
p. 188

SESSION EIGHT
p. 212

SESSION NINE
p. 240

SESSION TEN
p. 268

SESSION ELEVEN
p. 294

SESSION TWELVE
p. 325

HELP DECISION point become THE BEST VERSION OF itself

DECISION POINT is different from other programs in a hundred ways .

One way it is different is that it is always changing and improving.

We need your help with this.

Whether you find a typo or think of some fun way to improve the program, please email us and tell us about it so that year after year DECISION POINT can become even more dynamic.

feedback @ dynamiccatholic.com

{ To re-energize the Catholic Church in America by developing world-class resources that inspire people to rediscover the genius of Catholicism. }

{ To be the innovative leader in the New Evangelization helping Catholics and their parishes become the-best-version-of-themselves. }

■■ DynamicCatholic.com
Be Bold. Be Catholic.®

5081 Olympic Boulevard • Erlanger • KY • 41018
United States of America
Phone: 1–859–980–7900
info@DynamicCatholic.com